School-Based
FINANCING

TWENTIETH ANNUAL YEARBOOK
OF THE AMERICAN EDUCATION FINANCE ASSOCIATION
1999

School-Based
FINANCING

EDITED BY
Margaret E. Goertz
Allan Odden

CORWIN PRESS, INC.
A Sage Publications Company
Thousand Oaks, California

LB
2825
.G637
1999

For information:

Corwin Press, Inc.
A Sage Publications Company
2455 Teller Road
Thousand Oaks, California 91320
E-mail: order@corwinpress.com

SAGE Publications Ltd.
6 Bonhill Street
London EC2A 4PU
United Kingdom

SAGE Publications India Pvt. Ltd.
M-32 Market
Greater Kailash I
New Delhi 110 048 India

Printed in the United States of America

Library of Congress: sf 88019781

ISBN: 0-8039-6779-9

ISSN: 1054-1896

This book is printed on acid-free paper.

99 00 01 02 03 04 05 10 9 8 7 6 5 4 3 2 1

Corwin Editorial Assistant: Kylee Liegl
Production Editor: Denise Santoyo
Designer/Typesetter: Danielle Dillahunt

Contents

**PART II: Design and Implementation
of School Based-Financing Systems**

PART III: How Schools Allocate and Use Financial Resources

Preface

School-based financing concerns the policies districts and states use to allocate fiscal resources to schools and the ways in which schools allocate and use their resources. Although it is a central issue in many districts and states today, school-based finance was barely on the policy agenda a decade ago. Indeed, education finance in the 20th century has focused primarily on state-to-district funding and cross-district funding inequities. States created school districts to deliver education services in local communities and gave these districts taxing authority to raise local revenues to finance their educational operations. Although states created funding formulas to "equalize" for the differential ability of districts to raise local education revenues, districts have been the primary unit to raise or receive education dollars. Further, once total revenues were determined, districts made most decisions about how dollars were to be spent. They allocated principals, teachers, secretaries, janitors, books, materials, and supplies to schools that had little, if any, say over the level or use of these resources.

Beginning in the 1980s and accelerating in the 1990s, the school took on greater importance in the education program and finance system. First, schools were identified as the major unit for designing and implementing education improvement efforts. Although districts played key roles in reform, research showed that most substantive education improvement actions occurred at the school site level (Cohen, 1983).

Second, school-based management gained increased popularity as districts sought to change the way the education system was organized and managed, sometimes as a part of standards- and school-based education reform (Odden, 1992) and sometimes as part of general school "restructuring" (Murphy & Hallinger, 1993). As school-based management began to spread, research showed that giving schools control over their budget was a key element that helped make school-based management work (Clune & White, 1988; Wohlstetter, Van Kirk, Robertson, & Mohrman, 1997). Further, districts that began to adopt and implement whole school reforms designed by the New American Schools Development Corporation (Stringfield, Ross, & Smith, 1996) soon understood that schools needed budget authority to reallocate resources to the requirements of their chosen school models. In the process, districts realized that providing schools with a lump sum budget was a concomitant of providing this new fiscal authority to each school site (Bodilly, 1998; Odden, in press).

Third, emerging choice and charter legislation required states—for the first time—to consider how to fund schools as compared to school districts. Under public school choice programs, the district-based school finance structure became problematic when students could attend schools outside of the district in which they lived (Odden & Kotowski, 1992). Charter schools are public schools, but they are often not controlled by school districts. When districts chartered schools, the districts could provide funds as they would to any other site in the district. Problems arose, however, when these charter schools enrolled students who lived outside the district. But often charter schools were not linked to a district; that is, they received a charter from an entity that did not have any public school funding. States then had to determine how to fund such schools (Odden & Busch, 1998). Private school voucher programs, such as those in Wisconsin, raise similar issues. Though no state has done so, it could finance such a system as it would an independent charter school.

Finally, in 1998, a school finance court case placed the issue of school-based financing squarely on a state's policy agenda. The New Jersey Supreme Court's fifth decision in *Abbott v. Burke* required not only that the state equalize funding between its poorest urban and wealthiest suburban districts but that the affected districts use these dollars to implement whole school reform programs. The state, the districts, and their schools first determine whether site-level resources are sufficient to support whichever whole school reform program the school adopts, such as Roots and Wings/Success for All. In the short-term, districts allocate resources to schools through their traditional staffing formulas; schools must then reallocate and redeploy personnel and nonpersonnel resources to fund the whole school reform models. For the medium term, the state is working with the districts to develop a resource allocation system that will provide schools with a lump sum budget through a needs-based, per pupil funding formula. When such a system is in place, New Jersey will be the first state to link state-to-district and district-to-site funding formulas.

In sum, several policy initiatives during the past 10 to 15 years have raised the issue of how schools—as compared to school districts—could be funded. As states and districts have struggled with this imperative, it has become clear that this task is complex, is not easily accomplished, and raises a host of new issues not entailed in district-based education finance policy.

As researchers and policymakers paid more attention to the school site, interest also emerged in how districts had provided resources to schools in the past and how schools had used those resources. Researchers raised questions about how equitably resources were distributed at the school as well as at the district level (see, e.g., Berne & Stiefel, 1994; Hertert, 1995). Questions also were raised about how dollars were allocated and spent at the school site, and whether they could be used more productively (see, e.g., Miles, 1995).

These questions were difficult to answer because fiscal and other resource data were generally not collected or available at the school site. Fiscal systems were geared to the district level; the general ledger tracked details about districtwide uses of resources but generally did not provide similar data for schools. Indeed, when several researchers began to focus their attention on school-level fiscal issues in the late 1980s, they found insufficient and/or unreliable data at the school site (see Berne, Stiefel, & Moser, 1997; Busch & Odden, 1997; Cohen, 1997; Farland, 1997; Goertz, 1997; Picus, 1997; Speakman et al., 1997). Though some thoughtful studies were conducted on school-level resource allocation (see Chambers et al., 1993; Goertz & Stiefel, 1998; Stiefel et al., 1996), the researchers had to spend several months and thousands of dollars massaging district data systems to create school-level data sets for analysis. These research efforts showed that the lack of school-based funding policies had generally produced a lack of school-level resource data as well.

The impetus for this yearbook of the American Education Finance Association derived from the preceding issues and challenges. The idea for the book began as a way to bring together a set of papers commissioned by the Consortium for Policy Research in Education[1] as part of its research on school-based financing. Four of these papers, written by Robert Berne and Leanna Stiefel; Lawrence O. Picus; Quentin Thompson and John Lakin; and Brian Caldwell and Peter Hill, are included here. A fifth paper, by Paul Hill, James Guthrie, and Lawrence Pierce, is incorporated in Hill, Pierce, and Guthrie (1997). These and the other chapters address critical school-based financing issues facing state and district policymakers as they began to develop school-based funding policies and school-based fiscal and other resource data systems. This book also shows how school-based data can be used for research and analysis.

The book has three sections. The first section provides a conceptual overview of the different issues involved in designing, implementing, and evaluating school-based funding policies. The second section reports on the experiences of three countries that have enacted school-based financing policies: England, Australia, and Canada. The final section discusses different approaches to funding schools in the United States and provides some insights into how schools allocate and reallocate dollars.

A Conceptual Overview

The first section comprises three chapters. In Chapter 1, Robert Berne and Leanna Stiefel develop a framework for thinking about how financial decision making might be defined and implemented at the school level. Fiscal operations in any system involve four recurring functions—planning/budgeting, implementing, evaluating, and reporting—that are performed to accomplish three broad categories of goals: control, fairness, and accomplishment of results. The authors use this "function by goal" matrix to raise and discuss a number of design, policy, and research issues about the appropriate division of authority between schools and the central office under a site-based financing system.

Delegating more fiscal authority to school sites is a complex and difficult task. In Chapter 2, Lawrence O. Picus discusses the nuts and bolts of allocating personnel and nonpersonnel resources to schools, assessing the fairness of these allocations, and determining which functions should remain at the district level and which should be devolved to the schools. He also suggests what a restructured school business office might look like under site-based financing as it shifts from a control to a support agency.

Proponents of school-based financing argue that schools will make more efficient decisions about how to spend resources on site needs than the central office (see, e.g., Caldwell & Spinks, 1992). Yet, there is little agreement (or even discussion) about the way in which efficiency should be measured in K-12 education and the implications of applying any one of several alternative methods. Leanna Stiefel, Amy Ellen Schwartz, and Ross H. Rubenstein tackle these issues in Chapter 3. They review four methods for measuring school efficiency (production functions, data envelopment analysis [DEA], adjusted performance measures, and cost functions), describe their advantages and disadvantages, and discuss practical issues that each presents, such as how to choose inputs and outcomes. The authors caution us that there is no one best way of measuring efficiency. Different uses of efficiency measures—providing information, reorganizing schools, allocating resources to schools, and incentives for teachers—require different measures, methods, and/or interpretation.

Design and Implementation of School-Based Financing Systems

The three chapters in the second section describe the design and implementation of school-based financing systems in English-speaking democracies around the world. In the mid-1980s, Quentin Thompson and his colleagues at Coopers and Lybrand helped the English government conceptualize a decentralized management and finance system for education. The resulting legislation, the 1988 Education Reform Act, revolutionized how that country governs and finances its schools. Local education agencies (LEAs) now allocate most resources to schools through a block grant; schools are self-managed enterprises, with the oversight of a school governing board. In Chapter 4, Thompson and John Lakin examine how LEAs and schools responded to this major transfer of power, discuss issues that arose in the early years of implementation, and identify current implementation issues, such as the differentiation of funding between different levels of education and the treatment of special needs students. They are quite bullish about the results of the law, finding that the new system has created more responsive schools and a more transparent and open system of funding. Odden and Busch (1998) provide more detail on the English funding structure and describe formulas that several diverse local education agencies developed under this centrally defined budgetary framework.

In Chapter 5, Brian Caldwell and Peter Hill describe the experience one state "down under," Victoria, Australia, has had with school-based financing. Victoria has provided significant school decentralization, including some budgetary authority, since the early 1980s. A new liberal government elected in 1992 sought to make all schools self-managed, however, by granting them power and authority over virtually their entire school budget as well as the recruitment and selection of professional and nonprofessional staff. Within the context of a new curriculum and standards framework, including a new state student testing system, Victoria turned more than 1,700 schools into charter schools between 1993 and 1996. The authors, both central figures in the design of these "schools of the future," describe the rationale for and the structure of the state's decentralized funding structure, which sends nearly 90% of Victoria's education budget directly to individual schools. They also discuss implementation issues and the recommendations of a government commission, chaired by Caldwell, to enact a stronger needs-based, per pupil funding formula.

The final chapter in this section focuses on how one school system, the Edmonton (Alberta) Public Schools, managed the delegation of significant management and budgetary authority to its 190 schools between 1972 and 1989. In Chapter 6, Lloyd W. Ozembloski and

Daniel J. Brown describe the three phases of change—adoption, implementation, and continuation—and identify four clusters of factors that account for the successful enactment and institutionalization of Edmonton's reform. The authors suggest that the positive orientation of each of these clusters—sources of the policy initiative, support gathering, attributes of the decentralization initiative, and district context—is a necessary condition for a change to school-based management to take place. Policymakers (and researchers) will find this framework helpful in assessing the strengths and weaknesses of site-based management plans and in developing strategies to address potential problems.

How Schools Allocate and Use Financial Resources

The book concludes with three chapters that look at how schools, school districts, and states in the United States allocate and use financial resources. In Chapter 7, Allan Odden describes school-based funding formulas in five large districts in North America: Broward County (FL), Cincinnati (OH), Edmonton (Alberta, Canada), Pittsburgh (PA), and Seattle (WA). These formulas represent the state-of-the-art in school-based financing at the close of the 1990s and show how policymakers are beginning to link funding to district strategies to improve student performance, such as the adoption of comprehensive school reform models. The author uses a common framework to compare elements of the different programs: (1) basic pupil allocation; (2) curriculum enhancements, such as for magnet programs and language programs; (3) specific needs for students with disabilities, limited English proficiency, or socioeconomic disadvantage; and (4) specific school needs, such as small size. Odden also discusses how these five school funding systems address issues of equity, transparency, effectiveness, and assignment of functions to the schools versus the central office.

In Chapter 8, Carolyn D. Herrington examines the emergence of performance-based budgeting as a way of holding public agencies accountable for their use of tax dollars. Florida is a leader in this movement; it is one of only two states that have created formal mechanisms for imposing incentives and disincentives based on agency performance. Herrington provides an overview of performance-based budgeting in Florida and then describes the state's efforts to bring K-12 education into this process. She describes the assumptions guiding the development of a system of accountability and budgeting based on performance measures and identifies a number of design and implementation issues, including how to measure outcomes, determining who (which units) should be held accountable, and assessing the effect of incentive funding on the state's highly equalized school finance system. Herrington also weighs the costs of performance-based budgeting, particularly of collecting and analyzing data, against its potential benefits, such as more effective use of resources in schools and school districts.

Finally, in Chapter 9, Margaret E. Goertz and Mark C. Duffy analyze how reforming schools actually use educational dollars, a key issue in assessing the efficacy of school-based financing. School-based financing is a means to an end—better schools and higher levels of student achievement. Although many of the chapters in this book are concerned with the myriad technical issues related to funding schools fairly and adequately, an even more important issue is having schools use those resources in more effective ways, in ways that boost student performance. Goertz and Duffy examine how 24 school districts, selected for their reputation in pursuing innovative reforms to improve teaching and learning, allocate resources to their schools, and how a sample of elementary schools in 11 of these districts use these resources. They found that most of the districts in their study grant schools only marginal budgetary authority, usually for the use of federal Title I and state compensatory education dollars, professional development funds, and instructional materials grants. Schools used student performance data to inform the allocation of these discretionary dollars, and generally spent these funds on additional staff, particularly reading specialists and instructional aides. The few schools with school-based budgetary authority allocate their resources in the same way as schools with limited flexibility, raising questions of what factors facilitate and inhibit change under site-based financing systems.

Conclusion

These chapters address many aspects of school-based financing, and the authors bring a multiplicity of perspectives to the topic. Five sets of questions emerge from this work, however.

First, what services, expenditures, and management functions—if any—should be retained at the central level? The districts, states, and countries highlighted in this book devolve different percentages of their budgets directly to the school site, ranging from 49% in Seattle to nearly 90% in Victoria, Australia. This variation reflects differences in functions retained at the central office, such as transportation, capital expenditures, instructional and pupil support services, and services for special needs students. Similarly, districts differ in the extent to which they monitor school-site budget decisions and expenditures. What criteria should states and districts use in making these determinations?

Second, how do states and districts ensure equity in the allocation of resources and students' access to educational opportunities? What special student and school factors should be included in allocation formulas? How can formulas accommodate variations in student need across schools without creating perverse incentives to identify students for special programs (an issue raised currently in state funding formulas)? What criteria should be used to measure fairness?

Third, how should school-based funding systems be phased in? How long should states and districts allow for their implementation? At what point should schools become responsible for the actual cost of their staff? Which functions should be decentralized first? What support, if any, should the central office provide to schools? How can central offices restructure to support school-based budgeting?

Fourth, how much flexibility should schools have in spending their dollars? States currently impose numerous input and process requirements on their districts. Should these be extended to the relationship between districts and schools? For example, should districts set any minimum standards for the qualifications and kinds of staff employed in schools? If not, how does a district ensure that the state's requirements are met?

The fourth question is inexorably linked to the fifth and most important: How should states and districts hold schools accountable for the use of their dollars? The theory and practice of school-based management argue that schools know best how to teach their students and can make resource allocation decisions to do so. Explicit in all that is written is a movement away from input and process accountability to accountability for student performance. But in the final analysis, if the primary accountability mechanism is student performance, what happens with failing schools?

Acknowledgments

The Consortium for Policy Research in Education (CPRE) supported the preparation of five chapters of this book (Berne & Stiefel; Picus; Thompson & Lakin; Caldwell & Hill; Goertz & Duffy) through grant #OERI-R308A60003 from the U.S. Department of Education's National Institute on Educational Governance, Finance, Policymaking and Management. Opinions expressed in these chapters are those of the authors, and do not necessarily reflect the views of the National Institute on Educational Governance, Finance, Policymaking and Management, Office of Educational Research and Improvement, U.S. Department of Education or the institutional partners of CPRE.

We appreciate the administrative and editorial support provided by Lisa Armstrong at the University of Wisconsin and Anne Burns at the University of Pennsylvania. Doris Showers (University of Pennsylvania) also provided valuable secretarial support on this project.

Note

1. The Consortium for Policy Research in Education (CPRE) brings together researchers from five universities: the University of Pennsylvania, Harvard University, Stanford University, the University of Michigan, and the University of Wisconsin-Madison. CPRE conducts research on issues such as education reform, student and teacher standards, state and local policy making, education governance, school finance, teacher compensation, and student incentives.

References

Abbott v. Burke, 153 N.J. 480 (1998).

Berne, R., & Stiefel, L. (1994). Measuring equity at the school level: The finance perspective. *Journal of Education Finance, 16*(4), 405-421.

Berne, R., Stiefel, L., & Moser, M. (1997). The coming of age of school-level finance data. *Journal of Education Finance, 22*(3), 246-254.

Bodilly, S. (1998). *Lessons from New American Schools' scale-up phase: Prospects for bringing designs to multiple sites.* Santa Monica, CA: RAND.

Busch, C., & Odden, A. (1997). Introduction to the special issue—Improving policy and results with school-level data: A synthesis of multiple perspectives. *Journal of Education Finance, 22*(3), 225-245.

Caldwell, B. J., & Spinks, J. M. (1992). *Leading the self-managing school.* London: Falmer.

Chambers, J., Parrish, T., Goertz, M., Marder, C., & Padilla, C. (1993). *Translating dollars into services: Chapter 1 resources in the context of state and local resources for education.* Palo Alto, CA: American Institutes for Research.

Clune, W. H., & White, P. A. (1988). *School-based management: Institutional variation, implementation and issues for further research.* New Brunswick, NJ: Consortium for Policy Research in Education.

Cohen, M. (1983). Instructional, management and social conditions in effective schools. In A. Odden & L. D. Webb (Eds.), *School finance and school improvement: Linkages for the 1980s* (pp. 17-50). Cambridge, MA: Ballinger.

Cohen, M. C. (1997). Issues in school-level analysis of education expenditure data. *Journal of Education Finance, 22*(3), 255-279.

Farland, G. (1997). Collection of fiscal and staffing data at the school-site level. *Journal of Education Finance, 22*(3), 280-290.

Goertz, M. E. (1997). The challenges of collecting school-based data. *Journal of Education Finance, 22*(3), 291-302.

Goertz, M. E., & Stiefel, L. (1998). School-level resource allocation in urban public schools [Special issue]. *Journal of Education Finance, 23*(4).

Hertert, L. (1995). Does equal funding for districts mean equal funding for classroom students? Evidence from California. In L. O. Picus & J. L. Wattenbarger (Eds.), *Where does the money go? Resource reallocation in elementary and secondary schools* (pp. 71-84). Thousand Oaks, CA: Corwin.

Hill, P. T., Pierce, L. C., & Guthrie, J. W. (1997). *Reinventing public education: How contracting can transform America's schools.* Chicago: University of Chicago Press.

Miles, K. H. (1995). Freeing resources for improving schools: A case study of teacher allocation in Boston public schools. *Educational Evaluation and Policy Analysis, 17*(4), 476-493.

Murphy, J., & Hallinger, P. (1993). *Restructuring schooling: Learning from ongoing efforts.* Newbury Park, CA: Corwin.

Odden, A. (1992). *Rethinking school finance: An agenda for the 1990s.* San Francisco: Jossey-Bass.

Odden, A. (in press). Case study 3: North America (USA and Canada). In K. Ross & R. Levacic (Eds.), *Needs-based resource reallocation in education via formula funding of schools.* Paris: UNESCO, International Institute for Educational Planning.

Odden, A., & Busch, C. (1998). *Financing schools for high performance: Strategies for improving the use of educational resources.* San Francisco: Jossey-Bass.

Odden, A., & Kotowski, N. (1992). Financing public school choice: Policy issues and options. In A. Odden (Ed.), *Rethinking school finance: An agenda for the 1990s* (pp. 225-259). San Francisco: Jossey-Bass.

Picus, L. O. (1997). Using school-level finance data: Endless opportunity or bottomless pit? *Journal of Education Finance, 22*(3), 317-330.

Speakman, S., Cooper, B., Holsomback, H., May, J., Sampieri, R., & Maloney, L. (1997). The three Rs of education finance reform: Re-thinking, re-tooling, and re-evaluating school-site information. *Journal of Education Finance, 22*(4), 337-367.

Stiefel, L., Berne, R., Goertz, M., Sherman, J., Hess, G. A., Jr., Moser, M., Rubenstein, R., & Iatarola, P. (1996). *School-level resource allocation in urban public schools. Final report to the Andrew W. Mellon Foundation.* New York: New York University, Robert F. Wagner Graduate School of Public Service.

Stringfield, S., Ross, S., & Smith, L. (1996). *Bold plans for restructuring: The New American Schools designs.* Mahwah, NJ: Lawrence Erlbaum.

Wohlstetter, P., Van Kirk, A. N., Robertson, P., & Mohrman, S. A. (1997). *Organizing for successful school-based management.* Alexandria, VA: Association for Supervision and Curriculum Development.

About the Contributors

Robert Berne is Vice-President for Academic Development at New York University (NYU) and Professor of Public Administration in NYU's Robert F. Wagner Graduate School of Public Service. Previously, he was dean of the Wagner School and codirector of NYU's Institute for Education and Social Policy. His research has focused on school finance and education policy, with a particular emphasis on equity issues. He has written and edited numerous books and articles on education policy and government finance, including *The Measurement of Equity in School Finance* (with Leanna Stiefel) and *Hard Lessons, Public Schools and Privatization* (with Carol Ascher and Norm Fruchter). He was the lead editor of the 1994 AEFA yearbook, *Outcome Equity in Education.* He was also the director of policy research for the New York State Temporary Commission on State Aid to Local School Districts and executive director of the Temporary State Commission on New York City School Governance.

Daniel J. Brown is Professor of Educational Administration at the University of British Columbia in Vancouver. He has written books and articles on school district decentralization. His most recent book is *Schools with Heart: Voluntarism and Public Education,* and he is currently working on a study of traditional schools.

Brian J. Caldwell is Professor of Education and Dean of the Faculty of Education at the University of Melbourne. His interest in school-based financing spans more than two decades, commencing with his doctoral research in the mid-1970s on pioneering approaches in Alberta, Canada. His research on the links between school-based financing and educational outcomes laid the foundations for a publishing trilogy with Jim Spinks: *The Self-Managing School* (1988), *Leading the Self-Managing School* (1992) and *Beyond the Self-Managing School* (1998), the first two helping shape developments in several nations, notably Australia, Britain, Hong Kong and New Zealand. He has chaired committees of inquiry on school-based financing in Tasmania, Australia and Victoria, Australia, with the latter being the largest system of public schools anywhere to have decentralized more than 90% of funds to schools.

Mark C. Duffy is Research Specialist with the Consortium for Policy Research in Education (CPRE) at the University of Pennsylvania. Before joining CPRE, he did his graduate work in public policy at the Eagleton Institute of Politics at Rutgers University.

Margaret E. Goertz is Professor in the Graduate School of Education at the University of Pennsylvania and Codirector of the Consortium for Policy Research in Education. Previously, she was executive director of the Education Policy Research Division of the Educational Testing Service in Princeton, New Jersey. A past president of the American Education Finance Association, her research focuses on issues of education finance, state education reform policies, and state and federal programs for special needs students. Her current research activities include studies of standards-based reform in education and the allocation of school-level resources. She has written or edited several books, including *From Cashbox to the Classroom: The Struggle for Fiscal Reform and Educational Change in New Jersey* (1997) with William Firestone and Gary Natriello.

Carolyn D. Herrington is Associate Professor of Education Policy and Director of Florida Education Policy Studies at the Learning Systems Institute at Florida State University. Her research interests focus on educational policy and finance, public school governance, and the changing conditions of children. She is the coauthor with Catherine Emihovich of *Sex, Kids, and Politics: School-Based Health Services* (1997). She has written and edited numerous other articles, book chapters, monographs, and book reviews on education finance and policy. She has served on the board of directors of the American Education Finance Association and was recently appointed to the Policy Circle of the National Policy Board for Educational Administration.

Peter W. Hill is Foundation Professor of Leadership and Management, Head of the Department of Education Policy and Management, and Deputy Dean, Faculty of Education, University of Melbourne. He is Chair, Board of Directors, Australian Principals Center and a member of the Standards Council of the Teaching Profession. He was formerly Chief General Manager of the Department of Education in Victoria. Since joining the University of Melbourne, where he also serves as Director for the Centre for Applied Educational Research, he has provided the state education system with a powerful research base for school reform, especially for the early and middle years of schooling. His work with Carmel Crevola on early literacy has been taken up in Australia, Britain, Canada and the United States. This research-policy-practice link has helped shape approaches to the allocation of resources through schemes for school-based financing.

John Lakin is a Principal Consultant in the education and training group in PricewaterhouseCoopers (UK) and has managed all the firm's consultancy work in the schools sector in the United Kingdom over the last 7 years. He has extensive experience in school funding and management issues in the United Kingdom and has also worked for governments in several other countries on school reform projects. His professional background is as an economist, and he worked for 8 years for a local education authority in the United Kingdom before joining PricewaterhouseCoopers.

Allan Odden is Professor of Educational Administration at the University of Wisconsin-Madison and Codirector of the Consortium for Policy Research in Education (CPRE). He directs the CPRE Education Finance Research program and is the principal investigator for the CPRE Teacher Compensation Project. A past president of the American Education Finance Association, he worked with the Education Commission of the States for a decade, serving as assistant executive director, director of policy analysis and research, and director of its educational finance center. His current research is focused on school-based finance, school-based management, and teacher compensation. He has written widely, publishing more than 170 journal articles, book chapters, and research reports and 20 books and monographs. His most recent books include *Paying Teachers for What They Know and Do: New and Smarter Compensation Strategies to Improve Schools* (1997) with Carolyn Kelley, and *Financing Schools for High Performance* (1998) with Carolyn Busch.

Lloyd W. Ozembloski is Principal of the Holy Family School, a Roman Catholic K-9 school in Grimshaw, Alberta. A graduate of the Faculty of Education at the University of British Columbia, his dissertation concerned the change to school-based management in Edmonton and Langley, B.C.

Lawrence O. Picus is Professor in the School of Education at the University of Southern California, where he directs the Center for Research in Education Finance (CREF). CREF research focuses on issues of school finance and productivity. He is past president of the American Education Finance Association. He is the coauthor of *School Finance: A Policy Perspective* (1992) with Allan Odden, and of *Principles of School Business Administration* (1995) with R. Craig Wood, David Thompson, and Don I. Tharpe. In addition, he is the senior editor of the 1995 yearbook of the American Education Finance Association, *Where Does the Money Go? Resource Allocation in Elementary and Secondary Schools* (1995). He has published numerous articles in professional journals.

Ross H. Rubenstein is Assistant Professor of Public Administration and Urban Studies with a joint appointment in the School of Policy Studies and the College of Education at Georgia State University, where he heads the Education Finance Studies Project. He is coauthor (with Amy Ellen Schwartz and Leanna Stiefel) of a chapter on education finance in the *Handbook of Public Finance* (1988) and has published his research in the *Journal of Education Finance* and *Public Budgeting and Finance.*

Amy Ellen Schwartz is Associate Professor at New York University's Wagner School of Public Service, specializing in public finance, policy analysis, and applied econometrics. Her research spans a broad range in state and local public finance, focusing recently on issues in K-12 education. In addition to her work on measuring and improving efficiency and productivity in public schools, her current education-related research addresses both equity and efficiency considerations in the financing of education, intergovernmental aid, and the role of the private sector. Her work has been published in a variety of academic and professional journals, including *The American Economic Review, The Journal of Public Economics, The National Tax Journal, Public Finance Quarterly,* and *Regional Science and Urban Economics.*

Leanna Stiefel is Professor of Economics and Director of the Public and Nonprofit Management and Policy program at the Robert F. Wagner Graduate School of Public Service at New York University. Her current research on elementary and secondary education includes measuring equity of school-based finance systems, evaluating outcomes of school-based budgeting, and measuring efficiency and productivity at the school level. She is the author of *Statistical Analysis for Public and Nonprofit Managers,* and *The Measurement of Equity in School Finance* (with Robert Berne), as well as numerous articles and chapters in professional journals and books.

Quentin Thompson has been the partner in PricewaterhouseCoopers (UK) responsible for all the firm's education consultancy work in Britain for nearly 15 years. He has been responsible for over 300 projects in education and training in the United Kingdom, including the original study for the UK government in 1988 of the feasibility of introducing local management of schools. He holds two visiting professorships (London and Southern California) and is a member of a small panel directly advising the president of the World Bank on education policies. Prior to joining PricewaterhouseCoopers, he taught at all levels, and for 3 years was an advisor to the UK prime minister on education and training.

PART I

A Conceptual Overview

ONE

Issues in School Site-Based Financing in Large Cities in the United States

ROBERT BERNE

LEANNA STIEFEL

An emerging trend in school finance involves the ascendancy of the school as a decision-making unit, as contrasted with the recent past, when decision-making power was conceptualized and operationalized at the district and state level. The growing debate about charter schools, school-based governance, and management approaches in cities such as Chicago and Denver, and the steady increase in school choice programs in American cities, all place a greater emphasis on the school level than was the case even a decade ago. And in neighboring Canada, the success of site-based management in Edmonton, Alberta, has received significant attention.

To varying degrees, all these strategies presume that financial decision making takes place at the school level. Yet, remarkably, how financial decision making might be defined and implemented at the

3

school level is underdeveloped in the education finance literature. We hope to fill some of the gaps in this chapter.

We start with a basic question: What is school site-based financing (SSBF)? It is desirable to answer this question before discussing issues that may arise with its implementation, and we devote the first section of this chapter to describing general characteristics of a generic SSBF system. The second part of the chapter develops a framework for thinking about fiscal functions and goals; the framework is then used to discuss aspects of SSBF in the third section. The final section of the chapter outlines major empirical questions about SSBF that we believe need to be studied.

What Is School Site-Based Financing?

To finance schools, a variety of levels of organizations and governments must be involved in *raising, distributing,* and *spending* fiscal resources. SSBF could apply to any or all three of these stages. Schools could be responsible for *raising* revenues for their operations, as are schools run by private, religious, and nonsectarian nonprofit organizations in the United States. For public schools, this could resemble an enrollment-driven formula system or some kind of publicly financed voucher system, whereby revenues flow to a school based strictly on the number (and characteristics) of students in the school, perhaps with (or without) the addition of some privately raised funds. It could also mean giving schools control of some taxing authority in their catchment area, although this approach is much less likely. For purposes of this chapter, we will not address these more radical ways of changing the revenue raising functions of schools. Instead, we will assume that current public revenue raising systems, involving combinations of local, state, and federal revenue, with the state government ultimately responsible for the state's education system, remain in effect.

The traditional U.S. system of education finance relies on local education agencies (districts) as primary fiscal agents of the state (with a few exceptions, such as Hawaii). Once revenues are raised, presumably by the school districts, they must be *distributed* to the education production units. These units are usually considered to be schools, although other possibilities include divisions (elementary, middle, high, special education), subdivisions (community school districts, such as the ones in New York City), and houses, programs, or classrooms within schools. For now, we will use the term *school*, although what we discuss could apply to other possibilities below the district level.

The districts are responsible for distributing revenues to the schools consistent with various types of guidelines or regulations established by the states and federal government. In most cases, despite special, bilingual, and compensatory education regulations, districts have significant freedom to decide how to allocate revenues to their schools. In large part, this is because the greatest portion of funding to the district is composed of state general aid and locally raised revenues, which come with few restrictions on how they must be spread among schools. We assume that the way revenues are distributed to schools, including whether they could come directly from the state rather than through the district, is part of what is meant by SSBF.

Finally, revenues must be *spent*. How the funds are spent and which organizations have control over spending decisions have traditionally been the purview of districts, state and federal governments (through constraints on intergovernmental revenues), union contracts, the courts, and a myriad of informal interest groups. Districts have had considerable say both because they have traditionally centralized many functions (transportation, food service, capital, maintenance, and some curriculum decisions) and because they have kept tight budgetary control over objects of expenditures, not allowing schools to make reallocation decisions in the budgeting or implementation stages.

Regulations are important because they can specify which pupils must have special services and sometimes how those services must be provided. Unions have significant formal influence through contracts that often include specifications of class sizes, types of teachers that must be present in each school, and rules for hiring, firing, and transferring teachers. Rulings in court cases have been influential in how resources are spent to meet desegregation and special education goals. Interest groups composed of parents and other advocates are sometimes effective in influencing spending decisions. As a result of the effects of these forces, a discussion of SSBF needs to include how spending decisions will be different if made at the school rather than district level. Thus, our definition of SSBF focuses on how revenues are distributed to schools as well as how they are spent by those schools.

Framework for Understanding and Evaluating Fiscal Functions

Fiscal operations in any system involve four recurring functions: *planning, implementing, evaluating,* and *reporting.* The *planning* function is generally undertaken, if at all, during the budgeting process. Budgeting as a function is complex, uncertain, political, and may or may not be related well to an organization's goals. If the budget of projected revenues and expenditures is devised solely on the basis of previous budgets and uses unrealistic assumptions, then it may produce a poor planning document. If it is done with an effort to link resources with policy goals, it may serve the planning function well. *Implementation* is undertaken by agencies (in this case, schools) with a varying degree of control by a central organization. *Evaluation* is carried out more in the ideal world than in reality. Ideally, regular evaluation of budget and spending decisions would be undertaken and fed back into subsequent budget cycles. *Reporting* involves the production and dissemination of financial reports and statements, at various levels of detail, that show what was actually spent and raised. Often the reports compare actual expenditures and revenues to what is in the plan (budget).

These four functions are performed to accomplish three broad categories of goals: *control, fairness,* and accomplishment of *results* (including effectiveness and efficiency results). A fiscal system must be able to control finances to prevent deficits as well as fraud and abuse. In the school finance area, financial systems can be judged on the basis of the fairness of the allocation of resources among various stakeholders. Assessing fairness involves examining allocations of resources among states, districts, schools, other organizational units, and types of students. Accomplishment of results ties the fiscal functions to performance goals. Most recently, these goals have emphasized achievement of learning, often measured by test scores, as well as effectiveness and efficiency (Hatry, Alexander, & Fountain, 1990; Ladd, 1996a, 1996b).

Application of Framework
for Fiscal Functions to SSBF

Table 1.1 summarizes how the distribution and spending stages of SSBF fit into the matrix of functions and goals of fiscal systems. We next turn to a general discussion of the matrix, although we do not go into substantial depth for each of the 12 cells.

Planning or Budgeting

The planning or budgeting stage (Row 1 in Table 1.1) involves both the distribution of resources to the schools and the spending of resources at the school level. Two of the most important issues in budgeting and control are (1) which areas of distribution and spending should be site based versus more centralized; and (2) to what extent the budget should be built from the bottom up versus from the top down (Cell 1.1). Principles that could be useful for thinking about the site versus central decisions are economies of scale, externalities, and accountability. Certain functions, such as student transportation or textbook purchasing, may be more cost-effective if done (and thus planned) centrally. Planning and financing of major capital programs could be accomplished at lower costs if carried out by more central levels of the organization. For many other functions, it becomes an empirical question to decide exactly which functions are less expensive for similar quality when centralized.

Central control may be appropriate to avoid negative externalities. For example, in many urban districts, there is very high mobility of students between schools during the academic year. If curriculum goals are not standardized to some degree, mobile students will impose costs on stable students due to time spent trying to reorient new students to different curricula. But central control over too much curriculum may run counter to the basic premise of school autonomy for teaching and learning decisions. Answers to these kinds of questions about trade-offs need to guide the design of the budgeting process.

Finally, the area of accountability for results is also likely to be divided as to control, not only between the school and the district but also with the state playing a role. Accountability is one of the least

TABLE 1.1. Fiscal Functions and Goals

		Goals	
Function	Control	Fairness	Results: Performance and Efficiency
Planning (Budgeting)	D, S Central versus site Bottom up/top down	D, S Process Formulas Horizontal, vertical, equal opportunity equity	D, S What is accountability system? How is it used in planning?
Implementing	S Central versus site	S Who is involved?	S What decisions at what levels produce what results?
Evaluating	D, S Central versus site—which is efficient? How is it working?	D, S Values need to be specified Horizontal, vertical, equal opportunity (selected measures, selected years)	D Do incentives work? S How to measure results? How to know if results achieved? Why do results vary across schools?
Reporting	S Variance analysis How to teach public to read audit reports and financial statements?	D, S How much information and in what form?	D, S What reports? What is the effect of reports?

D = Distributing of funds
S = Spending of funds

well-developed of the planning activities, and currently links to the budget process are quite primitive. This area is crucial for the success of decentralization's performance goals, and thus it is a candidate for special attention by researchers.

Budgets can be constructed in a number of ways, ranging from complete bottom up to full top down. A true belief in the value of SSBF implies a fair amount of bottom-up budgeting, whereby sites propose and justify spending plans within broad guidelines from the district (center). The current practice in most urban districts in the United States is to notify the site about the size of its budget, perhaps without ever producing a site-based budget document at all.[1] Prior to SSBF, many urban schools had only limited authority for the planning of spending decisions. If SSBF is to become a reality, a necessary condition will be some movement of information and participation in the planning for distribution and spending decisions down to the school level.

Fairness in budgeting involves the distribution and spending functions (Cell 1.2). Issues to consider here are the processes and formulas used and the criteria to assess those processes and formulas. If both schools and the center play a role in budgeting, then a common approach across all schools may be useful for the assessment of fairness. What are some of issues involved in planning from a fairness perspective? We think that the framework we have used successfully at the district level works well at the school level as well—to look at horizontal, vertical, and equal opportunity issues with the student as the object of concern (Berne & Stiefel, 1984, 1994). For example, how is base funding, which is available to instruct all students, planned to be distributed to schools and spent on students (horizontal equity)? How are compensatory, bilingual, and special education monies to be distributed and spent with relationship to student needs (vertical equity)? How are different geographic areas of the district or different ethnic and racial groups treated in the distribution and spending processes (equal opportunity)? In addition, attention should be paid to the planning process to determine whether a fair and clearly understood method for distributing funds is in place. Obviously, value judgments about the relative importance of various kinds of equity will have to be made, and the process of making these judgments will certainly be complex, even more so if schools are actively involved in the distribution and spending processes at the budgeting stage. Historically, the distribution and spending functions have been centralized, and often the decisions are opaque, although not apolitical (Breslin, 1987; Division of High Schools, 1995-96; Stiefel, Berne, Iatarola, & Fruchter, 1998).

The third goal for budgeting involves planning for results (Cell 1.3). This is a relatively new area for school finance, with some promising research results becoming available (Ladd, 1996a, 1996b). To distribute funds at the school level and spend those funds to help promote results, accountability systems with clearly stated goals need to be in place. Specifically, to motivate schools positively and to encourage efficiency (ratio of outputs or outcomes to costs), the schools need to know what outputs or outcomes are expected of them and how those outputs and outcomes will be measured. The outcomes that have been most heavily researched are test scores (c.f., South Carolina and Dallas) and somewhat more elaborate school assessments (Kentucky). The question of how funding can motivate the achievement of the established goals is far from being known, however (Behn, 1997).

Implementing

The second row of Table 1.1 involves the implementation of fiscal functions, which in turn focuses on the actual spending (as opposed to planning for spending) of school resources. The control function is especially crucial here (Cell 2.1). Large districts with many schools traditionally have been leery of allowing much spending control at the local level for fear of fiscal mismanagement or incompetence that leads to budget overruns or spending out of compliance with district policies, court rulings, or state and federal regulations. In addition, there is fear of outright fraud or abuse. SSBF would surely involve more discretion for the school, giving school sites not only control over their budgeted lines but probably some control over moving funds between objects or programs to meet needs and conditions that change over the year. In other words, SSBF would probably involve much less micromanagement of the quotidian spending decisions than now exists.

Why would more site-based discretion over actual spending be desirable? With more control at the school, it would be possible to reward good performance. Or increased school-level discretion may be a way to promote experimentation in trying to reach goals where either there is incomplete knowledge on the most appropriate teaching and learning approach or local conditions are not known at the district level. In other words, under the theory that smaller units can be entrepreneurial in their decisions (e.g., substituting one seller or product for another as the opportunity arises during a year), or can know better when a particular use of funds for a program or group of students is yielding poor results (e.g., switching to a more promising method), site-based decision making could become an important ingredient to achieve better results. As a more specific example, if an English teacher resigns, perhaps a school would want to use the resources to purchase a part-time teacher and two aides rather than replacing the teacher, to give more small group attention to students in particular classes. Or perhaps a bilingual teacher would serve the school's needs better than an English teacher.

Control over budget overruns and fraud and abuse can be accomplished in ways other than strict centralized line-item control of expenditures. Variance reports comparing budget to spending can be generated regularly (even on-line, in real time) and investigated if and when they show significant deviations. Fiscal agents, such as business managers, can become professionalized. School fiscal reports can be audited by organizations outside the school system.

Fairness in implementing the actual spending decision addresses issues of process and equity (Cell 2.2). If control over spending is more site based, which individuals or groups will have a say over the implementation and how will the resources actually be spent? At present, in large districts, the principal is the only one likely to be involved in decision making, and sometimes the control is so tight that not even the principal is much involved (Stiefel et al., 1996). A fair process, which could vary from district to district and perhaps even across schools in a district, would need to be worked out among the major stakeholders. For example, it could involve teachers, parents, administrators, students, and community residents, along with the principal and perhaps a business manager. Beyond the process, the fairness of the actual spending may be addressed in the implementation stage, with information on spending equity disclosed as decisions are being made.

In terms of the nexus among implementation, spending, and results, we again need to ask how the theory of increased school-level spending authority promotes better outcomes or efficiency (Cell 2.3). One theory, expressed above, is that what works educationally depends so much on local conditions that school-level experimentation is desirable. For example, it is difficult to believe that a central spending policy will be ideal in New York City, with close to 1,100 schools. As long as there are adequate controls, diverse spending decisions may lead to workable strategies for accomplishing goals. Or, perhaps if more fiscal freedom is desired on the part of schools, such freedom could be a reward for good performance.

Evaluating

This function involves both distributing and spending resources across the three goals of control, fairness, and results (Row 3 in Table 1.1). Evaluation of the control function is particularly important because of the longstanding concerns that control will be effective only if maintained centrally. Now, with the advent of on-line, distributed computer systems, site-based decision making with effective controls is possible. Moreover, the same systems that support the school-based decision making can be used for evaluation. Management functions such as purchasing and personnel can be linked with finance to enable discretion at the school, and information can be used to determine the effectiveness of these operations.

Fairness in the distribution and spending functions is a complex issue to evaluate. Even if the three-part framework of horizontal, vertical, and equal opportunity equity is adopted, many choices need to be made to implement an evaluation. But, again, the computer systems needed to support school-based finance could be used to provide regular reports on equity, once choices about value judgments have been made (Rubenstein, 1998; Stiefel, Rubenstein, & Berne, 1998).

Evaluation of results entails both evaluations of outcomes achieved by schools as well as assessments of the causes of the variation in results, and in both cases, quantitative and qualitative approaches will be necessary. This area is the most underdeveloped of the three goals and will require substantial research support and creativity.

Reporting

SSBF systems require that good information be reported, both internally for managerial purposes and externally for accountability

(Row 4 in Table 1.1). In the control function, reporting would entail, at a minimum, regular variance reports and various financial statements and reports. Variance reports are generally used for internal control, showing both decentralized decision makers and central authorities how each unit is spending funds in comparison to the budget. Sophisticated reports that show causes of differences (variances) can be developed, but questions arise about the extent of reporting appropriate from a cost-effectiveness perspective. Additional questions arise surrounding the training needed to generate informed readers, particularly with external stakeholders such as parents. Finally, the issue of whether to standardize reports for all schools epitomizes the tension between central control and local autonomy.

Financial reports showing the actual expenditures of funds are likely to be an important part of SSBF. Governmental agencies and the Governmental Accounting Standards Board (GASB) could be helpful places to begin to look for models of reporting. GASB has been researching issues of how to report financial results so that they are both comprehensible and responsive to the informed public's needs (Berne, 1992; Hatry, Fountain, Sullivan, & Kremer, 1990). For both internal and external reporting, it is a complex task to decide what kind of information (by function, object, program, output, and/or outcome) is appropriate and at what level of detail. The disclosure objectives for external reporting are not always the same as the managerial and policy objectives for internal reporting, and, along with differences in reader knowledge and expectations, will make report design and issuance an important and potentially controversial topic.

To assess fairness, some of the work of the evaluation effort should be reported to the external stakeholders. Once again, the complex task of arriving at the right types and amount of information for various constituents will be a challenge. A complete research report could be overwhelming, and would probably be helpful to only a small segment of the interested public. Possibly selected indicators of equity (as well as results) could be reported with the financial information. Any consideration of external reporting should include the relationship with the media, because print and broadcast media appear to be increasing their coverage of educational issues.

Reporting about the results goal is particularly complex because the reports themselves may cause changes in the results. This could be good, if, for example, community pressure, perhaps through reporting in the media, were brought to bear on poorly performing schools, and that pressure led to improvements. The reports could be harmful if they were too narrowly focused and led to undue concentration on specific reported results or the neglect of other unreported ones. Reports can serve a variety of purposes, such as accountability, internal management, and regulation (Stiefel & Sparrow, 1996). The types of reports required and their effects on how schools respond will differ depending on purpose and audience.

Empirical Questions About SSBF: Research Needed

A large number of issues about SSBF arose as we examined the topics in Table 1.1. We identify several here, discussing why they are important and what methods might be available to address them.

Centralization Versus Decentralization

Clearly one of the overriding issues in SSBF is the most effective mix between centralization and decentralization, an issue being debated in other spheres, such as levels of governmental responsibilities in the United States and abroad, and private sector corporate governance and management. The criteria to judge this issue are complex and need to take into account several factors.

First, will outcomes vary with the greater decentralization that SSBF implies? This is one of those fundamental questions that many people in the field will answer without hesitation ("Yes, they will improve"), but social science research has yet to provide definitive answers. Perhaps decentralization will provide higher levels of outcomes in learning, but also a greater variation. Perhaps it is the avoidance of the low end of results that contributes to the staying power of centralization. (Witness the recent recentralization of some governance functions in the New York City elementary and middle school system, in response to both corruption and low performance in about one third of the 32 community school districts.) The question of how decentralization of financing functions will or can affect the performance of schools (mean, median, variance, etc.) is a highly underresearched question.

Second, what are the cost issues for centralized versus decentralized activities? And, equally important, how do the cost differences relate to the differences in outcomes? We have always assumed that many activities in school districts are more economically performed at the central level—hiring, curriculum development, purchasing, professional development for staff, transportation—but these assumptions may no longer hold true, especially given improvements in technology.

Issues of externalities also need to be considered in the centralization/decentralization debate. If full decentralization means that each school is so unique that movement from school to school is difficult, then arguments for the centralization of some aspects of district policies may have merit. But these concerns are likely to be analogous to the debate over district versus state control of educational issues, which has been ongoing for some time. Whether or not we can use research to help address these issues is an open question.

Finally, how the issue of accountability is resolved in the centralization/decentralization spectrum is likely to be fertile ground for research. Accountability is probably more talked about and less studied than any phenomenon in education policy today, and unless researchers can improve their own productivity and creativity in this area, public policy is likely to move ahead without the benefits of research.

*How Can or Does a Decentralized
System Handle Financial Issues of
Control, Abuse, and Fraud?*

One of the longstanding concerns about decentralized systems is the opportunities that they provide for fraud and abuse. Somehow, centralized systems are seen as more capable of preventing improprieties in areas such purchasing, hiring, and contracting. Whether this is true or not is certainly a researchable question, and one where the education field could probably benefit from private sector research on control systems.

Research could also investigate the organizational culture issues that support or impede decentralized systems. The work on private schools may be useful for developing both concepts and empirical evidence regarding what it takes beyond the technical systems for a decentralized organization to develop the expectations and checks and balances to prevent fraud and abuse (Hill, Foster, & Gendler, 1990).

Finally, the related issue of general expenditure control (compared to budget, shifting among lines, spending unused balances) needs to be understood for its own sake and also for its relationship to the other goals of fairness and results. Central control systems are often seen as constraints by those in schools. Whether they actually accomplish their narrow objectives and how they contribute or detract from these other objectives are worthy of additional research.

What Processes Are Necessary
for Real Decentralization to Occur?

Although we have viewed SSBF from a largely rational and technical perspective in this chapter, we know from research and experience that phenomena such as decentralization have strong organizational and political dimensions. Thus, even if we could work through all the technical and financial aspects of SSBF, a plethora of other issues must be addressed if decentralization is to meet its conceptual potential. The nature of these organizational and political concepts, how they are likely to be operationalized such that decentralization is supported, and how we can measure the presence and absence of these concepts will present real challenges for researchers.

We may be able to draw on research on decentralization in other countries to help us develop an understanding in education. For example, there were no more centralized worlds than the command and control systems that were in effect in the former Soviet Union. As those newly formed nations vary in their attempts at decentralization, research can help us understand the legal, political, social, and economic dimensions of this process (Smoke, 1996). Similar research in the corporate world may shed some light on what we can expect in education. But this type of research requires us to articulate and evaluate the goals and objectives and ultimately how we will measure the effectiveness of decentralization, which is a real challenge for research as well.

Finally, even if our research and experience suggest that decentralization is the right way to go, the issue of how such an approach will be implemented in the world of education that has been built around district power and control is not simple. Currently many stakeholders—principals, teachers, and even parents—are not anxious to change the status quo, and their reasons and behaviors can be better understood through research.

How Do We Learn How to
Report Effectively to the Various
Stakeholders in a Decentralized System?

A proposition adopted from the theory of freely competitive economic systems is that a decentralized system needs good information to function effectively. The analogy for a decentralized public K-12 education system would be that the various stakeholders need relevant information to participate in making the system work fairly, efficiently, and with high achievement for students. But what kinds of information are needed and at what level of detail and frequency are things we know little about. We do know that other levels of government continue to struggle with how to provide the public with useful information about what they are doing (e.g., the efforts at the national level resulting from the Government Performance and Results Act and the studies at the state and local level of GASB); that too much information is a bad as too little; and that large cities that are decentralizing will need to experiment and evaluate with various report formats and various dissemination methods. Some school districts in the United States are beginning to have some experience with school report cards, although not much is known about their effectiveness in changing behavior (Applebome, 1997). In addition to the type of information on report cards, decentralization would add reports on budgeting, spending, and fairness of the systems in place. In addition to good survey research involving the constituents for whom the reports are written, other more difficult research on the effects of such reports on changing behavior of schools and systems to promote more equity and high and less variable achievement among students will be a challenge.

How Do We Arrive at a Suitable Level of Checks and Balances in Newly Decentralized Systems?

Just as good information is an analogy for decentralization of K-12 education based on economic theory, a good system of checks and balances is an analogy based on political theory of federal systems. Of course, any public education system, centralized or not, will continue to function within the United States political structure. But how will the three branches of government (legislative, executive, and judicial) relate differently to a decentralized as opposed to a centralized system? If a system becomes truly decentralized, what role will the state and local legislatures play in monitoring the schools? Will state courts continue to rule on the basis of state systems of school districts, or will individual school performance or conditions become relevant to the courts? Will the executive branch want, need, or warrant more say at the individual school level in school districts that are not independent of their cities (e.g., New York City)? Most of these questions are normative, although research will play a role in documenting the various ways that systems across the states handle the issues. And the issues interact with the more technical ones of site versus central administration; whatever resolution of the site versus central issue that a locality evolves toward could be changed if the courts (legislature, etc.) begin to issue rulings (legislation) holding individual schools (central cities) responsible.

What Are the Factors That Change a School's Behavior, and Is SSBF One of Them?

The $64,000 questions: What are the factors that make an effective school, is SSBF one of them, and can the factors be replicated? Although the effective schools literature documented some of the key features found in well-functioning schools, there has never been a consensus about whether the research methods of that literature were adequate to their objective and, more important, whether any of the identified factors could be duplicated. Now we are about to add another factor—SSBF. This factor is certainly a complex one, because its definition and implementation will differ across localities and it will coincide (and thus be perfectly correlated) with more comprehensive types of decentralization of the education as well as the general local government system.

When large systems have an opportunity to set up experiments that are close to the ideal randomized ones, we advocate that they do so. This kind of experimentation may be inconsistent with the politics of rewarding good performance with additional budgeting flexibility, but we think it will pay off in the long run if a system wants systemic (almost all schools decentralized) rather than partial decentralization. Even choosing randomly among schools that volunteer to be among the first to try decentralized financing would provide good information about how hard or easy it will be to be promote it effectively and allow it in all schools.

Conclusions

Sometimes at the inception of a movement for change, it is important for the research community to remember that nothing in the real world works perfectly. It is certainly true that over the last few decades, highly centralized systems of K-12 education in large U.S. cities have failed many of the children they are meant to serve, and this is a powerful reason for trying something else. Still, we know very little about how a truly decentralized system would work. We know that changes that have taken place in schools that educate some of our most needy children have taken place on a decentralized, school-by-school basis (see Comer, 1992; Comer, Haynes, & Hamilton-Lee, 1987-88; Levin, 1994; Madden, Slavin, Karweit, Dolan, & Wasik, 1993). The evidence from the well-functioning school-by-school reforms provides some hope that a fully decentralized system could replicate their results. But if we move toward decentralized systems in our large cities, we in the research community should try hard to encourage research on questions where decisions could be affected by such efforts (e.g., cost-effectiveness of centralized vs. decentralized services of various kinds) and to encourage documentation and keen observation of those questions and issues where the outcomes will not depend so much on research as on values and political power (e.g., who should control the curriculum).

Acknowledgments

We gratefully acknowledge funding from the Consortium for Policy Research in Education (CPRE) and the Andrew W. Mellon Foundation. The statements made and views expressed are solely those of the authors.

Note

1. Chicago is a notable exception, at least with respect to state Chapter 1 monies.

References

Applebome, P. (1997, January 3). Prerequisite for better education: Accurate report cards on schools. *New York Times*, p. B4.

Behn, R. D. (1997). Linking measurement and motivation: A challenge for education. In P. W. Thurston & J. G. Ward (Eds.), *Improving educational performance: Local and systemic reforms* (pp. 15-58). Greenwich, CT: JAI.

Berne, R. (1992). *The relationships between financial reporting and the measurement of financial condition.* Norwalk, CT: Governmental Accounting Standards Board.

Berne, R., & Stiefel, L. (1984). *The measurement of equity in school finance.* Baltimore: Johns Hopkins University Press.

Berne, R., & Stiefel, L. (1994). Measuring equity at the school level: The finance perspective. *Education Evaluation and Policy Analysis, 16*(4), 415-421.

Breslin, S. (1987). *Promoting poverty: The shift of resources away from low-income New York City school districts.* New York: Community Service Society.

Comer, J. P. (1992). Organize schools around child development. *Social Policy, 22*(3), 28-30.

Comer, J. P., Haynes, N. M., & Hamilton-Lee, M. (1987-88). School power: A model for improving black student achievement. *Urban League Review, 11*(1-2), 187-200.

Division of High Schools. (1995-96). *High school allocation: Information, guidelines, and instructions.* New York: Board of Education of the City of New York.

Hatry, H. P., Alexander, M., & Fountain, J. R., Jr. (1990). Elementary and secondary education. In H. P. Hatry, J. R. Fountain, Jr., J. M. Sullivan, & L. Kremer (Eds.), *Service efforts and accomplishments: Its time has come* (pp. 97-118). Norwalk, CT: Governmental Accounting Standards Board.

Hatry, H. P., Fountain, J. R., Jr., Sullivan, J. M., & Kremer, L. (Eds.). (1990). *Service efforts and accomplishments: Its time has come.* Norwalk, CT: Governmental Accounting Standards Board.

Hill, P. T., Foster, G. E., & Gendler, T. (1990). *High schools with character.* Santa Monica, CA: RAND.

Ladd, H. F. (Ed.) (1996a). *Holding schools accountable: Performance-based reform in education.* Washington, DC: Brookings Institution.

Ladd, H. F. (1996b). Catalysts for learning. *The Brookings Review,* pp. 14-17.

Levin, H. M. (1994). The necessary and sufficient conditions for achieving educational equity. In R. Berne & L. O. Picus (Eds.), *Outcome equity in education* (pp. 179-188). Thousands Oaks, CA: Corwin.

Madden, N. A., Slavin, R. E., Karweit, N. L., Dolan, L. J., & Wasik, B. A. (1993). Success for all: Longitudinal effects of a restructuring program for inner-city elementary schools. *American Educational Research Journal, 30*(1), 123-148.

Rubenstein, R. (1998). Resource equity in the Chicago public schools: A school-level approach. *Journal of Education Finance, 23*(4), 468-489.

Smoke, P. (1996). *Designing and implementing public sector decentralization in developing countries.* Unpublished manuscript.

Stiefel, L., Berne, R., Goertz, M., Sherman, J., Hess, F., Moser, M., Rubenstein, R., & Iatarola, P. (1996). *Surveys and interviews from Andrew W. Mellon study of school level resource allocation in four large cities.* Unpublished manuscript.

Stiefel, L., Berne, R., Iatarola, P., & Fruchter, N. (1998). *The effects of size of student body on school costs and performance in New York City high schools.* New York: New York University, Institute for Education and Social Policy.

Stiefel, L., Rubenstein, R., & Berne, R. (1998). Intra-district equity in four large cities: Data, methods and results. *Journal of Education Finance, 23*(4), 447-467.

Stiefel, L., & Sparrow, R. (1996). *Measurement of output quality in U.S. nonprofit organizations.* New York: New York University, Robert F. Wagner Graduate School of Public Service.

TWO

Site-Based Management
A NUTS AND BOLTS APPROACH
FOR SCHOOL ADMINISTRATORS

LAWRENCE O. PICUS

One of the most profound and often implemented educational reforms of the last decade has been site-based management (SBM). Its popularity stems from many sources, most notably the desire of our school systems to operate more like businesses. The belief that our schools will improve through the delegation of more decision-making authority to local school sites is so prevalent that many state legislatures have mandated site-based decision-making mechanisms in local districts and schools (Picus, 1994). As a result of the intense interest in school-based authority and a belief that local decision making will improve our schools, many different models of SBM have emerged across the United States.

Much research has been conducted on the organizational aspects of SBM. Considerably less research has focused directly on the changes in school district fiscal systems needed to support SBM—even though early research by Malen, Ogawa, and Kranz (1990) identifies budgeting as one of the three major functions over which schools are given greater autonomy under SBM models. Given SBM's genesis in models designed to improve production in private business (Lawler, 1986), this is somewhat surprising. Yet, for any SBM model to succeed, the important functions of a school district's business office must be redesigned to shift authority and support for most fiscal decisions to school sites. As this chapter shows, such a change is much easier to discuss than to implement.

Discussions of education reform often ignore the school business office. Yet, the business office has responsibility for managing the vast sums of money spent for education. Moreover, the business office plays a crucial role in helping district policymakers allocate resources across the many competing demands of public education. The importance of the business office cannot be overstated. Regardless of who decides how to designate the funds—district- or school-level personnel—the business office will actually allocate the money and ensure that people get paid in a timely fashion, including the vendors who supply materials and services.

Educators' inadequate training in business and finance makes the situation more difficult; they often lack interest in acquiring the skills necessary to take responsibility for the fiscal management of a school. Thus, it has been easy for school-level personnel to leave the day-to-day fiscal management—and often by default decision making—to the central office. Moreover, given the importance of accounting for the proper use of public funds, it has been easier for districts to keep many, if not all, financial functions at the district office level, where it is easier to maintain control and take advantage of any economies of scale.

Many individuals have suggested that funding structures should bypass school districts entirely, and the funds should be sent directly to school sites. Others have argued for requirements that some percentage of total revenue (usually between 85% and 95%) be allocated to, and spent by, the schools in a district. Unfortunately, models containing this requirement are relatively easy for school districts to circumvent. Consequently, to facilitate school-site decision making requires dramatic changes and financial restructuring of traditional school districts.

Distribution of Resources

If schools are to have control over their available resources, it is essential that districts devise equitable ways to get those revenues to school sites. One alternative would be to distribute revenues to the schools on the basis of enrollment, giving a flat grant per pupil to each school site in the district.

A distribution system like this leads to several questions about the equity of the revenue distribution:

1. What percentage of total revenue should be directed to the school site? Similarly, should all services be "purchased" by the school, or should decisions regarding some services remain at the district?
2. Should distribution formulas be based entirely on dollars per unit, or in some instances (i.e., teachers and other personnel) should an alternative distribution formula be used?
3. How should such distribution formulas deal with differences in the age, location, and other characteristics of school facilities?
4. How should children with special needs, such as those with disabilities, be treated?
5. Should students at different grade levels and/or in schools with different organizational characteristics (i.e., elementary, intermediate, and high schools) receive differential levels of per pupil funding?

Sharing Revenue at the School Site

One of the goals of SBM is to shift authority over more resource decisions to the school site. Many schools have urged that a high percentage of district revenue be turned directly over to the schools. On the surface, this seems to be a good idea; however, without further definition, it is not clear whether this approach will succeed in achieving that goal.

Suppose that a state legislature mandates that "control over 85% of a district's revenues must be devolved to school sites." Although this sounds like a straightforward requirement, its exact meaning is hard to pin down. The vast majority of educational expenditures takes place at the school site. Consequently, most, if not all, districts in a state can probably claim that 85% of their expenditures are at the school level already. If one takes the word *control* as the operative goal, however, then it is unlikely that many schools across the United States can truly meet the 85% requirement.

Other issues complicate determination of whether or not the requirement has been met. First, how much money are we talking about? Second, what does control mean?

How Much Money Is 85%?

In the above example, schools have gained control of over 85% of a district's revenue. Does this refer to all district revenue or only to general revenues? The example is intentionally vague, but it is not that different from proposals before legislatures in many states. Specifically, how should state and federal categorical programs be treated? Although it is possible, theoretically if not politically, to roll state-funded programs into an 85% requirement, doing so with federal funds might, in some cases, result in the loss of federal support. This is a risk if the money were no longer distributed and used according to federal guidelines. Yet, Odden (1996) points out that one way schools can fund the relatively small additional costs of the New American Schools' whole school model is to use federal Title I money to fund the additional positions the models require. This brings up a related question: Will a fixed percentage rule change how money is spent?

The 85% Rule Change—
Will It Affect How or Where Money Is Spent?

Research in the allocation and use of resources has shown that instruction (teachers and instructional materials) accounts for approximately 60% of a district's total expenditures (Odden, Monk, Nakib, & Picus, 1995; Picus & Fazal, 1996). Although a goal of the hypothetical 85% requirement is to increase the proportion of resources devoted to instruction, it is not clear that this will happen. Today, the remaining 40% of school funds are used to provide support for operations and maintenance, pay utility bills, transport children to and from school, support school site administration and instructional leadership, feed children lunch (and in some cases, breakfast), and support the central office. In most cases, the goal of an 85% rule is to reduce the size of a district's central office, but it is not clear that this will happen either.

First, research indicates that central administrative costs amount to approximately 5% to 6% of total expenditures (Odden et al., 1995; Picus & Fazal, 1996), with the balance used to provide the other noninstructional services (listed above). This balance is generally directed toward school sites (e.g., utility bills, transportation of students from home to school, and noninstructional staff to operate and maintain school sites).

Moreover, not all central office functions are necessarily the result of a bloated bureaucracy. A number of district functions are still best handled centrally. These include preparing the overall district budget, handling fiscal management and accounting tasks, and managing the many details of the personnel system, including the payroll.

Finally, regardless of where funds for items such as pupil transportation and utility costs are budgeted and controlled, the money must be spent if the children are to get to school, and the school must provide an environment conducive for learning. Thus, simply moving 85% (or some other portion) of a district's total revenues to the school site, in and of itself, will not change how funds are spent. It may succeed only in changing where the accounting for them takes place. As explained next, the authority or control over resources at the school level is what really matters.

Staff Distribution Formulas

The second question has to do with how funds are distributed to school sites from the central district. As described above, school districts in the United States typically use a set of formulaic ratios to divert funds to school sites. For instructional personnel, teachers are typically provided to a school site based on the number of students at the school, for example, one teaching position for every 25 students.

Other personnel are generated on a variety of similar formulaic ratios based on numbers of students, other staff, or school characteristics.

The difficulty with using formulaic ratios for staff is they use *numbers* of personnel, not *cost* of the individual personnel assigned to the school site. Teacher salaries, for example, can vary by as much as two to one, depending on an individual's previous teaching experience and educational attainment. Thus, if a school site were to receive a dollar distribution (e.g., based on the number of students in the school), the composition of its teaching staff would affect how well it could stay within its budget.

As a result of the differential costs of staff, most districts allocate positions to schools on the basis of average cost. That is, a school site generates its staff positions without regard to the cost of the individuals employed at the site, and essentially pays the average cost for each type of individual. Whether this model leads to school-site control depends on the way it is implemented at the district level. For example, can a school site change the mix of personnel it wants to employ, trading an assistant principal for one-and-a-half or two teaching positions? If so, are there district employment rules that limit this flexibility, even if it is provided for in theory? More important, what flexibility does a school have to change the mix of professionals? If it is unlimited, the district must absorb the risk of suddenly having too many teachers, assistant principals, or counselors, and so forth on staff if different trade-offs are made by the school sites. If the district absorbs the risk, the effect is likely to be a higher average cost for each position and potentially fewer staff at each school site in total.

On the other hand, giving each school a fixed budget based on enrollments and letting the site allocate the funds across staff has its own problems. What happens to schools where the average cost of a teacher is above the district average? With a fixed per pupil budget, these schools will not be able to hire all the teachers they need, whereas a school with a relatively young teaching staff may be able to hire more teachers and reduce class size. Adding to this complexity is the effect of time, which will eventually lead to the retirement of experienced and expensive teachers and increased salaries of currently inexperienced teachers. Thus, a school that is advantaged today may be at a disadvantage in a few years.

Districts that want to use dollar formulas to allocate funds to schools must take these factors into account in distributing funds. One possibility is to adopt a model similar to that used by the Los Angeles Unified School District (LAUSD) under its consent decree for the *Rodriguez v. LAUSD* lawsuit (1992). The district was sued by plaintiffs seeking to equalize general fund per pupil expenditures across all the district's schools. The settlement recognized that a large component of the differences in per pupil expenditures is differential salaries of teachers due to variances in experience and education. The settlement calls for equalizing per pupil expenditures on teacher salaries over time by requiring school sites to hire teachers such that the average cost of a teacher is approximately the same as the average cost of teachers across the district. Thus, a school with a relatively expensive teaching staff must hire additional teachers with relatively low salaries (and consequently less education and experience), and a school with a relatively inexpensive teaching staff must hire new teachers who are relatively expensive (and thus have more education and experience). The goal is to equalize the educational and experience characteristics of teachers at each school site.

Rather than provide school sites more control over the characteristics of their teaching staff, the Los Angeles system seems to have put more constraints on school decision makers, forcing them to consider the price of a teacher as well as his or her qualifications. Similar pressures would exist in any system that gave school sites a fixed dollar amount per pupil for budget purposes. This may or may not be a good thing.

On one hand, principals and school-based decision-making councils feel that some of their hiring flexibility has been eliminated. On the other hand, forcing schools to have a teaching staff with mixed levels of education and experience may have long-term benefits in terms of consistent school leadership and instructional quality. In theory, there would always be a group of teachers at the school with knowledge and experience related to the school's goals and mission and a sense of history regarding what programs seem most successful.

Regardless of how a district resolves this issue, if school sites are held to total budget amounts, regardless of staff composition, then some kind of safety net will be needed to help schools deal with temporary highs and lows in teachers' salaries. The same issues need consideration in the employment of other certified and classified staff in schools. Differences in the unit cost of personnel, despite similar responsibilities, need to be taken into account if central districts are to continue to distribute funds to school sites.

Allocation of Nonstaff Resources

This section describes some of the difficulties school sites may encounter if they are given substantial responsibility for many of the functions now handled at the district level. It is not meant to be comprehensive, nor to be read as opposing SBM. It merely tries to describe some of the complexities of shifting the fiscal management to schools. For more information on individual topics and how they are managed in today's school business office, see Wood, Thompson, Picus, and Tharpe (1995).

Technology

One of the most frequently discussed and most expensive items facing schools is the purchase, maintenance, repair, and updating of tools for instructional technology, particularly computers. The cost of placing computers and Internet connections in classrooms or in computer labs is substantial. Once the investment in equipment has been made, the expense of maintaining that equipment is considerable. It also is expensive to provide technical training and support for teachers so that they make maximum use of the technology, and a plan must be established to keep both the hardware and the software up to date.

Providing equity for schools in making these purchases and then maintaining their investment is complicated. Moreover, unless schools are able to carry over funds from one year to the next, it may never be possible to establish a fund large enough to purchase enough computers to fund an entire computer lab at one time. This could lead to nonstandardization of hardware, further complicating the management of a school's technology program.

Transportation

The costs of transporting students to and from school vary with the distances children have to travel and the density of the population in the school's attendance boundaries. If school sites are held responsible for funding student transportation out of site funds, schools with fewer children to bus or shorter travel distances will have more money for alternative programs than schools with more expensive transportation needs. If the school is required to purchase transportation services from the district, why assign responsibility for this service to the school site? Why not simply make it a district service? And if that decision is made, what effect does that have on any attempt to establish an 85% rule?

Maintenance and Operations

Although few have suggested that authority for transportation be given to school sites, Hentschke (1988) does suggest shifting authority for utilities to school sites, assuming they can keep all or part of any savings they generate. Again, this will not work well if each school were to receive a flat amount per pupil (or per classroom or per square foot) for utilities. Older and less energy-efficient buildings might require substantially higher expenditures per student for utilities than newer and more energy-efficient schools. Thus, formulas to distribute funds to school sites need to take site characteristics into account.

Similar problems exist for the maintenance and repair of school facilities. Newer buildings require less expensive maintenance and repairs and are less likely to require expensive rehabilitation, such as roof repairs or the replacement of a boiler. It is important that either allocation rules take these differences into account or school-site decision makers have the foresight to establish reserves to pay for these items when they come due.

Risk Management

Another area critical to this discussion is risk management. For expenses on insurance and medical benefits, large risk pools are helpful in keeping costs down. There are some advantages to cooperative purchasing programs, across schools or districts. The advantage to letting school sites purchase their own benefit and insurance packages is that they can tailor their programs to meet the needs of their staff and students. The downside is that in smaller risk pools, the potential of one lengthy illness or catastrophic loss making future insurance very expensive is much greater. Thus, programs that provide more autonomy at school sites need to be structured very carefully so that these functions do not take away from funds available for direct instruction.

Food Services

Virtually every school in the United States provides food services for its students. In many schools, federal assistance pays for meals of low-income children. Although it is possible to shift authority for operation of food services programs to school sites, there may be little reason to do so. This is one area that frequently benefits from substantial economies of scale, particularly in the purchase of food. Moreover, it is unlikely that a school principal, or his or her staff, will have the skill and expertise to operate a food services program efficiently. Although school sites could consider contracting out for food services, again, there may be benefits of scale in allowing the district to handle this.

Purchasing

For years, districts have operated large purchasing operations, buying supplies in bulk and then distributing them to school sites. Although there are substantial savings in the purchase price of materials, the costs of maintaining inventory and distribution are significant. This is one area that, given today's market for office supplies, could benefit from decentralization. Rather than maintain large inventories and fleets of trucks and vans to deliver materials, why not simply give each school, or even each teacher, a credit card at one of the large office supply stores located in most areas? The credit card could have a fixed annual limit so that individuals would not overspend, and it would be straightforward to monitor purchases by having the store send the school or the district monthly reports of purchases.

This system would eliminate inventory storage and distribution costs, money that could be added to the value of the credit cards given to each teacher. The downside of this model is that it shifts the cost of distribution to individual teachers, who must now go shopping for supplies. Although this might be mitigated by delivery offers from various office supply companies, it is not clear whether teachers would welcome the trade-off of more flexibility, and possibly more money, in exchange for doing the purchasing themselves.

Dealing With Different Student Needs

Another issue in distributing resources to school sites is different student needs. A simple distribution based on the number of students does not account for children with disabilities and the additional costs special education programs incur, or provide additional resources to children from families with low incomes.

There are a number of models for distributing funds to school districts to compensate for the additional costs of educating children with special needs. These include full assumption of the costs, categorical grants, and weighted pupil distribution formulas. Similar models could be used within districts to distribute funds to school sites.

Full assumption of special education costs seems to be at odds with the concept of SBM, because that would imply placing more control at the district level. For example, in the LAUSD, the establishment of a separate special education unit within the district resulted in a system that operated almost as a school district within the district (Barber & Kerr, 1995). If the goal is to place more control at the school site and to provide inclusive environments for children with disabilities, then a model that places more funds and responsibility at the schools makes more sense.

Categorical grants give school sites additional funds to provide programs that meet the needs of their students. If grants could be provided that reward either cost-effective programs or those that meet the established priorities of the district, then schools would have incentives to establish programs aligned with district priorities, and possibly with national and/or state policies and laws.

If the goal was to provide as much revenue as possible to school sites without attaching any restrictions on how it should be used, a district wanting to recognize the additional costs of certain groups of children could establish a weighted pupil distribution model, providing additional resources for each child with specified conditions or needs. This would give school sites the most flexibility in determining how to meet each child's educational needs. Without some kind of system to provide support and knowledge about what kinds of programs are available and which ones work for children with particular needs, however, it would be difficult to ensure that schools would be capable of meeting these needs.

Dealing With Different School Organizational Characteristics

Another factor that has caused districts some difficulty is the differential costs of various school organizational structures. High schools with departmentalized instruction, where a teacher is responsible for teaching five classes a day and the average student is enrolled in six classes a day, require more teachers for a fixed number of students at a given average class size than do elementary schools with self-contained programs. As a result, in many districts, per pupil expenditures at the high school level are higher than they are at the elementary level, even when state funding is based on equal amounts of money per pupil regardless of grade level.

Today, there is a growing sense that children in the primary grades need additional instructional resources to be able to succeed. This effort has led to reduction in class size at the primary level, especially in Texas and California. Texas mandates that classes be no more than 22 students in grades K-4, whereas California has provided a financial incentive of $625 per student in K-3 classes of 20 or less. Most districts in California have opted to take advantage of the incentive funds, at least for grades 1 and 2. In Texas, any school with classes exceeding 22 students in grades K-4 is out of compliance with state guidelines.

Should internal district policies provide differential amounts of revenue per pupil to schools? Obviously, that is something that needs to be decided by individual districts. One could argue, however, that regardless of how much money finds its way to each school in a district with strong SBM, it is up to the individual school to determine exactly how large or small classes at various grade levels should be.

Thus, trade-offs between class sizes at different grade levels within a school might best be made by individuals at the school site.

The Elements of Restructuring

The previous discussion suggests that delegating more authority over fiscal matters to school sites is a complex and difficult task, but it does not mean it should not be considered. This section suggests what a restructured business office might look like under SBM. It deals with the traditional relationship between the business office and school sites, offers ways districts can implement budget procedures that give more authority to school sites, considers the implications of letting outside firms compete with the business office to provide services to school sites, and looks at which functions should be maintained at the district level and which should be devolved to school sites.

The School Site-Business Office Relationship

It is not uncommon for a school principal to tell his or her teachers or community advisory board that a proposal is impossible to implement because it violates district policy or state law or it costs too much. In the last case, blame is put squarely on the school business office for holding the purse strings so tightly. Similarly, school sites are required to follow detailed procedures to spend funds allocated to their site. Often, there is little flexibility to change plans midway through the year to take advantage of an unexpected opportunity or to modify plans on the basis of experience.

If school business offices want to support SBM, they must change the way they operate. The business office must provide more information and support services to schools and help facilitate decision making and implementation. Using the framework established previously, the business office must transfer its power over fiscal matters to school sites and provide site personnel with the knowledge necessary to make informed decisions. The most critical areas of change are budgeting, accounting, and cash management.

Budgeting

As already discussed, with traditional systems, there is very little, if any, discretionary money available at the school site. Financing school sites would turn this arrangement upside down. Rather than telling the school how much it has, the budget office would ask the school what it wants. Because the requests would undoubtedly exceed the district's anticipated revenues for the next year, the school would need to develop a system for establishing priorities. The most obvious would be to provide each school with some reasonable amount of money and let them do their own prioritization.

To do this, school sites must have decision-making power over how to use staff and other resources. They also need to be able to trade staff positions for money to purchase services such as professional development. This means that schools must be provided with the ability to understand how much money they have, what that money can currently purchase, and what the alternatives for those funds might be. Certainly, centrally organized systems do not find it easy to distribute information on a wide range of options and variations to school sites. But with today's computing tools, it is possible. One solution is to provide schools with simple spreadsheet applications to do their basic budgeting. Once the general budget has been established, then the data can be transferred, in the correct categories, to the district's budget system.

At that point, the role of the business office is to aggregate the budget for all the schools and to add the costs of any services being provided centrally. This represents a dramatic change for the business office. The staff of the business office would need to facilitate the development of accurate budgets that portray the mission and goals of each school and provide an estimate of the costs of the materials and personnel needed to achieve those goals.

Accounting

Once the budget has been approved, schools must live within their individual budgets. Without accurate, timely reports of the school's financial position, a sophisticated budgeting system is useless. The accounting system should provide school sites with on-line access to accounts and systems for preparing purchase orders for supplies and materials. If schools must manage the salary bill from their own resources (as opposed to paying average costs for personnel), then the system must also keep track of personnel expenditures on a weekly basis. Schools facing funding shortages near the end of the year might have to make adjustments in their use of substitute teachers or other part-time help. Given the consequences of mistakes, it is essential that the district's business office provide accurate and timely information on the status of each school's accounts.

It is critical that the system also allow the district to monitor school financial performance to make sure that individual schools are not spending beyond their budgets, and that if they are doing so, they are counseled immediately to prevent major financial problems at the end of the fiscal year. This watchdog function of a district business office would be one of the most important, yet among the most politically delicate.

Cash Flow

One of the problems in the management of any enterprise is matching income to outflow. This is particularly true for public agencies, where revenue is frequently accrued to the jurisdiction a few times a year. If spending needs don't match revenue streams, then the jurisdiction will need to borrow funds in the interim. The problem is exacerbated when the jurisdiction is small, is part of a larger organization, and competes with other jurisdictions for the available cash resources of the district. In some instances, schools may want to carry over funds from one year to the next to facilitate large purchases, such as hardware for a computer laboratory.

It is likely that a larger school district will have access to lower-interest borrowing than an individual school, particularly if the tax authority of the jurisdiction rests at the district level. In addition, if a school faces an unexpected expense, such as a major unplanned repair, it might be advantageous to use the reserves of the district to fund the repair, or at least to borrow the money to fund the repair. In short, the district could serve as an in-house bank, holding the carryover funds of some schools and providing short-term loans to schools faced with unanticipated expenditures in a given year. Although this service is currently in practice, a move to more site-based financing of schools would probably require the formalization of such banking functions.

Enhanced Competition

Business offices will have to allow schools to seek alternative sources of supply for various goods and services. Typically, school districts maintain lists of approved vendors with whom schools can do business or purchase goods and services. As SBM becomes more common, schools may want to make such decisions on their own. Rather than telling a school it can't purchase something from a particular firm, the business office will have to make sure that schools know how to find reputable vendors and help schools learn how to negotiate the best possible prices.

Moreover, schools may decide that many of the things currently being provided by the district and the business office can be purchased for less or at a higher quality from another vendor. For example, many companies provide payroll services to private employers. Many small firms take advantage of these services because it frees the firm from the complexities of handling a payroll and benefit system and offers an economy of scale that makes the service less expensive than doing it itself.

A school might discover that a private firm could handle its accounting or payroll needs for less money than the district's business office. It is even more likely that the school will find an organization or company that could provide food services or transportation services for less money than the business office charges. If such competition is allowed, certain services might be provided more efficiently if contracted out to other vendors, whereas those most expensive to operate will remain at the district or school level. The need to compete with private firms, and theoretically even other school districts, will make school business offices more efficient and help schools get the services they need at the lowest possible cost.

Site Versus District: What Goes Where?

Authority for the allocation and use of resources should be centered at the school site to the maximum extent possible. Taken to its logical conclusion, this means that each school would receive a lump sum budget with which to operate all its educational and support programs.

Although this model may seem far-fetched to some, it is essentially the model in use for most charter schools across the United States.

Charter schools have, in many cases, flourished with the additional responsibility for the fiscal management of their school site. Many of the services provided by central district business offices can continue to be purchased from the district, and in many cases, may be purchased elsewhere.

The problem with this model is not that it won't work, but that many school leaders are not ready to take on the added responsibility, out of fear or lack of training. There is likely to be considerable central office resistance to schemes that essentially make every school in the district an independent fiscal agency. Current state laws still hold districts accountable for the actions of their schools; consequently, districts will want to maintain some measure of control over what goes on at the school site.

Districts could restructure the central business office along the lines described earlier, shifting from a control agency to a support agency and allowing sites to make more real decisions about the use of resources. In some instances, this might result in giving schools authority to purchase some (if not eventually all) business services outside the district. This would force business offices to compete for school site business and encourage site leaders and managers to seek ways to reduce expenditures on noninstructional items so more resources could be devoted to teaching children.

All of this is, at best, a difficult and long-term transition. Given that, where should school officials focus their efforts? Clearly, leaders should look at areas most likely to improve student learning. Thus, more control over the way personnel resources are used, particularly teachers, seems the first step in the delegation of more fiscal authority to school sites. Because teachers and other personnel represent the single largest expenditure category in all districts, this action will go a long way toward meeting the goal of shifting the authority for resource allocation and use decisions to the school site.

This process is likely to be slow and at times painful. It is important to maintain standard accounting and management controls as schools take over more authority for fiscal management, and that central business offices continue to provide the training and support school site leaders will require.

References

Barber, L. S., & Kerr, M. M. (1995). *Chanda Smith v. LAUSD consultants' report.* Los Angeles: Los Angeles Unified School District.

Hentschke, G. (1988). Budgetary theory and reality: A microview. In D. H. Monk (Ed.), *Microlevel school finance: Issues and implications for policy* (pp. 311-336). Cambridge, MA: Ballinger.

Lawler, E. E. (1986). *High involvement management.* San Francisco: Jossey-Bass.

Malen, B., Ogawa, R. T., & Kranz, J. (1990). What do we know about school-based management? A case study of the literature: A call for research. In W. H. Clune & J. F. Witte (Eds.), *Choice and control in American education: Vol. 2. The practice of choice, decentralization and school restructuring* (pp. 289-342). Bristol, PA: Falmer.

Odden, A. (1996). *The finance side of implementing New American Schools.* Washington, DC: New American Schools Development Corporation.

Odden, A., Monk, D., Nakib, Y., & Picus, L. O. (1995). The story of the education dollar: No academy awards and no fiscal smoking guns. *Phi Delta Kappan, 77*(2), 161-168.

Picus, L. O. (1994). The local impact of school finance reform in Texas. *Educational Evaluation and Policy Analysis, 16*(4), 391-404.

Picus, L., & Fazal, M. B. (1996). Why do we need to know what money buys? Research on resource allocation patterns in elementary and secondary schools. In L. O. Picus & J. L. Wattenbarger (Eds.), *Where does the money go? Resource allocation in elementary and secondary schools: 1995 yearbook of the American Education Finance Association* (pp. 1-19). Newbury Park, CA: Corwin.

Rodriguez v. Los Angeles Unified School District, C611358 (Los Angeles County Sup. Ct. 1992).

Wood, R. C., Thompson, D. C., Picus, L. O., & Tharpe, D. I. (1995). *Principles of school business management* (2nd ed.). Reston, VA: Association of School Business Officials, International.

THREE

Measuring School Efficiency Using School-Level Data
THEORY AND PRACTICE

LEANNA STIEFEL

AMY ELLEN SCHWARTZ

ROSS H. RUBENSTEIN

Improving the efficiency of public schools has become the near-universal rallying cry of school reformers in the 1990s, appealing to a broad range of parents, educators, and policymakers alike. It may, in fact, be difficult to find someone who disagrees with the notion that schools should use their resources to educate children in the most efficient manner possible. Despite the widespread support and almost irresistible appeal of efficient provision, there is little agreement about (and often little thought given to) the way in which efficiency should be measured and the implications of adopting any one of several alternative methods. Measures of the efficiency of public schools are used currently for a variety of purposes, including to provide incentives for teachers and principals, among others, for better performance (e.g., schoolwide, teamwide, or individual teacher bonuses); to guide the reorganization of schools (e.g., school restructuring); to inform parents and students about school performance (e.g., through report cards or published reports); and to inform policymakers on where resources need to be allocated and could be effectively applied. These uses are quite different from one another, and the method of measuring efficiency, as well as its specific application, needs to be aligned to the proposed use.

In this chapter, we review the various methods available for measuring school efficiency, describe their relative advantages and disadvantages as well as relationships among them, discuss the practical issues each presents, and illustrate with examples of applications where possible. More specifically, we consider efficiency measurement based on (1) the statistical estimation of production functions; (2) the nonstochastically derived production frontiers found through data envelopment analysis (DEA); (3) adjusted performance measures derived from regression analyses; and (4) the statistical estimation of cost functions. We begin with the production function approach because it provides much of the underlying conceptual framework for the remaining methods. Thus, the theoretical discussions in the second through fourth sections build on the theoretical discussion in the first section. The last section provides concluding remarks. Our goal is to provide an overview of the most common approaches, with an eye toward implementation in K-12 schools in the United States.

Production Functions

Theory and Conceptual Framework

At the heart of most measures of efficiency, whether in education, health care, or automobile production, is the conceptual framework developed to describe a firm's production possibilities. The *production function* measures the maximum amount of output that can be produced from a given quantity of inputs.[1] In its general form, it can be represented as

$$(1) \qquad\qquad Q = f(X_1, X_2, \ldots \ldots X_n)$$

where Q represents the quantity of output, $X_1, X_2, \ldots \ldots X_n$ are the n inputs to production, and $f(.)$ is the transformation linking them, summarizing the technology of production. The results obtained from the estimation of the production function and the interpretation of those results are critically determined by the way in which Q, X_i, and f are specified and the level of aggregation of the data—that is, whether the unit of analysis is the school (where school-level data are available), the student (where student-level data are available), or perhaps something in between, such as classes or grades.

Increasingly, contemporary analyses rely on school-level data to gauge performance of public schools.[2] Although (1) can be estimated using a single cross-section of data, using panel data (i.e., using data on a cohort of schools over several time periods) provides significantly greater opportunity to investigate school efficiency using the production function. A fully specified production function, in simple linear additive form, with panel data on schools (within a state), can be represented as

$$(2) \qquad TS_{sdt} = \alpha_0 + \alpha_1 TS_{sdt-1} + \alpha_2 ST_{sdt} + \alpha_3 P_{sdt} + \alpha_4 SC_{sdt} + \\ \alpha_5 DT_{dt} + \alpha_6 T + \alpha_7 D + \alpha_8 S + \varepsilon$$

where TS_{sdt} is the output of school s in district d at time t, TS_{sdt-1} is the same output one period earlier, ST is a vector of student characteristics, P is a vector of peer characteristics, SC is a vector of school inputs, DT is a vector of district characteristics, T is a vector of time dummies, D is a vector of district dummies, and S is a vector of school dummies and ε is an error term (or several error terms) with the usual statistical characteristics.

Efficiency in an equation such as (2) could be measured two ways: by the α_8 coefficients on the school dummies, where the size of the α_8 coefficients represents the efficiency of schools relative to each other in the sample; or by the α_4 coefficients on school inputs, where the α_4 coefficients measure the marginal productivity. The first method uses the α_8 coefficients as measures of technical efficiency—the α_8s measure the residual variation in school output unaccounted for by variation in inputs, peer characteristics, and so on, that is systematically related to a given school.[3] In the specific case where the variables in (2) are measured in logarithms, it can be shown that the α_8 coefficients are measures of multifactor productivity. Similarly, the relative efficiency of school districts might be gauged by the size of the α_7 coefficients.

The advantage of the method that uses the fixed effects (the α_8s) is that efficiency is distinguished from the effects of different student and peer characteristics and accounts for differing resource patterns of schools. In addition, not all residual variation is attributed to efficiency, as it is in the adjusted performance measures discussed below. Rather, the error term picks up the random variation. The disadvantage of the method (and the adjusted performance and DEA ones as well) is that the α_8s are *black boxes* and, in fact, are likely to reflect more than just differences in efficiency or productivity. They are, in some sense, measures of our ignorance, capturing the systematic variation in output by a school across time that is unexplained by any of the included variables.

Notice that the inclusion of school dummies, S, precludes the inclusion of any time-invariant school-level variables in ST, P, or SC—both those that are truly fixed such as location and those that are infrequently measured or slow to change, such as physical capital—because they would be collinear with the dummies. Thus, the estimated fixed effects will, in part, reflect the effect of all the time-invariant school-level variables that might have been included. Similarly, including district dummy variables, D, means that variables describing district characteristics can be included only if they vary across time. Thus, the district dummies will capture the effect of all the time-invariant characteristics of districts; again, both those that are truly time invariant and those that are infrequently measured or slow to change.[4] The different effects could, in principle, be disentangled by specifying the school effects as random, rather than fixed, effects or, more generally, by using a random coefficients specification.[5]

The second method of measuring efficiency is to use the α_4 coefficients to obtain the marginal productivity of the school inputs and then to compare these marginal productivities to the input prices faced by each school. This is a measure of allocative efficiency because it combines technical efficiency (marginal productivities) with market prices or, implicitly, a budget constraint. Recall that one requirement for economic efficiency is that the ratio of the marginal products of any two inputs (i.e., teachers, aides) used is equal to the ratio of their prices. Thus, to the extent that different schools face different input prices or different marginal products, efficient production would require different combinations of inputs.[6] One application would be to simulate the cost savings of reallocating resources if the ratio of the prices is unequal to the ratio of marginal products. (See Levin, 1970, for an example of cost-effectiveness analysis based on an estimated production function.)

Student-level data could be used analogously to school-level data in a hierarchical model (students within schools within districts). Such a model can be represented in simple linear form as

$$(3) \qquad TS_{isdt} = \beta_0 + \beta_1 TS_{isdt-1} + \beta_2 ST_{isdt} + \beta_3 P_{isdt} + \\ \beta_4 SC_{isdt} + \beta_5 DT_{idt} + \beta_6 T + \beta_7 D + \beta_8 S + \beta_9 SI + \psi$$

where all variables are defined as for the school-level model except for individual student i in school s in district d at time t; SI is a student-level dummy and is ψ the error term (or terms). Because the data and computing demands for estimating a model with an indi-vidual student-level dummy would be prodigious, in practice we would expect to omit at least the student fixed effect (SI).

Once again, the school efficiency in such a model could be estimated two ways—by the relative size of the β_8 coefficients on the school dummy variables or by the marginal productivities of school inputs compared to their prices, using β_4 coefficients.

What are the differences between equation (2) and equation (3)? Equation (3) looks at the mean school-level effect after adjusting for individual-level differences. The student differences have not already been aggregated to the school level, and the equation has a chance to adjust statistically on the basis of more variation within the schools. If we think that the individual student is the right starting point for evaluating school behavior, then equation (3) provides better infor-maticn for us. On the other hand, if we think that schools are better represented by a summary measure of student output (such as the mean, median, 25th percentile), then (2), which already aggregates to the school, is better. A priori it does not seem that the statistics can decide this issue. For some purposes, we may want to go to the school level. An argument could be made that decisions within the school about which students to encourage and so on are appropriate school-level decisions. The evaluation of a school would then not question these decisions, but instead look at summary outcome measures. On the other hand, if the school is a convenient aggregation unit and it is actually each individual student who counts, then the student is the more appropriate unit.

Whether school-level or student-level data are used to estimate the efficiency coefficients on the school dummies and/or the marginal productivities of school inputs, a number of important assumptions and alternatives, alluded to above, require some additional discussion. First, the estimation of a production function assumes that schools allocate resources, make policy decisions, and so on in an effort to maximize output. This is, at best, a dubious assumption for most public schools in the 1990s. To the extent that they do not act to maximize output, then the equations should be interpreted as reflecting average behavior, and our efficiency measures reflect a school's efficiency relative to other schools in the sample, because all schools may be off the production frontier.

Second, we have proceeded based on the assumption that TS is adequately agreed on as an output, and the only one, against which to gauge efficiency. Although test scores are the most common measure of TS, schools clearly produce other outputs, and it is unlikely that consensus on which test score, among the many available, will be easily achieved. Third, there are likely to be measurement errors, both in the independent and dependent variable, that may cause significant bias in the estimated coefficients (see Ladd, Roselius, & Walsh, 1997, for a longer discussion). Finally, the linear specifications in the previous equations may be too restrictive, and they may not appropriately capture the educational production process. Instead, more flexible functional forms, such as a logarithmic specification, may be more appropriate and more useful for evaluating efficiency in public schools. These issues will be dealt with in greater depth in the following sections.

Choosing and Measuring Outputs

Perhaps the most controversial part of specifying an education production function is the choice of an output measure. Although test scores are commonly used, there are alternatives, such as dropout rates, retention rates, earnings of graduates, and college-going rates (especially for high schools). Further, test score data typically offer a variety of alternative metrics with which to measure output—raw scores, grade equivalent scores, and percentage of students achieving minimum competency are just a few. In addition, scores on more than one test are usually available for any grade in any one year—spanning different subject areas or using different testing philosophies, such as criterion versus norm referenced.

Clearly, schools serve many purposes, and therefore produce many outputs, only some of which are readily used as output measures for production functions.[7] Further, although there is rarely an easy consensus in the school community of teachers, administrators, and parents on which are the most important outputs, the production function framework does not easily lend itself to consideration of multiple output measures.[8]

The ramifications of the choice of output measure are important. To the extent that the output measure inadequately measures "true" output, or is poorly correlated with other outputs schools seek to produce, the efficiency measures will be biased, probably toward finding greater inefficiency. As an example, if reading scores are used to measure output, but significant resources are allocated to the acquisition of math skills, then resources will be shown to be inefficiently deployed in the production of reading. In practice, high correlation in test scores may make the choice between reading and math scores less critical, but to the extent that test scores will be uncorrelated with other relevant outputs, such as reductions in dropout rates, the problem may be significant.

Finally, output can be measured in levels, for example, using the reading scores for the year or as the change from last year. The latter specification creates a "value-added" type of production function where school efficiency is gauged based on the effect of the resources on the gain in student performance. According to one view, the value-added specification is more appropriate, reflecting the notion that schools should be held accountable for that which they can affect—that is, a single year's education—and not for their "client mix." On the other hand, the implication, decried by some, is that schools with low overall scores may be identified as equally or more "efficient" than schools with high overall scores depending on how poorly their students performed last year. An alternative method for addressing this problem is to include prior year output data as an input variable, as discussed below.[9]

Choosing and Measuring Inputs

Although there is some agreement about the broad groupings of factors that are inputs to education production functions, there is considerably less consensus about how to measure specific variables within each group. Broadly, inputs can be divided four ways: student and family characteristics, peer characteristics, school inputs, and district or state characteristics. This last category is relevant only if the unit of analysis is one that crosses district or state lines.

Variables describing students and their families usually include some measure of the ability of students, marital status of parents, educational attainment and income of parents, number of siblings, native language, sex, race, and ethnicity. Missing from most studies are measures of student motivation. In addition, there is not much precision on which kinds of family background matter, perhaps due to limitations imposed by data. For example, some researchers would like to include mother's education alone or birth order, but these refinements are usually not possible. Finally, there is typically no consideration of inputs purchased by parents or students outside the public schools, such as after-school classes or computers, that might increase output.

Many production functions include variables that describe the peer group of the students. The general idea is that the students with whom an individual interacts will influence the level at which classes are taught, the depth of classroom discussions, the ethos of how impor-tant achievement is, and other intangibles. Although there is intuitive appeal to the idea, precise measurement of peer effects is difficult both conceptually and in practice. For example, are the relevant peers ones in the classroom, the school, the neighborhood, or the circle of friends? Usual measures include average characteristics of all students in a school or district. More detailed data sets, such as the National Education Longitudinal Study (NELS) from the U.S. Department of Education, include more detailed information about characteristics of peers in the classroom and allow more precise measurement.

Increasingly, input variables include some measure of previous period output. In this way, the performance of students (or the school) in the previous year is controlled for and school efficiency is measured based on the gain or value added. (This is an alternative to measuring output as the change in scores between periods, discussed above.) Whether or not this is the appropriate specification depends on whether the intention is to hold schools accountable for improvement or for level of performance. If improvement is the answer, then the output level from a previous period needs to be included in the production function either as part of the output or as an additional input variable that controls for a previously achieved level of output. Researchers generally seem to agree that the improvement or value-added specification makes the most sense for most purposes to which efficiency measures are put. (See Bifulco & Duncombe, 1998, for a discussion of the distinction between performance and performing.)

Variables that describe the inputs provided by schools are always included in production functions. Such variables ideally include measures of teachers, staff, buildings, computers, books, and so on. Conceptually, it is important to distinguish the quality of such inputs from their quantity, but in practice, this is difficult to do. For example, teachers vary in their quality, but how the relevant qualities should be measured is not clear, and, at least equally important, detailed data on characteristics suspected to be important, such as verbal ability, knowledge of subject matter, and experience with particular types of students, are rarely available. Although the list of teacher characteristics should, perhaps, be quite detailed, the data generally permit distinctions based only on certification, years of education, and experience, although some progress is being made as the importance of good measures becomes clear. (See Ferguson, 1991; Kain & Singleton, 1996; Murnane, 1991; or Murnane, Singer, Willet, Kemple, & Olsen, 1991, for more on this.)

Data on physical plant are usually incomplete at best, and details on other inputs, although sometimes available, are often measured not in physical quantities but in dollar terms. As an example, "expenditures on staff support" is used rather than "number of support staff." These expenditure numbers "weight" the inputs by their market prices, so, to the extent that such prices indicate quality or marginal productivity differences of teachers, the expenditure numbers may help solve the issues involved in differing quality of inputs. These measures cannot be counted on to solve the quality problem entirely, however, because of the monopoly that most districts have over public school provision and the effects of unionization on prices of personnel inputs. Finally, there is typically little detail in the report of input data, so it is difficult to examine the different effects of different types of inputs. As an example, number of teachers may be reported, but it is less usual to have data on the number of teachers by grade or subject taught.

Finally, if production functions are estimated with data that cross district or state boundaries, it may be important to include measures that distinguish policies or resource availability and use at these levels.

Correctly specifying the inputs to production is critical to efficiency measurement. If important school inputs are omitted from the production function, that is, if there are unobserved school variables, then the estimated fixed effect (or the marginal productivities) that forms the basis for efficiency measurement will reflect the effect of those unobserved variables and confound the interpretation of the fixed effects as efficiency measures.

Choosing a Functional Form

To estimate a production function empirically, a specific functional form must be specified. The simplest ones are additive or multiplicative (logarithmic), but as data sets with more observations become available, researchers are experimenting with interaction terms and polynomial forms. (See Clotfelter & Ladd, 1996, for a discussion of the South Carolina approach.)

The logarithmic specification is particularly attractive both because of its ease in estimation (it is linear in its parameters) and because of its properties as a production function. More specifically, these properties are as follows:

1. The coefficients on the inputs are elasticities, rather than marginal products (i.e., α_4 is $(\Delta TS_{it}/\Delta SC)*(SC/TS_{it})$). Elasticities allow the marginal products to vary with the levels of input use and output in different schools or time periods and allow the estimated production function to exhibit diminishing marginal products, both of which are intuitively appealing.

2. The interpretation of the fixed effects for schools as a measure of efficiency (or productivity) can be more clearly derived from the specification of the production function. In a simple logarithmic (Cobb-Douglas) production function, the intercept measures multifactor productivity. The school fixed effects provide a school-specific estimate of multifactor productivity.[10]

Finally, production functions can be estimated in more sophisticated ways as parts of larger systems of equations and/or as related to their dual cost functions, for example. These methods are intended to address some of the issues discussed above and to allow greater flexibility (i.e., impose fewer restrictions) on the shape of the production function.

Data Envelopment Analysis

Theory and Conceptual Framework

DEA is a nonstochastic technique developed expressly to measure technical efficiency. It is well suited to analyzing the relationship between inputs and outputs in schools and can help overcome several of the shortcomings associated with regression-based production function analyses. Specifically, it permits the inclusion of multiple input and output measures, explains productivity without a priori specification of the functional form relating inputs to outputs, and allows the relative weights of inputs and outputs to vary across decision-making units (DMUs). These advantages allow researchers to avoid difficult issues such as choosing (or constructing) a single measure to capture a school's multidimensional performance, specifying a single functional form to explain the production process in all schools, and assigning weights to outputs based on value judgments regarding their relative importance.

Moreover, whereas regression analysis compares each school's production relative to the average, DEA measures efficiency relative to the most efficient results actually achieved by schools in the data set. This extremal orientation may be particularly appropriate for analyzing efficiency because outlier schools—those on the production frontiers—are likely to provide the most useful information for identifying best practices in the allocation of resources (Charnes, Cooper, Lewin, & Seiford, 1994b).

DEA has been used to analyze efficiency in a wide range of settings, from banking (Sherman, 1984) to baseball (Mazur, 1994). Applications of the DEA methodology to examine public sector efficiency have become quite common, particularly in the area of education (see, e.g., Bessent, Bessent, Kennington, & Reagan, 1982; Chalos & Cherian, 1995; Fere, Grosskopf, & Weber, 1989; Grosskopf, Hayes, Taylor, & Webber, 1997; Mayston & Jesson, 1988; Ruggiero, 1996). These studies of educational efficiency typically rely on district-level data, although researchers have occasionally conducted intradistrict, school-level analyses (Arnold, Bardhan, & Cooper, 1994; Bessent & Bessent, 1980).

The term *data envelopment analysis* encompasses an assortment of mathematical programming models, each taking a slightly different form. The first DEA formulation, developed by Charnes, Cooper, and Rhodes (1978), sets out the basic analytic framework. The model measures relative efficiency by constructing a production frontier from the observed inputs and outputs of the units in the data set. The production frontier represents the most efficient use of resources actually achieved by the DMUs. All units operating on the frontier are deemed efficient and receive an efficiency score of one. Units operating below the frontier receive a score between zero and one, with lower efficiency scores indicating greater degrees of inefficiency (Charnes et al., 1978). The model can also estimate "slack" values for all inefficient DMUs, specifying the reduction in inputs that would be possible without causing a decline in output values.[11] For all technically efficient units, these slack values will be zero.

Later work extended the basic model to incorporate constant and variable returns to scale (Banker, Charnes, & Cooper, 1984), the use of categorical variables (Banker & Morey, 1986), and a myriad of other extensions and adaptations. The original Charnes et al. (1978) model treats all inputs as discretionary; that is, as being within the control of the DMU itself. Early work using this technique produced results indicating, for example, that some schools may be inefficient because they serve too many students from low-income families (Bessent & Bessent, 1980). Current models are able to distinguish between discretionary and nondiscretionary inputs, an essential requirement if analysts hope to produce DEA results useful for managerial decision making.

Because DEA calculates relative efficiency based on the actual results achieved by units in the data set, the analysis will always rate at least some units as efficient. If, in fact, all units operate below their actual production frontiers, the assessment of efficiency may produce misleading results. In low-achieving districts, for example, some schools could be deemed efficient despite producing levels of student outputs that the community generally finds unacceptable. Even in such cases, DEA may be useful for identifying those schools most in need of assistance.

DEA need not be used as a stand-alone analytic technique. Numerous researchers have employed DEA in combination with other methods to further understanding of efficiency in educational organizations. For example, Duncombe and Yinger (1997) simulate the effects of an outcome-based state aid program on district-level efficiency—as measured by DEA—for New York state districts. Lovell, Knox, Walters, and Wood (1994) employ OLS regression in a two-stage approach exploring the determinants of school-level efficiency as calculated by a modified DEA procedure, whereas Chalos and Cherian (1995) use probit analysis to examine the relationship between efficiency and the results of tax levy referenda in Illinois school districts.

Choosing and Measuring Outputs

As described above, a primary advantage of DEA is its ability to include multiple output measures in a single model. Although data availability will inevitably constrain the choice of outputs, the inclusion of multiple outputs (e.g., scores in reading, math, science, and social studies) allows explicit consideration of the trade-offs between schools' many, sometimes competing, outputs and goals. Noncognitive output measures may also be included (if available), as well as the other school-level outputs and outcomes described earlier. Although most DEA applications in education have used test score levels as outputs (either raw numbers or percentage reaching a specified level), variables may also be specified as improvements in performance over some time period (see Lovell et al., 1994). DEA's ability to include multiple outputs also helps avoid the possibility that schools could be rewarded for investing disproportionate resources in certain subject areas or grades to maximize a limited number of outputs, or for improving their test scores by allowing low-performing students to drop out.

DEA requires no a priori specification of variable weights. Instead, weights may vary across units, and are calculated so as to maximize each DMU's efficiency rating. If exogenously determined judgments about school goals can be imposed on the analysis (e.g., a district-level focus on reading scores), however, such judgments should be incorporated into the mathematical program (see Charnes, Cooper, Lewin, & Seiford, 1994a) or should guide the selection of output measures.

Choosing and Measuring Inputs

Conceptually, DEA approaches school processes in much the same manner as a production function, linking multiple inputs to an array of school outputs. The DEA inputs are categorized as discretionary if the level of the input is within the control of the individual DMU or another relevant decision-making authority, or as nondiscretionary if they are not easily manipulated. The discretionary inputs should include broadly defined measures of school resources. These are likely to consist of various expenditures, although data on pupil-teacher ratios, teacher characteristics, and physical school inputs may be available. Nondiscretionary inputs reflect student and school characteristics commonly thought to make the attainment of high outputs relatively more or less difficult (e.g., student poverty, limited English proficiency, or disabilities). Previous test scores can also be included among the nondiscretionary inputs to approximate a value-added approach to performance measurement.

Although DEA can help researchers avoid many of the difficulties described in the review of production functions, it should not be used to enter all available data indiscriminately into a poorly defined model. For example, the inputs and outputs included in the model should be associated in some way, the direction (positive or negative) of the relationship should be understood, and the input variables should display as little multicollinearity as possible (Charnes et al., 1994a). Variable selection is particularly critical because the number of DMUs rated as efficient will tend to rise as the number of included variables increases (Chalos & Cherian, 1995). An analysis in which nearly all schools are deemed efficient will have limited practical use for accountability purposes, or for analyzing resource allocation practices.

Choosing a Unit of Analysis

In conducting DEA of school systems practicing traditional district-centered budgeting, the appropriate level of analysis can be difficult to determine because schools may have primary responsibility for producing outputs (defined in various ways), whereas district personnel may control resource allocation decisions. In a district practicing school-based budgeting, though, schools have the responsibility and the discretion to link resource allocation decisions to student performance. Therefore, school-level (rather than more aggregated) data are especially appropriate for DEAs in decentralized districts because schools are the units at which fundamental resource allocation decisions may be made.

Although cross-sectional data have been most commonly used in DEA analyses of schools, panel data can also be incorporated through a technique called *window analysis* (Charnes et al., 1994a). The procedure uses a moving average of DMU performance across different time periods to compare each DMU's performance to itself over time, and to that of other DMUs, to assess the consistency of results over time.

An Application

The analysis presented here examines school-level efficiency using 1994-95 data for all public elementary schools in Chicago. (For an equity analysis based on the same data set, see Rubenstein, 1998.) The DEA includes three types of variables: outputs (test scores), nondiscretionary inputs, and discretionary inputs. The nondiscretionary inputs include measures of student poverty,[12] students with language needs,[13] student mobility,[14] and school size.[15] The discretionary variables include general fund resources, state Chapter 1 funding, federal Title I funding, and desegregation funding (all per pupil), as well as average teacher salaries. Although the school itself may not have discretion over the level of these inputs, it would be possible (in theory) for federal, state, and district authorities to alter funding levels and formulas to make more productive use of scarce resources. The output variables are average school test scores on the Illinois Goals Assessment program's (IGAP) third and sixth grade reading and mathematics exams.[16]

The model seeks to minimize the level of discretionary inputs used to produce observed levels of outputs, given observed nondiscretionary inputs. An alternative approach would attempt to maximize outputs given observed levels of discretionary and nondiscretionary inputs. Considering the uncertain nature of educational production, as well as ongoing budget constraints, it may be more feasible to reduce inputs rather than maximize outputs to achieve efficiency. Therefore, this study uses the input-minimization orientation. This decision is not intended to imply a policy preference for minimizing school resources rather than maximizing outputs, but rather reflects the uncertainty about how inputs can be used to maximize outputs in inefficient schools.

Efficiency scores are computed for 399 elementary schools reporting IGAP results for each test. Approximately one quarter of the schools (99) are rated as efficient. The remaining 300 schools achieve a mean efficiency rating of .73, indicating that these schools, on average, could reduce some combination of inputs by about 27% without adversely affecting test scores.

Table 3.1 displays differences in the mean level of resources (discretionary inputs) available to the groups of efficient and inefficient

TABLE 3.1.   Average 1994-95 Chicago Elementary School Discretionary
                Resource Levels

Discretionary Resource Variables	Efficient School Mean	Inefficient School Mean	Difference
General fund	$2,818.88	$3,002.01	-$183.13
State Chapter 1	607.91	677.42	-69.51
Federal Title 1	252.88	467.46	-214.58
Desegregation	318.33	354.47	-36.14
Total funding	4,854.49	5,412.07	-557.58
Average teacher salary	37,914.62	38,464.97	-550.35

schools. As one might expect, the efficient schools tend to have lower average funding from all sources, as well as slightly lower average teacher salaries. Table 3.2 lists average outputs and nondiscretionary inputs for the two groups of schools. The efficient schools have higher proportions of students for whom English is not a native language, as well as larger enrollments and higher student mobility. The inefficient schools have a slightly higher proportion of students from low-income families. Despite the similarities in these environmental characteristics, Table 3.2 shows that the efficient schools as a group produce much higher average scores on each IGAP test.

Although the DEA model presented here includes resource levels as discretionary inputs, the results can also be used to explore differences in resource allocation patterns between efficient and inefficient

TABLE 3.2.   Average 1994-95 Chicago Elementary School
                Nondiscretionary Inputs and Outputs

Nondiscretionary Inputs and Outputs	Efficient School Mean	Inefficient School Mean	Difference
Percentage limited English proficiency	25.06	10.15	14.91
Percentage from low-income families	78.30	80.91	-2.61
Student mobility	33.02	28.30	4.72
School enrollment	703.64	657.22	46.42
Third grade reading IGAP	211.23	170.41	40.82
Third grade math IGAP	242.22	196.80	45.42
Sixth grade reading IGAP	210.88	181.20	29.68
Sixth grade math IGAP	235.73	197.99	37.74

TABLE 3.3. Average 1994-95 Chicago Elementary School Functional Spending Patterns

Proportional Spending by Function	Efficient School Mean	Inefficient School Mean	Difference
Total Spending			
Percentage on instruction	63.80	61.74	2.06
Percentage on instructional support	10.16	11.16	-1.00
Percentage on administration	6.47	6.05	.42
Percentage on operations	18.23	19.10	-.87
State Chapter 1 Spending			
Percentage on instruction	65.19	65.04	.15
Percentage on instructional support	16.52	16.96	-.44
Percentage on administration	14.59	14.21	.38
Percentage on operations	2.64	2.89	-.25

schools. Analyses of school-level spending patterns may yield particularly useful insights in a decentralized district such as Chicago, in which a large number of schools make resource allocation decisions. To explore the relationship between spending patterns and efficiency, Table 3.3 displays the proportion of the total budget and state Chapter 1 resources devoted to each of four functional areas (instruction, instructional support, operations, and administration)[17] for the groups of efficient and inefficient schools.

Excessive spending for administration and other noninstructional purposes is often blamed for perceived inefficiencies in the provision of public education (Bennett, 1988). The results presented in Table 3.3 only weakly support this hypothesis. Efficient schools as a group spend a higher proportion of their total resources on instruction (63.8% to 61.7%) and spend a slightly lower proportion of total resources on operations. Efficient schools also spend a larger share of their resources on administration, although the difference is extremely small. Given the higher level of total per pupil funding available in the average inefficient school ($5,412 as compared to $4,854), these results do suggest that inefficient schools tend to spend more money per pupil in noninstructional areas, although the proportional differences are small.

Table 3.3 also displays differences in spending patterns for Illinois state Chapter 1 funds. State Chapter 1 funding is the largest source of discretionary money under the control of school-level personnel, representing approximately 12% of the average elementary school's budget (Hess, 1994). Given the discretion schools have over these resources, it may be surprising to find, as Table 3.3 shows, that functional spending patterns are virtually identical across the groups of efficient and inefficient schools. Though this pattern may suggest that the resource allocation decisions of school-level actors have little effect on the measured efficiency of their schools, it is important to note that such aggregate spending analyses could mask important school-to-school variations in the specific programs and efforts supported by these dollars. Consequently, more microlevel analyses may be needed to identify the determinants of efficiency accurately within these schools.

Adjusted Performance Measures

Theory and Conceptual Framework

Adjusted performance measures are constructed based on the same conceptual framework summarized in the production function—the output of a school is viewed as depending on student characteristics, school inputs, and the like. Adjusted performance measures then proceed to distinguish between variables that are outside a school's control, such as student poverty levels, and those that are within a school's control, such as class size.[18] When linked to analysis of school-level resource patterns, adjusted performance measures provide another tool for exploring relative efficiency across schools.

Adjusted performance measures are constructed based on an equation such as

$$(4) \qquad\qquad TS_{sdt} = \gamma_0 + \gamma_1 Z_{sdt} + v$$

where TS_{sdt} is the output of school s, in district d, in year t; Z_{sdt} is a vector of uncontrollable factors and v is an error term. Z would typically include variables similar to those in the production functions such as TS_{sdt-1}, ST, P, DT, and D and may include some of the SC. The

prediction error for each school is the adjusted performance measure—
that is, the difference between the value of the performance measure
predicted by the regression equation for that school and the actual
value realized—and can form the basis for a comparison of schools'
relative performance. At the simplest, a residual greater than zero
indicates that the school has produced a level of output greater than
predicted, suggesting better than average performance. Residuals less
than zero suggest lower or poorer performance. The residuals can be
compared (and subjected to greater statistical analysis) to provide
more insight into differentiating high- and low-performing schools.

An alternative specification of the performance model might also
include a set of variables that could be controlled under some circumstances, or are controllable by some authority even if not by the school
itself. Such variables might typically describe the resources available
to schools. Such a model can be represented as

$$(5) \qquad TS_{sdt} = \gamma_0 + \gamma_1 Z_{sdt} + \gamma_2 X_{sdt} + \Theta$$

where all variables are the same as in equation (4), with the addition of
a vector of resource variables for school s, in district d, X_{sdt}, and a different
error term, Θ. The X_{sdt} might include the variables in SC not already
included in the Z. If resource variables are included, however, the residuals must be interpreted differently. Here, they capture the extent to
which the school's performance differs from that of other schools with
different levels of resources. This approach may be particularly appropriate if the resource variables are susceptible to policy intervention by a governing body (district, state, etc.) above the school itself.

Notice that the school dummies are in neither Z nor X. Typically,
adjusted performance measures are formed using only a single year
of data, precluding the estimation of the school effect.[19]

Practical Considerations

Although creating adjusted performance measures addresses potential shortcomings of raw performance measures, a variety of difficulties needs to be addressed before relying on them for decision

making. These are similar to those posed by the production functions, reflecting the relationship between the two. They include choosing between alternative raw performance measures; using existing data for performance measures; choosing independent variables; adjusting for initial conditions (or not); and other technical issues. Again, it is unlikely that any single measure will adequately capture all dimensions of performance, and the choice between available options is difficult. Choosing explanatory variables is also difficult. As described thus far, these should be variables describing the particular characteristics of schools and their students that are typically outside the control of individual schools. These independent variables are included to capture the relative difficulty (or ease) that the school has in earning high levels of measured performance, compared to other schools in the sample.[20] Which variables are uncontrollable? In analyses of schools, socioeconomic ones are usual, although data availability may limit the choices. Income level or poverty, the fraction of the students with limited English proficiency, race, and ethnicity variables are commonly included.[21]

As described above, variables that are either controllable in principle or could be controlled by some governing authority other than the school itself may be included. The typical candidates for inclusion are variables capturing the resources used by the school. The most commonly used resource variables are measures of class size, pupil-teacher ratios, or various types of spending per pupil.

Under what circumstances should resource variables be included? If the production function were explicitly specified, the answer would be all of them. Notice that equation (5) may, perhaps, be viewed as a "poor man's production function," depending if the X and Z are specified to have all the same variables as the production function. In the pragmatic world of adjusted performance measures, however, frequently they are not all included. If they are not, the coefficients of the included socioeconomic variables will reflect not only their direct effect on performance but also an indirect effect through their effect on resources. That is, if resources are omitted, then the coefficient on an included variable such as limited English proficiency (LEP) will reflect both its direct effect on performance and the indirect effect caused by the additional resources that might follow students who are not native speakers of English. If resources are included, then these effects will be somewhat disentangled. To the extent that higher-performing schools are also better able to attract funding (perhaps by attracting private sector support or through more effective use of public funding programs), the inclusion of resource variables may introduce endogeneity into the equations and, therefore, bias the coefficient in an unknown direction.[22]

For the purpose of evaluating the effect of budget allocations in schools where overall resources are not easily controlled by the schools, including resource variables in estimating performance equations is warranted and allows the disentangling of the effects of patterns of allocations from the effect of levels of resources.

Again, it is unclear whether (or how) information on prior performance should be included. Because prior performance is typically a powerful predictor of the subsequent year's performance, the fit of the equations improves dramatically when the prior performance is included. Alternatively, changes between periods may be used as the performance measure. In either case, controlling for prior performance may mean that other included variables become less significant. The answer about how to treat prior performance cannot be resolved statistically, but should reflect the policy definition of performance— is it level or an improvement?

A series of additional decisions needs to be made. As before, the theory of performance adjustment puts no particular bounds on the form of this function. Variables might be specified in logarithms, allowing the estimation of elasticities rather than marginal contributions, and/or interaction variables could be included. The list could be much longer. In this chapter, we illustrate the simplest functional form.[23]

An Application

To assess efficiency, the adjusted performance measures may be used to evaluate the relative merits of varying resource allocation patterns found across groups of high- and low-performing schools. Schools producing higher performance than others using the same level of resources may be assumed to be operating more efficiently. Policymakers and educators are interested in determining the extent to which altering the allocation of resources, holding constant overall resource levels, can improve performance and, therefore, efficiency.

For the purpose of understanding resource allocations, we are interested in examining aggregate (rather than individual) patterns across subsets of high- and low-performing schools. These high and low subsets could be selected by identifying groups of schools whose mean residuals differ significantly from zero, or, preferably, differ significantly from each other. This latter procedure would be analogous to a t-test for the difference of means between two samples, one with high residuals and one with low residuals.

Rather than turning to a statistical test, we turn to a more intuitive approach. Thresholds can be chosen based on various criteria, such as the size of the residual (e.g., schools whose standardized residuals have an absolute value greater than 2)[24], or the distribution of the residuals (e.g., quartiles). Notice that the choice of a threshold will determine the number of schools in each group, and a threshold should be selected within the framework of the application. If the purpose of the analysis is to identify groups of schools to examine resource allocation patterns within the groups and differences between them, lower thresholds will produce larger subsamples for subsequent analyses. A trade-off between sample size and precision is inevitable; however, lower threshold levels produce larger groups, but also less confidence that the observed values in each group are truly outliers.

An alternative approach would involve the estimation of a second regression in which the performance measures are regressed on the variables describing the allocation patterns. This is, in fact, quite similar to including the allocation patterns in the performance regressions themselves. The two-stage approach adopted here, however, allows us to create multipurpose performance measures and also to focus on the allocation relationship in isolation.

The application presented here uses the 1994-95 Chicago data set employed earlier. The regression model includes five independent variables to adjust for uncontrollable factors that may affect school-level test scores (percentage of students from low-income households, percentage of students with limited English proficiency, student mobility, total school enrollment, and parent involvement).[25] Total per pupil spending is also included to disentangle spending levels from subsequent analyses of spending patterns.[26]

Although achievement gains cannot be directly measured with the available data (which are for 1 year), a pretest approach can be approximated using third grade scores as independent variables in models to predict fourth grade scores from the same year.[27] To the extent that the current third grade strongly resembles the previous third grade (the current year's fourth grade) in characteristics and performance, prior student performance will be controlled for. Chicago schools administer reading and mathematics tests—the most commonly used indicators of student performance—in the years prior to administration of the social studies and science examinations. Therefore, social studies and science scores are the only scores available for use as dependent variables in models with previous grade scores.

Ordinary least squares (OLS) regressions with linear functional forms are estimated using fourth grade social studies IGAP scores to measure performance. Table 3.4 shows the parameter estimates from the adjusted performance models. The percentage of students from low-income families has a significant negative effect on school outputs, whereas higher student enrollments produce lower scores. As expected, third grade scores have a significant positive effect on fourth grade scores. Standardized residuals are calculated to measure the difference between each school's actual output and that predicted by the model.[28]

The purpose of the analyses presented here is to examine differences in resource allocation patterns across groups of high- and low-performing schools. Therefore, thresholds should be selected to ensure that the subsamples are large enough to facilitate the analysis of allocation patterns. We classify all schools with standardized residuals greater than 1 as high-performing schools, and those with negative residuals smaller than -1 as low-performing schools, producing subsamples of 49 and 46 schools respectively.

Table 3.5 lists the mean values for the groups of high- and low-performing schools on each of the independent and dependent variables in the performance measurement equations, and for several resource allocation variables. As expected, few differences in the independent variables emerge between the groups. Surprisingly, the high-performing schools have a higher average rate of student poverty and higher student mobility. Low-performing schools receive higher average

TABLE 3.4.   Results of Adjusted Performance Measurement OLS
Regressions: Fourth Grade Social Studies IGAP Score as
Dependent Variable

Independent Variable	Coefficient (se)
Constant	109.24**
	(17.94)
Percentage limited English proficiency	.100
	(.091)
Percentage from low-income families	-.527**
	(.093)
Student mobility	-.148
	(.094)
Parent involvement	-.048
	(.103)
School enrollment	-.015**
	(.006)
Total funding per pupil	.000
	(.001)
Third grade math IGAP	.123*
	(.054)
Third grade reading IGAP	.569**
	(.066)
N	426
F	160.92**
R^2	.755

**Significant at the .01 level
*Significant at the .05 level

levels of funding. Although the two groups have virtually identical
mean scores on the pretests (third grade reading and math), the mean
fourth grade score is 90 points (63%) higher in the high-performing
than the low-performing group. That is, high-performing schools
produced substantially larger achievement gains between third and
fourth grades.

Table 3.5 also shows the average proportion of total school spending
and Illinois state Chapter 1 spending allocated to each of the four
largest functions across high- and low-performing schools. As in the
previous comparison of efficient and inefficient schools, the differences for total spending are small. Low-performing schools spend an

TABLE 3.5.   Difference of Means—High- and Low-Performing Schools
(standardized residual > |1|)

	Low N=46	*High N=49*	*Difference*
Variables in Regression			
Percentage limited English proficiency students	10.75	10.89	-0.14
Percentage low-income students	73.01	78.10	-5.09
Student mobility (percentage)	28.69	30.76	-2.07
Percentage parent involvement	92.07	93.06	-.99
School enrollment	620	597	23
Total budget per pupil	5794	5527	267
Pupil-teacher ratio	15.68	16.19	-0.51
Third grade reading score	194.35	195.61	-1.26
Third grade math score	220.43	219.61	.82
Fourth grade social studies score	143.89	234.33	-90.44
Patterns of Total Expenditures			
Percentage spent on instruction	60.73	62.01	-1.28
Percentage spent on instructional support	12.77	10.27	2.50
Percentage spent on administration	6.11	6.30	-0.19
Percentage spent on operations	18.66	19.74	-1.08
Patterns of Chapter 1 Expenditures			
Percentage Chapter 1 on instruction	61.97	66.93	-4.96
Percentage Chapter 1 on instructional support	20.10	16.95	3.16
Percentage Chapter 1 on administration	14.52	12.84	1.68
Percentage Chapter 1 on operations	2.41	2.77	-.36

average of 2.5 percentage points more on instructional support, whereas high-performing schools spend slightly more in the other three areas.

Again, these relatively minor spending differences may reflect the limited discretion that even schools in Chicago have over their full budgets. Focusing on discretionary money may yield more insight. In contrast to the comparison of DEA-efficient and inefficient schools, the bottom panel of Table 3.5 shows several differences between high- and low-performing schools in the allocation of discretionary spending across functions. This is consistent with the belief of many proponents of school-based budgeting that fiscal decentralization will result in more diverse spending patterns as schools target their resources to meet individual school needs.

Notice that high-performing schools average almost 5 percentage points more Chapter 1 spending on instruction and less on instructional support and administration. Although the cross-sectional nature of the data limits causal inferences, these results indicate that schools producing higher student outputs tend to target a larger share of their discretionary resources toward direct instructional expenditures. Of course, without more detailed analysis of individual school needs in relation to their spending patterns, we should not conclude that low-performing schools budget their resources inappropriately.[29]

Alternative Methods:
Cost Functions

A final method that has been used to assess efficiency of public schools relies on the estimation of a cost function for education, rather than the estimation of the production function. To date, this method has been applied almost exclusively using only district-level data, due, in large part, to the dearth of school-level cost data (see, e.g., Downes & Pogue, 1994; or Duncombe, Ruggiero, & Yinger, 1996). As school-level spending data become available, researchers and policymakers are likely to be interested in the application of cost-function-based methods for assessing school efficiency. Although these cost-function-based methods have some attractive features as outlined below, serious practical and conceptual issues need to be addressed in applying these techniques at the school level to assess efficiency.

According to economic principles, a cost function for education would measure the minimum cost of producing some level of output, given the set of input prices. In fact, production functions and cost functions can be closely related—given a specific production function, a related (or dual) cost function can be derived that captures the minimum costs of producing output via the technology summarized by that specific production function and given input prices.[30] In its general form, it can be represented as

(6) $C = f(w_1, w_2, \ldots, w_n, Q)$

where C represents cost, $w_1, w_2, \ldots, w_n$ represent the prices of the inputs to production, and Q represents output.[31]

A simple, linear cost function might be represented by

$$
\begin{aligned}
(7) \qquad \text{COST}_{sdt} = {} & \beta_0 + \beta_1 TS_{sdt} + \beta_2 ST_{sdt} + \beta_3 P_{sdt} + \\
& \beta_4 W_{sdt} + \beta_5 DT_{dt} + \beta_6 T + \beta_7 D + \beta_8 S + \kappa
\end{aligned}
$$

where COST_{sdt} measures costs in school s in district d at time t, W_{sdt} represents the vectors of the prices of the school inputs and all other variables are as previously defined.[32] (Note that SC, the vector of school inputs, is not included. Instead W, the vector of input prices, is.) Again, the coefficients on the school dummies, β_8, capture efficiency differentials between schools.

In general, different assumptions and restrictions govern the estimation of cost and production functions. First, a production function treats output as endogenous and input quantities as exogenous, whereas a cost function treats costs and input quantities as endogenous and input prices and output quantities as exogenous. Thus, to the extent that the prices of inputs are determined by district administrators or officials, rather than school administrators or officials, input prices may be appropriately viewed as exogenous and the cost function may be considered more appropriate. Second, because output is specified as a regressor in a cost function, multiple output measures can be readily included.

Although cost functions have an undeniable appeal, there are some serious impediments to their use—most important, data that purport to measure school-level costs rarely do. Instead, the cost data may be more appropriately viewed as expenditure data or budget allocation data, which may merely reflect a politically driven allocation of district spending to the schools. As demonstrated by Downes and Pogue (1994), a district-level analysis of expenditure data can disentangle cost factors by employing an explicit model of public expenditure determination by school districts. Intuitively, in such a model, public expenditures are viewed as resulting from the interplay of factors determining voter demand for education services and the costs they face in producing them. Cost factors can, then, be identified in a model that includes variables explaining costs that do not also explain the demand for public education.[33] Although the model of expenditure determination may be readily applied to school districts, the process by which school-level costs are determined likely bears little similarity to the process described by typical district models, where the median voter formulation is most often employed. Are schools appropriately viewed as acting to minimize costs? If not, how important is the bias that would be introduced by assuming so? In a world in which schools are typically allocated teacher lines, rather than wielding any direct real control over their budget or spending, applying this model to understanding school efficiency may require some additional thinking and adaptation.

Concluding Comments

Running through the discussion of alternative methods for measuring school-level efficiency are a number of recurring issues whose importance depends in part on the use to which the efficiency measure will be put. The introduction identifies four broad uses of measures: providing information, reorganizing schools, allocating resources, and providing incentives. In this section, we highlight issues in relationship to each proposed use of the measure.

For purposes of providing information to parents and students about school performance, it is particularly important to choose the output measures carefully, whichever method of measuring efficiency is employed. Given the dearth of evidence about the relationship between results generated by the different measures and the lack of consensus about the importance of the different outputs, efficiency measures will have to be gauged based on a wide variety of measures to inform parents, students, and communities adequately. The DEA or cost-function-based measures—which allow the simultaneous consideration of multiple outputs—are attractive methods to consider. Alternatively, production function or adjusted performance measures can be applied to multiple measures seriatim. Both value-added and level measures of performance will be useful for reporting purposes— allowing users to form appropriate expectations about final outcomes and annual improvement. In fact, if the information is intended for use by individuals choosing a school, then matrixes of information showing outcomes and value added by alternative beginning levels at different schools may be most useful (e.g., see Meyer, 1996).

If the information is to be used to reorganize schools, care must be taken to construct measures that can reasonably be used to evaluate the effectiveness of the reorganization. Although it is reasonable to hold schools responsible for what they do over a school year and thus to use value-added measures, it is possible that significant improvement will still result in levels that are unacceptably low. Thus, both levels and changes are needed to address issues of restructuring. If productivity and efficiency measures change significantly across years, there will be particularly difficult problems for reorganization efforts, because the political and real resources needed to restructure are large and should not be deployed without evidence of persistent problems. Finally, the level of resources may be a significant part of the reason why some schools fail, and thus decisions about whether such resources are held constant or not in the productivity measure will be important. If they are not held constant, then the implication for a failing school is that it does control its resources, and even with this control, it could not succeed. Holding constant the resources, on the other hand, would imply that a solution for a failing school might be found by increasing its resources.

When using efficiency measures to allocate resources to schools, it will be particularly important to know how much choice school administrators have in allocating resources and whether they face any incentives to maximize any specific outputs. At one extreme, if schools do not have freedom to choose levels or patterns of resource use and no incentives to maximize outputs, then allocations by central authorities based on school-level efficiency measures will not be helpful in promoting efficiency. Instead, the central authority will need to devise incentives to which schools will respond. The efficiency measures in such a situation will depict average behavior in response to unknown and perhaps varying incentives, many of which could include patronage, political, or bureaucratic incentives.

Using efficiency measures as incentives for teachers, principals, or other participants provides perhaps the greatest challenge for these measures. Stakes are high because getting the measure wrong can lead to disillusionment on the part of crucial participants and/or gaming behavior that uses resources but produces no results. Value-added-type measures seem to make the most sense for providing incentives, but the unresolved technical issues about output measures, functional forms, appropriate risk factors, or stability of measures mean that implementation is difficult. In addition, more complex models, which may be more accurate, are often less transparent or understandable to administrators and teachers. The advantage is that gaming would be less common, but the cost is that an opaque system may seem arbitrary.

Thus, no matter what the particular use of performance measures, the state of knowledge is not adequate to be confident that we will achieve the desired results using any of the currently available methodologies. We are confident, however, that given the pace of research in this area, we will know quite a bit more within 5 years, and hopefully enough to be able to use the appropriate method for the desired purpose.

Acknowledgments

The authors are listed in reverse alphabetical order. All contributed equally to the writing of this paper. We thank Andrew Reschovsky and Margaret E. Goertz for helpful comments on the paper and the Andrew W. Mellon Foundation for funding some of the work on the paper. All statements are the authors' alone.

Notes

1. See Schwartz, Stiefel, and Rubenstein (1998) for a discussion of education production functions in the context of financing K-12 education.

2. Although education production functions have traditionally been estimated using district-level data, school efficiency—in contrast to school district efficiency—cannot easily be measured without more disaggregated data (see Hanushek, 1986, for a review). The choice has been largely dictated by data availability rather than on conceptual or statistical grounds, and, as disaggregated data become available, school- and student-level analyses are becoming more common. In general, district-level production functions yield estimates of the efficiency of both the schools and the school district as one unit. A district-level analysis precludes the disentangling of inefficiencies due to characteristics of the district—say, due to poor or wasteful administration—from inefficiencies in the schools. Estimates of school efficiency can be derived from district-level data only if one assumes that all schools in the district are characterized by identical production functions, efficiency properties, and the like.

Alternatively, one could approximate school-level data from district-level data by using only those districts containing a single school of the kind being analyzed, say, only one high school. To the extent that there are variations in the production characteristics of schools within districts and/or there is interest in schools in larger districts, this approach will be unsatisfying. Because contemporary data sets more routinely include school and student-level data, which do not present these same limitations in estimating school efficiency, we do not include a discussion of the use of district-level data to measure school efficiency.

3. The distinction between productivity and efficiency is discussed below.

4. This means that bias on the coefficients of the included variables due to unobserved variables would be reduced. See Holtz-Eakin (1986) for a discussion of the importance of unobserved variables.

5. Alternatively, hierarchical linear modeling (HLM) could be employed to much the same effect. See Bryk and Raudenbush (1992) for examples of HLM applied to schools.

6. Although the linear specification in (2) would yield constant marginal products across schools, other specifications, such as the logarithmic specification, would yield different marginal products for inputs for different schools. Alternatively, school variables could be interacted with district dummies to allow variations across districts, which might realistically reflect the invariance of input prices within a district.

7. Some of the outputs produced by schools are closely associated in time to the education process. These include acquisition of knowledge and skills, social development, and commitment to good citizenship. Other outputs occur some time after schooling ends and are less closely tied to the schooling experience. These include individual lifetime earnings, health and social behavior (such as voting or committing crimes), and satisfaction with life. Currently, the most commonly used outputs in empirically estimated production functions are test scores and earnings, due, in large part, to the relative ease of obtaining these data and their appeal to the school community. Hanushek (1986) and Burtless (1996) provide good summaries of two strands of literature on tests and on human capital.

8. It is possible to model the joint production of multiple outputs or to develop output indexes that incorporate several outputs, but these present practical and conceptual difficulties that significantly complicate the estimation of the production function and assessment of school efficiency.

9. See Bryk, Yeow, Easton, and Luppescu (1998) for a thoughtful discussion of how to incorporate both levels and changes into a measure of school productivity.

10. Efficiency and productivity are distinct, but related, concepts. Efficiency in production occurs when "there is no way to produce more output with the same inputs or to produce the same output with less inputs" (Varian, 1992, p. 4). Increases in productivity (output per unit of input employed) occur due to increased efficiency in the use of the inputs to production or when costs are minimized for a given level of output.

11. This discussion refers to the input minimization model, which seeks to minimize inputs given observed outputs. An alternative approach, the output maximization model, specifies the increase in outputs that should be possible given observed inputs (Charnes et al., 1994b). The two orientations produce identical sets of efficient DMUs, while inefficient DMUs will be projected to different points on the production frontier.

12. Percentage of students in the school who are eligible for free and reduced price lunch or whose families receive public assistance.

13. Percentage of students with limited proficiency in English.

14. The number of students who transfer in or out of the school during the year, divided by total school enrollment.

15. Total school enrollment.

16. The IGAP tests are a series of state-administered subject-area examinations given yearly in selected grades. They are scored on a scale ranging from zero to 500, with 250 representing average performance.

17. Instruction consists of expenditures associated with direct instruction of students in classrooms, including teacher salaries and benefits; instructional support expenditures are those used to provide teacher, student, and program support, including professional development, guidance, health, library, and media services; administration expenditures are those used for principal and assistant principal salaries and for attendance and security services; and operations consist of noninstructional expenditures associated with the maintenance of the school building and lunchroom services.

18. This approach has been usefully employed in other applications. See Stiefel, Rubenstein, and Schwartz (1998) for a discussion of this approach in budgeting. See Bradbury, Ladd, Perrault, Reschovsky, and Yinger (1984) for a description of a Massachusetts's intergovernmental aid formula based in part on an estimate of costs of local services, where costs are adjusted for uncontrollable community environmental factors. Duncombe et al. (1996) develop an intradistrict education cost index involving uncontrollable factors (as well as other features).

19. If, instead, multiple years of data are available, then an estimate of the school effect can be formed based on averaging the estimated performance measures for a single school over multiple years.

20. Although this chapter focuses on adjusted measures, there is a case for excluding factors that are not controllable under prevailing circumstances, because their inclusion may lead to lower standards for schools serving vulnerable populations. Use of growth rates or changes in performance measures, rather than the levels themselves, may ameliorate this problem, as discussed in greater detail below.

21. See Ferguson and Ladd (1996) for a specific example involving black males.

22. This will matter less, however, when using added-value performance measures and/or the resources change little between the years.

23. See Goldstein and Spiegelhalter (1996) for an example of the use of adjusted performance measures for evaluating the performance of individual organizations in health care and education.

24. Assuming a normal distribution, standardized residuals will have a mean of approximately zero and a standard deviation of approximately one. Therefore, selecting a threshold standardized residual of 2, for example, can be expected to eliminate approximately 95% of the units from the sample.

25. Parent involvement is measured as the percentage of students whose family made at least one contact with the school during the year.

26. Alternative specifications of the model included pupil-teacher ratios in place of per pupil expenditures and produced similar results.

27. The schedule for administering the IGAP tests raises several difficulties for assessing performance using a pretest approach. First, same subject-area tests are administered at intervals of two or three grade levels. Therefore, it is not possible to examine differences in student performance in specific subject areas for the same cohort of students from one year to the next. In principle, achievement gains could be measured across several years (e.g., between third and sixth grade, or between sixth

and eighth grade). Unfortunately, only schoolwide averages are available in Chicago, not student-level performance data. High student mobility in Chicago makes changes in test scores across several years an unreliable indicator of school performance.

28. By standardizing the unit of measure, residuals from multiple output measures with different scales can be compared and aggregated. Although the residuals' units of measure may be standardized in other ways (e.g., by studentizing), the intuitive appeal and relatively simple calculation of the standardized residual (the simple residual divided by its estimated standard deviation) broadens its appeal for policy applications.

29. Low-performing schools may, for example, tend to have greater needs in noninstructional areas due to greater student or physical plant requirements.

30. For more on the duality between cost and production functions see, for example, Varian (1992).

31. This method has been applied to child care providers. See Mocan (1995).

32. Economic theory places some restrictions on the cost function; as an example, it should be linearly homogenous in the input prices. See Varian (1992) for more on the properties of cost functions.

33. See also Reschovsky and Imazeki (1998) for another application of this approach to Wisconsin school districts.

References

Arnold, V. L., Bardhan, I. L., & Cooper, W. W. (1994). *DEA models for evaluating efficiency and excellence in Texas secondary schools.* Austin: University of Texas, IC2 Institute.

Banker, R. D., Charnes, A., & Cooper, W. W. (1984). Some models for estimating scale and technical efficiencies in data envelopment analysis. *Management Science, 30*(9), 1078-1092.

Banker, R. D., & Morey, R. (1986). The use of categorical variables in data envelopment analysis. *Management Science, 32*(12), 1613-1627.

Bennett, W. J. (1988). *American education: Making it work.* Washington, DC: Department of Education.

Bessent, A. M., & Bessent, E.W. (1980). Determining the comparative efficiency of schools through data envelopment analysis. *Educational Administration Quarterly, 16*(2), 57-75.

Bessent, A., Bessent, E., Kennington, J., & Reagan, B. (1982). An application of mathematical programming to assess productivity in the Houston Independent School District. *Management Science, 28*(12), 1355-1367.

Bifulco, R., & Duncombe, W. (1998, March). *The identification and evaluation of low-performance schools: The case of New York City.* Paper presented at the annual meeting of the American Education Finance Association, Mobile, AL.

Bradbury, K., Ladd, H. F., Perrault, M., Reschovsky, A., & Yinger, J. (1984). State aid to offset fiscal disparities across communities. *National Tax Journal, 37,* 151-170.

Bryk, A. S., & Raudenbush, S. W. (1992). *Hierarchical linear models.* Newbury Park, CA: Sage.

Bryk, A. S., Yeow, M. T., Easton, J. Q., & Luppescu, S. (1998). *Academic productivity of Chicago public elementary schools.* Chicago: Consortium on Chicago School Research.

Burtless, G. (Ed.). (1996). *Does money matter? The effect of school resources on student achievement and adult success.* Washington, DC: Brookings Institute.

74   SCHOOL-BASED FINANCING

Chalos, P., & Cherian, J. (1995). An application of data envelopment analysis to public sector performance measurement and accountability. *Journal of Accounting and Public Policy, 14*, 143-160.

Charnes, A., Cooper, W. W., Lewin, A. Y., & Seiford, L. M. (1994a). Extensions to DEA models. In A. Charnes, W. W. Cooper, A. Y. Lewin, & L. M. Seiford (Eds.), *Data envelopment analysis: Theory, methodology and application* (pp. 23-48). Boston: Kluwer.

Charnes, A., Cooper, W. W., Lewin, A. Y., & Seiford, L. M. (1994b). Introduction. In A. Charnes, W. W. Cooper, A. Y. Lewin, & L. M. Seiford (Eds.), *Data envelopment analysis: Theory, methodology and application* (pp. 3-22). Boston: Kluwer.

Charnes, A., Cooper, W. W., & Rhodes, E. (1978). Measuring the efficiency of decision-making units. *European Journal of Operations Research, 2*, 429-444.

Clotfelter, C. T., & Ladd, H. F. (1996). Recognizing and rewarding success in public schools. In H. F. Ladd (Ed.), *Holding schools accountable* (pp. 23-63). Washington, DC: Brookings Institute.

Downes, T. A., & Pogue, T. F. (1994). Adjusting school aid formulas for the higher cost of education disadvantaged students. *National Tax Journal, 47*(1), 89-110.

Duncombe, W., Ruggerio, J., & Yinger, J. (1996). Alternate approaches to measuring the cost of education. In H. F. Ladd (Ed.), *Holding schools accountable* (pp. 327-356). Washington DC: Brookings Institute.

Duncombe, W., & Yinger, J. (1997). Why is it so hard to help central city schools? *Journal of Policy Analysis and Management, 16*(1), 85-113.

Fere, R., Grosskopf, S., & Weber, W. L. (1989). Measuring school district performance. *Public Finance Quarterly, 17*(4), 409-428.

Ferguson, R. F., (1991). Paying for public education: New evidence on how and why money matters. *Harvard Journal on Legislation, 28*(2), 465-498.

Ferguson, R. F., & Ladd, H. F. (1996). How and why money matters: An analysis of Alabama schools. In H. F. Ladd (Ed.), *Holding schools accountable* (pp. 265-298). Washington, DC: Brookings Institute.

Goldstein, H., & Spiegelhalter, D. J. (1996). League tables and their limitations: Statistical issues in comparisons of institutional performance. *Journal of the Royal Statistical Society, 159* (Part 3), 385-443.

Grosskopf, S., Hayes, K. J., Taylor, L. L., & Webber, W. L. (1997). Budget—Constrained frontier measures of fiscal equality and efficiency of schooling. *Review of Economics and Statistics, 79*(1), 116-124.

Hanushek, E. A. (1986). The economics of schooling: Production and efficiency in public schools. *Journal of Economic Literature, 24*, 1147-1177.

Hess, G. A., Jr. (1994). School based management as a vehicle for school reform. *Education and Urban Society, 26*(3), 3-17.

Holtz-Eakin, D. (1986). Unobserved tastes and the determination of municipal services. *National Tax Journal, 39*(4), 527-532.

Kain, J. F., & Singleton, K. (1996). Equality of educational opportunity revisited. *New England Economic Review*, 87-114.

Ladd, H. F., Roselius, B. L., & Walsh, R. P. (1997, November). *Using student test scores to measure the effectiveness of schools.* Paper presented at the annual conference of the Association for Public Policy Analysis and Management, Washington, DC.

Levin, H. M. (1970). A cost-effectiveness analysis of teacher selection. *Journal of Human Resources, 5*(1), 25-33.

Lovell, C. A., Knox, L. C., Walters, C., & Wood, L. L. (1994). Stratified models of education production using modified DEA and regression analysis. In A. Charnes,

W. W. Cooper, A. Y. Lewin, & L. M. Seiford (Eds.), *Data envelopment analysis: Theory, methodology and application* (pp. 329-352). Boston: Kluwer.

Mayston, D., & Jesson, D. (1988). Developing models of educational accountability. *Oxford Review of Education, 14*(3), 321-339.

Mazur, M. (1994). Evaluating the relative efficiency of baseball players. In A. Charnes, W. W. Cooper, A. Y. Lewin, & L. M. Seiford (Eds.), *Data envelopment analysis: Theory, methodology and application* (pp. 369-391). Boston: Kluwer.

Meyer, R. H. (1996). Value-added indicators of school performance. In E. Hanuschek & D. W. Jorgenson (Eds.), *Improving America's schools* (pp. 197-223). Washington, DC: National Academy Press.

Mocan, H. N. (1995). *Quality adjusted cost functions for child care centers.* Cambridge, MA: National Bureau of Economic Research.

Murnane, R. J. (1991). Interpreting the evidence on "does money matter?" *Harvard Journal on Legislation, 28*(2), 457-464.

Murnane, J., Singer, J., Willet, J., Kemple, F., & Olsen, R. (1991). *Who will teach?* Cambridge, MA: Harvard University Press.

Reschovsky, A., & Imazeki, J. (1998). The development of school finance formulas to guarantee the provision of adequate education to low-income students. In W. J. Fowler, Jr. (Ed.), *Developments in school finance, 1997* (pp. 121-148). Washington, DC: Department of Education, National Center for Education Statistics.

Rubenstein, R. (1998). Resource equity in Chicago public schools: A school-level approach. *Journal of Education Finance, 23*(4), 468-489.

Ruggiero, J. (1996). Efficiency of educational production: An analysis of New York school districts. *Review of Economics and Statistics, 78*(3), 499-509.

Schwartz, A. E., Stiefel, L., & Rubenstein, R. (1998). Education finance. In F. Thompson & M. Green (Eds.), *The handbook of public finance* (pp. 447-482). New York: Marcel Dekker.

Sherman, H. D. (1984). Improving the productivity of service business. *Sloan Management Review, 25*(3), 100-112.

Stiefel, L., Rubenstein, R., & Schwartz, A. E. (in press). Using adjusted performance measures for evaluating resource use. *Public Budgeting and Financing.*

Varian, H. R. (1992). *Microeconomic analysis.* New York: Norton.

PART II

Design and Implementation of School-Based Financing Systems

FOUR

Local Management of Schools and School Site-Based Financing

THE EXPERIENCE IN ENGLAND AND WALES SINCE 1988

QUENTIN THOMPSON

JOHN LAKIN

Since 1988, there has been a revolution in the management of schools in England and Wales. Most powers and responsibilities, which were previously the duty of locally elected bodies, have been either decentralized to schools or centralized to central government. This chapter explores these changes, the general reactions to them, the difficulties that were predicted at the outset, and some of the issues that have subsequently arisen.

The chapter draws on the initial work we did for the central government in 1988, where we reported on the practical implications of the proposed changes and the potential barriers to their success—indeed, we coined the term *local management of schools*, which the government subsequently adopted. This chapter also draws on the many sub-

sequent projects that we conducted for government and for the locally
elected bodies responsible for implementing the changes.

Background

From the original development of state education at the end of the
19th century until very recently, the responsibility for developing and
managing schools in England and Wales has been that of local education authorities (LEAs), of which there are just over 100, varying in
population size from under 200,000 to over 2 million. (The average
LEA contains around 200 schools, but the range is very wide, from less
than 50 to over 500 schools.) These LEAs were a democratically elected
part of the system of local government and employed professional
officers to run the school system in their areas. By contrast, the role of
central government was very limited, with more power to exhort than
to dictate.

The LEAs appointed heads of schools (the term used for school
principals in England and Wales), determined the numbers of teaching and nonteaching staff for each school, and controlled virtually all
expenditures. Each school had a "governing body" of people, generally composed of a mix of local politicians and other lay individuals
appointed by the LEA to take a particular interest in the school. But,
with the head of the school responsible for the internal discipline of
pupils and the conduct of staff, governing bodies had few powers and
acted mainly as a sounding board for the head and the LEA.

The 1988 Education Reform Act changed all this. It required each
LEA to submit to central government for approval a scheme for local
management of schools (LMS), under which schools would be funded
by a formula largely driven by pupil numbers and the resulting
budgets delegated to schools as a single block. At the same time, and
through a separate part of the legislation, central government took
responsibility for what was taught in schools by introducing a common national curriculum. A summary of the requirements for an LMS
scheme is shown in the Appendix in this chapter. Odden and Busch
(1998, chapter 5) describe in greater detail both the centrally defined
budgetary framework that structures each LEA's school financing
system and the precise formulas created by several diverse LEAs.

This control over the details of the LMS scheme by central government has been used to remove control of the day-to-day running of schools from LEAs and hand it over to the governing body of each individual school. Now the governing body appoints the head, decides the number of teaching and nonteaching staff, and makes decisions on most other aspects of expenditures. Central government also altered the constitution of each governing body so that the majority of members are now elected by parents at the school rather than being LEA appointees.

In addition, the 1988 act introduced "open enrollment" for schools, meaning that parents could choose which school their child would attend without reference to catchment areas or any other restrictions LEAs had previously sought to impose. The only restriction now was whether the school had sufficient places to meet parental demand.

It is not the purpose of this chapter to explain in detail why central government wished to instigate these changes, but a brief reflection may help in understanding their influence. Three pressures had led central government to wish to reduce the powers of LEAs (and local government more widely). The first was the change in the sources of finance for LEAs. One hundred years ago, almost all the costs of running schools were met by local taxes; today, central government grants meet 80% of LEA expenditure. Central government has therefore increasingly come to the view that it cannot allow locally elected representatives—often of an opposing political party to that of central government—to make decisions on expenditure that is now funded mostly by national taxes.

The second pressure was the growing view that the performance of schools is a national concern and not a local one. Central government has increasingly expressed worries about the outputs of schools and the diversity in the range and quality of decision making in the different LEAs. This pressure was also largely responsible for the introduction of the common national curriculum.

The third pressure was the wish of central government to use consumer pressure as a driver to increase quality in schools. To do this, parents needed the freedom to choose schools, and schools needed the ability (and the budget) to react to these market pressures. The standardized approaches of LEAs in their own local areas was therefore seen as a barrier to the development of a full education market place.

Thus, it is important to understand that LMS in England and Wales was not simply a means of funding schools in a more rational and transparent way; it was also an integral part of the transfer of powers away from LEAs (and local government more generally) toward central government upward and individual schools downward.

LEA Reactions to LMS and School Site-Based Financing

Because the introduction of LMS was part of a transfer of power, it is interesting to consider how the LEAs, widely perceived to be losers in the transfer, reacted. A distinction between the elected representatives and the professional officers can be made. Elected representatives exhibited a variety of responses at the outset. Some elected representatives perceived LMS as a major transfer of power away from LEAs, and were hostile to the change for this reason. Others recognized the extent of the change, but actively welcomed the move, seeing it as in line with their own policies of decentralization. But the majority of elected representatives probably failed to perceive the scale of the change and merely set their minds to working within the legislation to produce an LMS scheme that was tailored to meet the individual nature of the schools in their areas.

The officers within LEAs reacted slightly differently. There were two broad reactions. Senior LEA officers had traditionally been recruited from the teaching profession, with some having had experience as a school head before making the transfer to work for a LEA. For such officers who had moved into a LEA to influence the decisions of schools, the LMS proposals represented a loss of power that they found hard to accept. They looked for ways of retaining their influence over schools outside the LMS scheme. Many sought to establish a new relationship with schools that they called "partnership" but that, in reality, often concealed a paternalistic approach to heads of schools. Schools quickly made it clear that a partnership on these terms was not acceptable. But other officers, particularly those who had not sought day-to-day control over schools, saw the introduction of LMS as an exciting challenge. They welcomed the opportunity to extricate the LEA from detailed management at the school level to focus more on strategic issues and planning functions.

Today, LEA reactions are similarly divided, although far more elected representatives and officers are supportive of LMS than at the outset. Most have now accepted this reduced but more strategic role, and some even welcome the loss of what they saw as mundane tasks. Indeed, much to central government's surprise, many LEAs have pressed LMS further and faster than required by the legislation. For example, some have delegated responsibility for more of the centrally held services (and their budgets) than the government required; some delegated to small schools before the requirement from the government to do so; and some have delegated to all schools faster than the timetable set by government. But there remains a minority of LEAs that continue to resent the loss of power over schools that LMS entails. This group of LEAs has delegated only what central government has required according to the required timetable.

In our advice to central government at the outset of LMS, we argued that LEAs should be encouraged to move to a more strategic role, concentrating on planning the local school system, setting objectives, and monitoring educational outcomes. In the intervening period, many LEAs have attempted to make this transition, but few have achieved it entirely successfully. This is for a number of reasons. One is a cultural reason: Few LEA elected representatives and officers had traditionally operated in this way, preferring detailed administration and control to strategic management and influence. It was thus a learning process for them and their schools.

There are also more practical reasons: Two other changes made by central government at the same time as the introduction of LMS have undermined the strategic role of LEAs. The first was the opportunity for schools to become directly funded by central government, outside LEA influence altogether. Thus, any school that did not approve of the actions of its LEA could opt to become a "grant-maintained" school, with its budget provided (on a formula basis) from central government. This severely inhibited a LEA from acting in a way that was contrary to the interests of any one school, even if such actions were in the interests of schools in the area as a whole (e.g., the closure of a school to remove surplus places).

The second change was to create a national system for the inspection of schools, which had the effect of downgrading the role of LEAs in monitoring the performance and outcomes of schools. The funding to create the national inspection system was deducted from government grants to LEAs, such that LEA inspectors had to bid to government to carry out inspections of schools according to the national program rather than according to the priorities of their LEA. Thus, LEAs found themselves employing inspectors who now worked, in effect, more for central government than for the LEA.

School Reactions

The reactions of schools have been crucial to the implementation of LMS. We stressed at the outset that the success of LMS would depend on heads, governors, and teachers adopting a positive attitude toward the change. We also stressed how important an adequate training program would be to the successful introduction of LMS. A key factor in the initial attitudes of schools was their view of the additional workload that would result at the school level. Our advice to central government was that, although heads and governors of larger schools would accept the trade-off of an increased workload in return for greater decision-making power, it was unlikely to be as attractive to heads and governors of small primary schools. This was because the flexibility that LMS offered to small primary schools was so much less than for larger schools, given that the nonstaffing element of their budgets was very small and the staffing element difficult to change.

Central government decided to allow LEAs to exclude primary schools with fewer than 200 pupils from LMS if they wished, and many LEAs took advantage of this option initially. This caution was bolstered by the attitude expressed by many heads that they "had trained to be teachers, not accountants." The reality of the change over time has changed this perception almost universally; however, heads quickly saw that LMS did not require them to gain complex accountancy skills and that the freedoms of LMS far outweighed the additional workload. Moreover, the heads could normally delegate the extra workload to other management or administrative staff within the school, and many LEAs increased the general funding available to schools to allow them to appoint or enhance such posts.

For many heads, their newfound status as managers of their schools was little short of a revelation, and most relished their ability to take decisions without reference to an LEA officer. Indeed, such was the enthusiasm for LMS that even heads of small schools began to press for delegation. This led many LEAs voluntarily to delegate budgets to schools with fewer than 200 pupils. Eventually, this also led to central government amending the legislation to require the remaining LEAs to do likewise so that presently no schools are excluded from LMS (including specialist schools for pupils with severe physical or learning difficulties, to which a particular form of LMS was later extended).

Implementation Issues

In addition to a general concern about the reactions of LEAs and schools to LMS, we identified a number of implementation issues as likely to cause specific concerns: (1) the basis of the factors to be used in the formula; (2) the basis of the charges made to schools for their teachers; (3) the development of a formula based on need rather them historic expenditure; (4) the position of advisory and inspection services; and (5) the phasing in of delegation. We discuss each of these in more detail below before considering the new issues that have arisen subsequently.

Factors in the Formula

We argued at the outset that the bulk of a school's budget should be determined by pupil numbers, weighted to take account of relevant factors. The initial debate was therefore around the extent of weighting that should be given to pupil numbers for the factors of age, social deprivation, and special educational needs (SEN). In fact, central government decided to insist that at least 75% of all funds should be allocated to schools on the basis of pupil numbers weighted by age alone, with the remaining (up to 25%) for LEAs to distribute on some other basis. Thus, although LEAs were free to take account of differences between pupils as a result of social deprivation or SEN, this was more constrained than their ability to reflect differences in age.

Many LEAs argued at the time that this gave them insufficient flexibility to reflect differences in social deprivation and SEN. But this has not proved to be the case for two reasons. First, although some LEAs have schools with high levels of social deprivation and/or SEN, this is a problem in formula funding terms only if the same LEAs also contain schools with very low levels, too. Thus, it is the diversity within an LEA that causes the funding difficulty; an LEA with a high level of social deprivation or SEN across all its schools can simply fund all pupils at a higher level without needing to use special factors—and most LEAs in urban areas are small enough for this to be the case. Second, when central government subsequently increased the minimum percentage of funds that must be allocated by pupil numbers from 75% to 80%, it allowed weightings for social deprivation and SEN to be included alongside age weightings within this target. So, LEAs were free to increase their weightings for these factors without restraint, though few did.

At a more detailed level, the identification of the indicators to measure social deprivation has also caused debate. Some LEAs sought to use national census measures of poverty, such as overcrowded housing or low car ownership. But these factors are collected every 10 years and so can be very out of date. They also tend to relate to geographical areas rather than pupils, and so fail to differentiate between a school in a poor area that is providing for pupils in that area and a school in a poor area but admitting large numbers of pupils from more affluent surrounding areas. In the end, the general practice has developed of using the numbers of pupils eligible for free school meals as the measure for social deprivation. This benefit is income related and is part of the national benefit system across England and Wales. It is also based on reasonably accurate and up-to-date information on parental income levels. If consensus has emerged on the best indicator to measure social deprivation, there is less consensus on the amount of additional funding that pupils experiencing social deprivation should receive. This is a matter for each individual LEA to determine in its formula, and varies widely across the country.

The issues around SEN are more complex. Many LEAs were muddled about the distinction between social deprivation and SEN at the outset; even those that were not found it difficult to make the choice of appropriate indicators to identify pupils with SEN. Thus, many LEAs, for pragmatic reasons, opted to use the same factor to weight pupil numbers for SEN as for social deprivation (i.e., free school meals), even though they recognized that the causal relationship between poverty and SEN was unproven—and even unlikely for at least some types of SEN. Their defense was that there was a rough statistical correlation between schools with social deprivation and schools with SEN, even though not all pupils on free school meals had SEN (or vice versa).

The difficulty of sustaining this argument led several LEAs to develop more accurate ways of identifying pupils with SEN through regular audits of pupils in schools. This approach was encouraged by central government, and many LEAs now operate such a practice. The costs of these audits are high, however, and have led some LEAs (including several that pioneered the original audit approach) to look for methods that are cheaper and less burdensome for LEA officers and schools. New approaches for identifying SEN that mix indicators such as free school meals with occasional audits are now emerging.

Charges for Teachers

Another major issue was the basis for charging the salaries of teachers to the budgets of schools. This became known as the "average/actual salaries debate," and revolved around whether schools should be charged for the actual costs of the specific teachers they employ or for the average cost of teachers within that LEA. This issues arises because the basic pay scale in England and Wales for teachers includes a very long series of annual increments paid automatically within the same grade; these can vary the cost of an individual teacher by up to 40%. A formula that allocates money largely by pupil numbers could therefore result in some schools, staffed by older teachers, having insufficient money to pay their teachers, whereas another school with the same number of pupils but with younger teachers might have money in hand. The danger of this happening is related to the size of a school, however; the larger the school, the more likely it is to have a mix of staff of different ages and salary levels and so gravitate toward the average.

Our advice to government was that schools should be charged on the basis of actual rather than average salaries but be given a long transitional period (up to 10 years) in which they could adjust their staffing complements to take account of their position. To do otherwise, we argued, would take away from a school the freedom (and desirability) to balance experience against cost when appointing staff. It would also disadvantage schools that traditionally have taken recently qualified teachers, either out of choice or out of circumstance (given that some less popular schools do not attract a strong field of experienced applicants for vacant posts)—and advantage schools with many senior, experienced staff.

The government decided to act on our advice, but to allow a transition period of not more than 5 years. It argued that a longer transition period was unnecessary and would create other difficulties.

LEAs lobbied more vigorously on this issue than on any other. The government at first conceded that very small schools could be charged average rather than actual salaries for their teaching staff, but it later allowed LEAs to introduce averaging arrangements for all schools below 330 pupils in size—which, in effect, meant that the vast majority of primary schools in the country could be protected in this way.

The position today is that some LEAs have taken full advantage of this for all their schools below 330 pupils, whereas others have not. Each group of LEAs holds strong views on the issue, and there is little sign of movement. Those schools protected by the averaging of salaries show no wish to change, whereas heads in LEAs that chose no such protection are equally clear that their LEA got it right.

The views of heads in LEAs that did not introduce the protection are interesting. In general, they feel more able to manage the budgets of their schools because they can influence the costs of the teaching staff by appointing less experienced teachers if they wish and using the extra money for other things, such as teaching materials. Because, in a primary school, some 80% of the costs of running the school are salary costs, they wonder why other heads would want to take on the workload of LMS but, at the same time, give up the chance to influence 80% of the budget.

Needs-Based Versus Historic Expenditure

In our report, we recommended that LEAs should look to develop a funding formula for schools that was needs-based rather than a mere reflection of historic spending. This advice was echoed in central government advice to LEAs. Even those LEAs that were sympathetic to this message found the advice difficult to act on, however. The problem was twofold. First, LEAs had few reference points to develop a needs-based approach other than the historic pattern of spending (which, some claimed slightly disingenuously, was an accumulation of previous policy decisions and so, by definition, represented need). Second, the pressure on LEAs from their schools to produce a formula that produced the fewest "winners" and "losers" (and hence the closest match to the historic pattern of spending) was very great.

LEAs approached the task of developing the formula in one of two ways. About one third worked top down: They tried to analyze the policies behind the current expenditure pattern and then produced relatively simple formulas. Typically, they divided the total budget to be delegated to schools into a number of blocks on a percentage basis, and then allocated these blocks by relevant factors. The school, of course, simply received one aggregated block sum. Thus, a typical top-down formula might be as follows:

- A block (typically 75% of the total budget) to be allocated by pupil numbers weighted by age (with age weightings typically ranging from 1.0 for primary school pupils to 1.6 for secondary school pupils under 16 years of age and to 1.9 for secondary school pupils over 16 years of age)
- A block (typically 5%) to meet social deprivation (normally allocated on the basis of the numbers of pupils in receipt of free school meals)
- A block (typically 5%) to meet SEN (sometimes again allocated on the basis of free school meals or an audit of pupils in schools)
- A block (typically 5%) to provide a lump sum to all schools to cover fixed costs and to protect small schools with high overheads
- A block (typically 10%) to be allocated to meet premises costs (i.e., heating, lighting, cleaning), usually based on the floor space of the school buildings

The advantage of this approach was its simplicity and transparency and the likelihood that it would be based more on need than history.

But the disadvantage was that it was likely to produce financial turbulence for some schools in the initial period as they adjusted their expenditure up or down to meet their new budget allocations. In other words, there could be a great deal of winners and losers among schools, with the losers more vocal than the winners.

It was for these reasons that about two thirds of LEAs preferred to develop their formulas by working bottom up from the historic expenditure pattern on schools. In this way they attempted to match the previous spending pattern as closely as possible through a series of intricate subformulas for each item of spending (i.e., for teaching staff, nonteaching staff, heating, lighting, cleaning, and so on), although again the school received a single block sum.

The advantage of this approach was that it had an initial appearance of greater fairness to schools because it led to fewer winners and losers. Moreover, schools could check the various subformulas to see whether the LEA had taken account of all relevant factors and not short-changed schools in the transition to LMS by underfunding some aspect of school expenditure. The disadvantage was the huge complexity of the exercise and the fact that it did not question whether the historic pattern of expenditure was based on real need or not.

Over the years, the top-down approach has proved more durable, and many LEAs that initially opted for a bottom-up approach have looked to simplify their formula and lose the detailed subformulas. Four main problems with the bottom-up approach emerged. First, the detailed subformulas became increasingly anachronistic as schools changed their expenditure patterns under LMS to reflect their needs, leaving the LEA the choice of either continuing to fund them using subformulas based on the old expenditure pattern or amending the subformulas to keep up with the new pattern. Second, it gave LEA elected representatives the mistaken idea that they still controlled detailed school expenditure and that schools should be held to account if they did not spend the sums allocated by the subformula on the items in question. Third, schools wishing to maximize their own budget allocations from the formula argued for extra subformulas to take account of their own particular circumstances (e.g., high ceilings, which made some classrooms more expensive to heat, heating systems that were particularly expensive to maintain). This led either to arguments between schools and LEAs or to the LEA trying to develop ever more complex (and sometimes absurd) subformulas. Fourth, as the LEA officers and heads who had designed the original formula moved on, the reasoning behind the various subformulas became lost in time and less relevant to their successors.

Regardless of which approach an LEA adopted for developing its formula, a more recent development has been the search for more genuinely needs-based formulas. This has usually taken the form of an analysis of activities at the school level to determine exactly how much a school needs to spend to educate pupils of different ages and abilities. The results typically show a much narrower range of age weightings for pupils than most LEA formulas had assumed. In particular, the current differential of funding between primary and secondary school pupils is rarely supported by the exercise. Such work is at an early stage even in the minority of LEAs that have started it; still fewer have attempted to amend their formula to reflect the results.

Advisory and Inspection Services

In our original report, we suggested that the new relationship between the LEA and its schools with respect to the provision of goods and services should be one of contractor and customer, with schools acting as the customer. In this way, schools would determine the goods and services they required and choose the most appropriate supplier, which might or might not be the LEA, depending on price and quality.

We recognized, however, that this relationship would be most difficult to achieve in terms of the LEA teaching advisory service, which offers advice to schools on curriculum and professional leadership issues. The problem here was that this service advised the LEA as well as schools on these issues, and also inspected and monitored the performance of schools on behalf of the LEA. Thus, the advisory service was a contractor both to the LEA and to schools, with dual functions that could not easily be disentangled. For this reason, we suggested that many LEAs would want to hold this service centrally and not delegate it to schools until the service could be reviewed and the different roles identified.

Most LEAs followed this practice initially, but some have now separated the service into two groups: a small group to advise the LEA with its costs retained centrally, and a larger group to advise schools with its costs delegated and schools choosing whether to buy it back. Other LEAs have not sought to divide the service into two groups, but simply established it as a business unit, either inside or outside the LEA, that must earn its income by selling its services to schools and to the LEA. This latter development has been accelerated by the establishment of a national schools inspection system (contrasting with the plethora of local inspection arrangements that existed previously), which has required the service to bid to central government for contracts to carry out national inspections of schools.

Whatever approach adopted, the experience of professional staff in the advisory service has been chastening. Many believed themselves to be highly regarded by schools and as having recent and relevant experience that schools would readily wish to buy back using their delegated budgets. But the general experience has been that schools have purchased much less advice than was provided (at no charge) to them previously, causing a rapid loss of posts in the advisory service. This reflects not only the more selective approach that schools display as customers when they are footing the bill, but also the fact that the high regard schools previously appeared to have for advisers lay as much in the advisers' power and influence within the LEA (which too has declined) as in their professional expertise.

Phasing of Delegation

A final implementation issue on which there were choices for LEAs concerned the phasing in of delegation to schools, for which LEAs were allowed a period of 3 years. We identified two main options: (1) delegate the money for all functions to some schools and then increase the number of schools to which full delegation applied each year; and (2) delegate the money for some functions to all schools immediately and then increase the range of functions each year until full delegation was reached.

Most LEAs chose the former course, starting with full delegation to secondary schools in the first year, extending it to large primary schools in the second year, and then bringing in small primaries in the third year. This allowed LEAs to manage the delivery of training for heads, schools administrators, and governors over a 3-year period.

A minority of LEAs chose the latter course and phased in delegation by function. This usually meant starting with the delegation of funds for books and materials in the first year, then extending it to costs for premises in the second year, and on to staffing costs in the third year. In retrospect, this course was much less successful, both for schools and for LEAs, for the following reasons. First, confusion arose over the demarcation between expenditure heads. Second, accountancy problems occurred because a school might wish to use the money delegated for one function for another that had not yet been delegated. Third, heads complained that they were not fully in control of their budgets until the end of the program. This made the extra workload of LMS more apparent to them than the extra freedoms that were promised. It also put heads at a disadvantage in career terms in comparison to heads in LEAs that had moved to full delegation much earlier.

Some LEAs also accelerated their timetable for phasing in delegation once it became apparent that schools wanted to make the transition quickly. For example, several LEAs decided to phase over 2 years rather than make use of the full 3 years that the legislation allowed. The general lesson appears to be that the phasing in of delegation is best done swiftly, provided that adequate training and preparation has been carried out. A long or complex transition period merely creates uncertainty and delays the full realization of potential benefits.

New Issues

A number of issues concerning LMS have emerged since 1988, some as a result of subsequent changes in legislation or attitudes. Four of the main issues are (1) the differentiation in funding between different levels of education; (2) the treatment of special educational needs; (3) the maintenance of central services; and (4) the growth of market pressures on schools and the implications for the role of the LEA.

Funding Different Levels of Education

The development of funding formulas for schools within a common framework by LEAs has allowed comparisons of funding levels to be made between different levels of education. The main areas of debate have been the differential between primary and secondary schools pupils within LEAs, the differential between 16- to 19-year-old pupils in schools and in further education colleges, and the differential between similar pupils in different LEAs.

The fact that there is a differential between the funds LEAs allocate for primary and secondary pupils is a long established aspect of school management in England and Wales. Its justification has been in the lower class sizes and pupil teacher ratios that secondary school education has always enjoyed (and in the higher salaries that secondary school teachers tend to receive). The full extent of the differential in favor of secondary schools was rarely apparent before the development of LMS, however.

LEAs have therefore come under pressure from primary schools to justify the differential on the basis of need rather than historic precedent. Moreover, the arguments of primary schools have been strengthened by the introduction of a common national curriculum that requires subject specialists in primary schools for the first time (a factor that was previously used to justify part of the secondary school differential) and by increasing research evidence that suggests that greater investment in the early years of primary education is the most likely guarantee of future pupil achievement.

As a result, a few LEAs have committed themselves to reduce the differential over time, and some have embarked on research to determine what factors continue to have relevance in supporting the differential. The latter approach normally takes the form of an activity-based analysis of schools and generally supports a narrowing of the differential.

A problem LEAs face in reducing the primary/secondary differential is the potential reaction of secondary schools to any change. Although many secondary school heads accept the fact that primary schools have been underfunded historically, they do not believe that this should be addressed by shifting resources away from secondary schools (which they argue are also underfunded). Moreover, they are able to hold over their LEAs the threat that they will opt to become grant maintained (i.e., funded directly by central government) if any change is made to the status quo. This has led many LEAs to state that the differential can be addressed only when extra resources are available, which may be some considerable time in the future given the prospects for increased public expenditure in England and Wales.

Another differential that has been exposed is that between 16- to 19-year-old pupils in schools and further education colleges. Historically, the divide in role between schools and colleges for this age group was that academic pupils remained in schools beyond the compulsory school age of 16, whereas vocational pupils entered colleges at 16 years of age (or entered work directly). This educational apartheid has broken down in recent years as the wisdom of categorizing pupils and qualifications in such a way has been questioned. Thus, many schools now offer vocational courses for this age group, and most colleges also provide a full range of academic qualifications. This means that students of the same age can be found in schools and in colleges studying for the same qualifications but being funded by different methods.

The advent of formula funding for schools by LEAs and formula funding for colleges by central government (albeit a different kind of formula) has allowed a direct comparison of funding levels to be made for the first time. This has revealed a funding differential of between 5% and 10% in favor of schools, although the figures are fiercely disputed by college principals, who claim it is a much wider differential.

Whatever the true level of the differential, the net result is to fuel the argument that all 16- to 19-year-olds should be funded on the same basis, via a transfer of responsibility for the funding of this age group in schools from LEAs to central government. There is also debate around whether the funding mechanism for such a change should be via a national formula that would directly fund schools and colleges or via a publicly funded voucher system that would put purchasing power in the hands of individual pupils.

The final differential that has been exposed by LMS is that between similar pupils in different LEAs. Early work we carried out showed a funding differential of as much as 30% between different LEAs for pupils of a similar age that could not be explained by factors other than the policy decisions of LEAs. This has led schools in relatively low-funded areas to argue for an increase in funding. Moreover, central government has increasingly come to question whether such differentials are acceptable in a national schools system that has introduced common approaches in so many other areas (e.g., a national curriculum, national inspection system, and national salary structure for teachers).

This questioning of local diversity has also been championed by schools that have opted to become grant maintained (i.e., directly funded by central government). To date, their budgets have been calculated by reference to what they would have been had they remained with their former LEA, but there are now plans to produce a national formula for these schools to divorce them entirely from LEA comparisons. For many commentators, it would be a relatively small step to extend the national funding formula being developed for these schools (which are currently around 20% of secondary schools and 5% of primary schools) to all schools, thus removing the LEA influence over school funding entirely (and perhaps the need for LEAs at all).

Treatment of Special Educational Needs (SEN)

We have already commented on the problems LEAs have had in developing ways of identifying pupils with SEN in their funding formulas for schools. This has been compounded by two developments: (1) the introduction of a new legislative framework for SEN in 1991 that placed new duties on LEAs and gave greater rights to parents of pupils with SEN; and (2) an increase in the numbers of pupils identified as having SEN of all types.

Although neither of these developments may at first sight seem related to LMS, all are in practice inextricably linked. For example, LMS is credited with having made schools think about pupils in financial terms for the first time, such that each extra pupil was now seen as being worth a certain sum of money to the school. Likewise, the higher costs of educating pupils with SEN also became apparent to schools, such that they become reluctant to teach "expensive" pupils unless adequate additional resources were made available. Thus, schools lobbied LEAs to make sure that additional resources were available for pupils with SEN and then looked to maximize the income they received by identifying all such pupils. At the same time, changes in legislation introduced a common framework across LEAs for the management of SEN for the first time and gave parents the right to appeal against LEA decisions. Thus, parental pressure on LEAs to provide more generous resources to SEN has also increased.

The net effect of these changes has been a rise in the number of pupils identified as having SEN and in the resources allocated for them. LEAs have responded in a variety of ways, but most have looked to contain the increase in some way, usually either by strengthening their criteria for identifying SEN so that only higher levels of need receive extra resources, or by making it clear to schools that any increase in expenditure on SEN pupils will be met by a corresponding reduction in the resources allocated for non-SEN pupils (such that the total budget for schools remains unchanged).

Maintenance of Central Services

We have already commented on the experience of advisory services in LEAs. A similar fate has befallen many other LEA services; when their budgets have been delegated to schools, many schools have not bought budgets back in sufficient volume to maintain these services at their previous level. In many respects, this can be viewed as a success of LMS in that it constitutes a reallocation of resources away from services that schools believe to be adding less value to the education process and toward activities that they take to have a higher value. The scale and speed of the change has caused disruption in many LEAs, however.

There is also a range of support services, such as music tuition, school library services, and outdoor education, that are particularly vulnerable to small changes in the level of demand from schools. For example, the high fixed cost of assembling and maintaining an adequate book stock for a LEA-wide school library service means that it is viable only if the vast majority of schools buy into the service. Thus, the loss of one or two schools as customers can result in the viability of the whole service being thrown into question.

LEAs have sought to overcome these problems by developing service agreements with their schools in which schools are invited to enter into long-term commitments to buy services. Few schools have been willing to commit themselves to any agreement that extends beyond 1 or 2 years, however. As an alternative, therefore, some LEAs have resisted delegating funds for vulnerable services and instead delegated service entitlements within which schools can choose from a menu of possibilities.

This approach, which is often called *devolution* rather than delegation, allows schools to use their entitlement in different ways, but not to convert it into cash that could be used for other purposes. Thus, it allows schools to exert some power as customers but without the ultimate sanction of refusing to purchase the service altogether. It also has the advantage that it gives service providers a guaranteed level of demand into the future. Doubts remain, however, about whether such alternatives will prove durable into the future. For some commentators, they are merely a stepping stone toward full delegation that will be achieved once providers and schools have refashioned the services in question. For others, they represent the end of the journey, and one from which LEAs and schools will not seek to move.

Market Pressures on Schools
and the Role of LEAs

As we stated at the outset, LMS was one of a number of changes designed to put greater market pressure on schools to improve their quality and responsiveness. Other changes were the introduction of a common national curriculum, regular national inspection, reports, open enrollment, and the publication of comparative data on pupil achievement in tests and exams (creating "league tables" of schools published in the national press). The result of this has been to create a more diverse school system, with schools seeking to identify and promote their most favorable characteristics. Thus, many schools have invested in promotion and marketing activities, and there has been a corresponding reduction in many local areas of collaborative arrangements between schools (particularly at the secondary school level).

In the light of open enrollment for admissions, some popular schools with a high demand for places have sought to increase their share of high-ability pupils (whose subsequent performance is more likely to enhance the school's league table position); they are selecting pupils on the grounds of ability and aptitude, a development that the government has encouraged by relaxing the controls LEAs previously had to prevent selection of pupils by schools on these grounds. Similarly, schools have become more ready to expel pupils for disruptive behavior, thus creating a larger pool of pupils for which LEAs must cater to out of school.

Although these changes have undoubtedly improved the performance of some schools (as measured in test and exam results), it has created a greater number of "failing schools." These schools find themselves trapped in a downward spiral, where their poor published results lead to difficulties in attracting sufficient pupils (and particularly sufficient high-ability pupils) to maintain or improve their position. Prior to LMS, LEAs would have intended to assist such schools, but they now have fewer powers and resources to do so. Thus, a school is more likely to progress to a crisis stage before intervention is triggered. This raises the wider question of whether LEAs are, in reality, any longer able to effect change and improvement in their school systems, or whether their role has become weakened to the point of irrelevance.

In the next few years, we are likely to see either a strengthening of the role of LEAs to allow them greater powers of intervention in schools or, alternatively, an acceptance that they no longer serve an important role in the schools system in England and Wales.

Conclusion

The experience of the last 8 years of local management of schools, formula funding, and delegation of budgets has generally been positive. It has created more responsive schools and a more transparent and open system of funding in which previous assumptions have been challenged. Schools have reacted positively to the change, and LEAs have accepted their new reduced role. The transition period was generally well managed by LEAs, and central government has been pleased with the results.

A number of new issues have emerged as a result of subsequent developments, some of which now cause concern. It remains to be seen whether these lead to further changes, either a strengthening of the role of LEAs in managing the new education market place or a move to even greater school autonomy in which the need for an intermediate body between schools and central government is further questioned.

Appendix:
Summary of the LMS Funding Formulas Requirements

The regulations laid down by central government for the construction of LMS schemes allowed LEAs to construct their own formulas, but within a common framework that constrained their scope for retaining control over schools' detailed expenditures.

The regulations set down minimum requirements for each scheme. All money made available for schools by LEAs had to be delegated to schools except for a limited number of exceptions. The main exceptions were (1) capital works and major structure maintenance; (2) home-to-school transport; (3) some central services for pupils with SEN; (4) professional advice and support; (5) provision of school meals; and (6) central administrative costs.

All the remaining money had to be delegated to schools by a formula. The formula had to delegate at least 75% of this remaining sum on the basis of pupil numbers that could be weighted by age. (This was later increased to 80%, but allowed weighting by age, social deprivation, and special educational needs.) The formula was allowed to allocate the balance of the remaining sum to take account of (1) protection for small schools where their overhead costs were abnormally high; (2) premises costs; (3) social deprivation; (4) special educational needs; and (5) actual/average salary costs in schools under 200 pupils (later increased to schools under 330 pupils).

All money used formerly by the LEA to meet the costs of the following had to be delegated to schools in a single block for schools to use as they wished: (1) teacher costs; (2) nonteaching staff costs; (3) costs of books, materials, furniture, and equipment; (4) examination fees; (5) internal buildings maintenance; (6) grounds maintenance; and (7) fuel and water costs.

Reference

Odden, A., & Busch, C. (1998). *Financing schools for high performance: Strategies for improving the use of educational resources.* San Francisco: Jossey-Bass.

Recent Developments in Decentralizing School Budgets in Australia

BRIAN CALDWELL

PETER HILL

This chapter provides an account of developments in three school systems under conditions of school-based management. Particular attention is given to Victoria, where the Schools of the Future program implemented since 1993 involves a higher level of decentralization than any other state. Indeed, Victoria is the largest system anywhere to have decentralized as much as 90% of a public authority's school education budget to schools. The extended account of experience in Victoria is preceded by brief reference to Tasmania, which for many years provided the benchmark for school-based management of resources; and to practice in one of the largest nongovernment systems, Catholic schools in the Archdiocese of Melbourne, where there is a relatively high level of school-based management.

Tasmania

Tasmania is the smallest of the Australian states, but it moved relatively quickly to decentralize funds to schools following the work of the Australian Schools Commission in the 1970s. Indeed, this state furnished the model for self-managing schools that has proved helpful in a number of other settings (see Caldwell & Spinks, 1988). By 1997, funds to cover almost all nonstaff expenditure were decentralized to schools.

The School Resource Package in Tasmania, which allows high flexibility as far as deployment is concerned, has four components: general support grant, maintenance grant, energy, and student assistance scheme. The general support grant is disbursed with 67% of the total being a per capita allocation, 25% according to educational needs, and 8% for rurality needs, with relativities across grades being 1.00 primary (grades K-6), 1.25 secondary (grades 7-10), and 1.45 senior secondary (grades 11-12). The maintenance grant comprises four components, with 40% allocated on the basis of a building needs index, 45% on a per capita basis, 7% for educational needs, and 8% for rurality needs, with relativities across grades being 1.0 for primary (grades K-6) and 1.6 for secondary (grades 7-12).

Educational needs are assessed using a composite measure involving the Ross Index of Educational Disadvantage and the proportion of students in receipt of an income-tested government assistance allowance. This index was developed in 1983 by Kenneth Ross, then at the Australian Council for Educational Research (see Ross, 1983), joined later by Stephen Farish, then at the Education Department of Victoria. Ross developed his index using 44 variables derived from Australian Bureau of Statistics census data; these were reduced to six to provide a measure of disadvantage reflecting the capacity of students to take advantage of educational facilities: occupation, income, accommodation, education, family structure, and transiency. An index was obtained for each school by mapping the school's catchment area for students in grade 4 (primary) and grade 8 (secondary). Scores on the index were converted into a scale with 16 levels of disadvantage.

Rurality needs in Tasmania are determined by distance from a major city and the size of the center where school is located, with relativities according to grades of schooling. Teaching and nonteaching staff are allocated according to a range of school and student characteristics, with little local flexibility and some district discretion for school by school variation.

Catholic Schools in Melbourne

Approximately 30% of all students are educated in nongovernment schools, mostly in systems of Catholic schools. No account of efforts to implement needs-based funding under conditions of decentralization would be complete without reference to approaches in such systems. The model adopted by the Catholic Education Commission of Victoria for schools in the Archdiocese of Melbourne provides a good illustration of these approaches. Five principles underpin the model (Doyle, personal communication, May 27, 1997) and the commission's commitment to promoting equality of opportunity by (1) ensuring that no Catholic child is excluded from a Catholic school because of financial incapacity; (2) ensuring that each member school has sufficient finances to operate at a basic standard of recurrent resource usage; (3) promoting diversity of curriculum within each member school and among neighboring schools; (4) preserving autonomy of action of member schools in servicing the needs of the local area; and (5) ensuring a balanced improvement in standards in meeting the relative needs of member schools.

As in Tasmania and formerly in Victorian government schools (see below), the resource model in its application uses the Ross Index of Disadvantage. All primary and secondary schools receive a total budget that reflects the principles listed above and placement on the 16-point Ross index. A proportion of funds is retained centrally for such expenditures as school support, teacher development, and long service leave. Of particular interest is the manner in which state and commonwealth recurrent grants are combined and provided to the schools, from which sum is deducted an expected local contribution of private income. This last item is essentially a fee paid by parents, also determined on the 16-point scale, with provision for exemptions for parents unable to pay.

Schools of the Future in Victoria

Victoria is a state with a population approaching 5 million people, with a government school system serving some 520,000 students in approximately 1,700 schools. Almost 90% of the state's education budget is decentralized to schools. This is the highest proportion allocated by any system in Australia, and for this reason alone warrants particular attention. It should be noted that New South Wales planned to move in this direction in the late 1980s and early 1990s, but the opposition of the New South Wales Teachers Federation to including a salaries component in the school budget meant that the scheme fell well short of intentions.

Schools of the Future

The reform of schools in the public sector in Victoria has reached an advanced stage, particularly as a result of the implementation of the current government's Schools of the Future program. In line with trends in comparable nations, the broad features of the Victorian government schools reforms involve the establishment of frameworks within which schools can be self-managing. The Schools of the Future program is built around frameworks for curriculum, people, resources, and accountability. Consistent with efforts to restructure the public sector, there has been substantial downsizing of central and regional agencies, leaving a small but powerful strategic core to "steer" the system.

Content and performance standards for student learning in eight key learning areas (arts, English, health and physical education, languages other than English, mathematics, science, studies of society and the environment, and technology) are determined centrally (curriculum). Although personnel for the most part remain centrally employed, there is capacity and flexibility at the school level to select new staff and determine the mix of professional, paraprofessional, and support arrangements (people) as positions become vacant. Schools have their own budgets in a process variously described as global budgeting or school-based budgeting, allowing discretion in deployment at the local level according to a mix of school and state priorities (resources). In Victoria, this is embodied in a school charter that provides a framework for planning and accountability over a 3-year period (accountability).

The first steps toward the concept of a school global budget were taken in Victoria in the early 1980s with the introduction of program budgeting and the further empowerment of school councils to set policy and approve budgets for certain nonsalary operating costs, which amounted to about 5% of total recurrent expenditure. These developments were stalled in the late 1980s as a result of the opposition of teacher unions and parent organizations, but were moved forward in dramatic fashion following the landslide election of the Liberal/National Parties Coalition government in Victoria in September 1992 (see Caldwell & Hayward, 1998, for an account of the design and implementation of the Schools of the Future program).

Principles Underpinning
the Delegated Schools Budget in Victoria

Having determined that about 90% of the state's budget for school education would be allocated directly to schools through a mechanism known as the school global budget (delegated schools budget), the newly elected government sought to establish a mechanism for allocating the available funds. To assist in this task, a committee was set up to advise the minister for education on the development and implementation of new funding arrangements. The committee's recommendations as contained in its first two reports (Education Committee, 1994, 1995) were accepted and implemented. These recommendations set down the principles underpinning the school global budget and a mechanism for allocating funds involving per capita core funding supplemented by needs-based allocations for students at educational risk, students with disabilities and impairments, rural and isolated students, English as a second language (ESL) students, and certain priority programs. The committee's final report (Education Committee, 1998) and the response of the Department of Education were relatively recently released and most of the recommendations have not been implemented at this stage. On the other hand, a number of decisions have been taken by the government, and these are discussed in the final sections of this chapter.

Central to the education committee's deliberations were a set of six principles that the committee believed should guide decisions about funding for schools:

1. *Preeminence of educational considerations:* Determining what factors ought to be included in the construction of the delegated schools budget and their relative weighting are preeminently educational considerations.

2. *Fairness:* Schools with the same mix of learning needs should receive the same total of resources in the delegated schools budget.

3. *Transparency:* The basis for allocations in the delegated schools budget should be clear and readily understandable by all with an interest. The basis for the allocation of resources to each and every school should be made public.

4. *Subsidiarity:* Decisions on resource allocation should be made centrally only if they cannot be made locally. Decisions on items of expenditure should be excluded from the delegated schools budget only if schools do not control expenditure, if there is excessive variation of expenditure, if expenditure patterns are unpredictable, if an expenditure is once-off, or for expenditures for which schools are payment conduits.

5. *Accountability:* A school that receives resources because it has students with a certain mix of learning needs has the responsibility of providing programs to meet those needs, has authority to make decisions on how those resources will be allocated, and should be accountable for the use of those resources, including outcomes in relation to learning needs.

6. *Strategic implementation:* When new funding arrangements are indicated, they should be implemented progressively over several years to eliminate dramatic changes in the funding levels of schools from one year to another.

The committee concluded that the differential in per student funding provided to primary and secondary schools, which was 43% in favor of secondary schools, was not warranted if due regard was given to the first principle (preeminence of educational considerations). The committee also concluded that because this was not an immediate prospect. In its final report (Education Committee, 1998), the committee placed considerable emphasis on the principle of strategic implementation and moving toward the full implementation of its recommendations over a number of years and as additional funds became available, assuming an improvement in the economic environment.

Consideration of the first principle also led the committee to the conclusion that there was no educational rationale for adopting one rate of funding for primary schools (grades K-6) and another for secondary schools (grades 7-12), but rather that allocations should reflect needs at different stages of schooling (grades P-4, 5-8, and 9-12). In adopting this stages of schooling approach to funding, the committee was greatly influenced by research on school and classroom effectiveness, especially that relating to the early grades and to ensuring success in literacy, and research relating to the middle years and addressing problems of student alienation and lack of engagement in learning.

In its final report (Education Committee, 1998), the committee concludes that it is important to make explicit two further principles, in addition to the six identified above:

1. *Effectiveness:* Relativities among allocations in the delegated schools budget should reflect knowledge about school and classroom effectiveness.
2. *Efficiency:* Allocations in the delegated schools budget should reflect knowledge about the most cost-effective ways of achieving desired outcomes in schooling.

Adopting these definitions acknowledges that efficiency is also affected by the state of knowledge on effectiveness and the rate of take-up of this knowledge in schools. Thomas (1996) contends that efficiency is constrained by knowledge and the capacity to apply knowledge of what will yield a higher output, and, for this and other reasons, suggests that there are limits to efficiency in schools. That this should be so turns primarily on the absence of a convincing or wholly adequate theory of learning—a prerequisite for specifying clear technical relationships as a predictive basis for the relationship between inputs and educational outcomes. There is the added difficulty that schools are multipurpose organizations, and the achievement of some goals is not always compatible with others (Thomas, 1996).

Thomas (1996) proposes that schools should seek to become more cost-effective, an efficiency-related concept, engaging in a cost-effectiveness analysis that "compares alternative ways of achieving the same objective: the most cost effective will be the least costly of alternatives being compared, which is not necessarily the cheapest possible method of attaining the objective" (p. 35).

Structure of the Delegated Schools Budget

The structure of the delegated schools budget (school global budget) as first implemented in Victorian government schools in 1996 is summarized in Table 5.1. The total schools budget, excluding capital expenditure, for school education in the 1995-96 financial year was $1.360 million, of which a little over 5% ($72 million) was spent on state administration, including the salaries of centrally and regionally based staff, administration and office accommodation costs, and a proportion of the costs of operating the board of studies.[1] Thus, a sum of $1.288 million, or just under 95% of the total budget for school education, was made available for expenditure at the school level.

A further $108 million, or 8% of total recurrent funds, was excluded from the delegated schools budget, even though the costs were incurred at the school level. In line with the principle of subsidiarity, these funds were excluded because schools were not in a position to control their expenditures, or it was anticipated that there would be unavoidable and excessive variation of expenditures from school to school, or expenditure patterns were likely to be unpredictable. These included the costs of busing students, which is the responsibility of another government agency; distributing an education welfare allowance to poor families to assist them with unavoidable costs of schooling, such as uniforms and books; meeting the salary costs of replacement teachers where there was an extended absence of the regular teacher; and the costs of providing school support services, such as speech therapists and psychologists who serve several schools. Essential retentions thus totaled $182 million or 13% of the total schools budget. This left a total of $110 million or 87% of the total schools budget for school education, which was provided directly to individual schools as the delegated schools budget.

Table 5.2 amplifies the summary provided in Table 5.1 and gives a more detailed specification of components, dimensions, and indica-

TABLE 5.1.   Structure of the Total Schools Budget in Victoria: 1995-96
                   Financial Year (excludes capital expenditures)

Component	$ Million	% of Total
School-Level Allocation		
Delegated schools budget		
1. Basic pupil allocation: core funding	986	72.5
2. Curriculum enhancement: priority programs	32	2.4
3. Pupil specific		
a. Disabilities and impairments	42	3.1
b. Special learning needs	16	1.1
c. Non-English speaking background	18	1.3
4. Specific school factors		
a. Rurality and isolation	12	0.9
b. Premises	74	5.4
Total delegated schools budget	1,180	86.7
Essential exclusions related to school expenditure	108	7.9
Total school-level allocation	1,288	94.6
Nonschool-Level Allocation		
Essential exclusions related to system administration	72	5.3
Total schools budget (excluding capital expenditure)	1,360	100

tors. What follows is an account of how these components were developed and the directions for further development as proposed by the education committee of the School Global Budget Research Project and as implemented by the department of education.

Component 1: Basic Pupil Allocation

For the 1995-96 financial year, funding to cover salary and operating costs within schools was based on a single per capita rate for primary students and a single rate for secondary students. The rate for secondary school students was set at a rate that was approximately 43% higher than for primary students. Following extensive investigation of the actual pattern of internal allocation of funds within schools, and after consideration of research evidence regarding the educational needs of students in different stages of schooling, the education committee recommended that a system of per capita funding be adopted based on different weights at each grade level. The proposed weights were set at levels that reduced the differential between funding levels for students in primary and secondary schools, particularly at the point of transition between the two levels of schooling.

For the first three grades (K-2), the committee concluded that per capita funding levels should be at least 20% higher than in grades 3 and 4 to enable the implementation of best practice programs, including smaller class sizes, especially in kindergarten (see Blachford & Mortimore, 1994) and the implementation of an effective intervention program based on one-to-one tutoring in grade 1, such as Reading Recovery (Clay, 1991, 1993; Clay & Watson, 1982).

To obtain accurate estimates of program cost-effectiveness, a 3-year, longitudinal Early Literacy Research Project was initiated in a large sample of disadvantaged schools. The design elements incorporated into this project were based broadly on Slavin and colleagues' Success for All design (Madden, Slavin, Karweit, Dolan, & Wasik, 1993; Slavin et al., 1994; Slavin, Madden, Karweit, Livermon, & Dolan, 1990), although the details of each element, particularly the details of the classroom teaching programs, were developed locally to reflect the Australian context. The project involved a matched, control group of schools and extensive annual pre- and post-testing using a large number of measures of literacy achievement (see Crévola & Hill, 1998).

A consideration of the literature related to provision for the middle years of schooling, which in the Victorian context spans the final grades of primary education and the first two or three grades of secondary education, led the committee to conclude that traditional models of primary and secondary education provision typically fail to meet the educational and developmental needs of young adolescents (Australian Curriculum Studies Association, 1996; Capelluti & Stokes, 1991; Carnegie Council, 1989; Eyers, 1993; Hargreaves & Earl, 1990; Schools Council, 1993). Although an examination of best practice approaches to middle schooling within the Australian context (see, e.g., Cumming & Fleming, 1993; McKenzie & Taylor, 1995) reveals no one best way, it points to certain common elements of which the most important as far as funding levels are concerned involve interdisciplinary teams of teachers working with as few students as possible across as many subjects as possible. Accordingly, proposed weights for grades 5 and 6 (1.2) were set at a higher level than those for grades 3 and 4 (1.0) to enable common planning time for teachers in the final

TABLE 5.2. Relationship Among Components, Dimensions, and Indicators in the Delegated Schools Budget in Victoria, Australia in 1996

Component	Dimension	Indicator Measured for Each School
1. Basic pupil allocation		
a. Common allocation	Core funding with weighting: 1.00 for primary schools 1.43 for secondary schools	Number of students in the school with size adjustment factor for small schools
b. Grade-level supplement	Refinement to core funding proposed by the education committee of the School Global Budget Research Project would involve different weights for each grade level within three stages of schooling: K-4 5-8 9-12	Number of students at each grade level
2. Curriculum enhancement	Priority programs for statewide initiatives and special purpose programs, including instrumental music, languages other than English, programs for Aboriginal students, teacher professional development, school restructure	Numbers of students or teachers engaged in program or per school allocation, as relevant

two grades of the primary school. This also meant that the disparity in per capita funding for students in grade 7 (the first year of secondary school) as compared to grade 6 (the last year of elementary school) would be greatly reduced. A steadily increasing gradient was nevertheless built into the proposed set of weights for grades 5-8 in recognition of the increasing teacher assessment and preparation time involved and the additional operating costs inherent in specialist areas such as science, during the middle years.

TABLE 5.2. *Continued*

Component	Dimension	Indicator Measured for Each School
3. Pupil-specific factors	a. Students with disabilities and impairments	Assessed on educational needs questionnaire, with six levels of funding according to level of need
	b. Students with special educational needs	Index based on student-level measures of poverty, occupation, language spoken at home, family structure, Aboriginality, and transience, and applying an eligibility threshold so that funds are allocated only to the 30% of most disadvantaged schools
	c. Non-English-speaking-background students	Number of students in each category defined by stage of schooling (P-4, 5-6, 7-8, 9-12) and recency of arrival in Australia (0-2< years, 2-< 5, 5-< 7)
4. Specific school factors	a. Rurality and isolation	Equally weighted combination of distance from Melbourne, distance from provincial center of more than 20,000, distance from nearest primary or secondary school that is not eligible
		Location index funding = base funding + (location index score x student enrollment x $ rate)
		Rural size adjustment factor for primary schools < 200, secondary schools < 500
	b. Premises	Per school allocation with two elements:
		• Cleaning: total floor area and number of students
		• Maintenance and minor works allocation weighted 50% area, 25% type of materials in construction, 25% relative condition

A significant feature of schooling for older adolescents and young adults in grades 9-12 is the provision of a range of curricular choices, allowing students to explore and develop specific areas in depth and to pursue personal interests and strengths. Schools in Victoria typically provide a wide range of optional subjects in grade 9 and 10. In the final two grades (11 and 12), subject choice becomes even more significant as students select a relatively small number of subjects (typically six in grade 11 and five in grade 12) that they study in depth and are examined on. Choice and the availability of a full range of vocational pathways translate into significantly increased costs for schools. These costs arise from providing a comprehensive range of subjects despite relatively low enrollments in many (e.g., languages other than English) and the need for relatively small class sizes in others (e.g., the performing arts and laboratory and workshop-based subjects). In addition, costs relating to tutoring, counseling, and remediation are higher than average during the later grades of schooling, but increase significantly in grade 11 and yet again in grade 12 as demands increase for career counseling, assistance with study skills, home support, monitoring progress, and one-to-one or small group tutoring and guidance. Preparation and correction loads also increase as students prepare for their grade 12 examinations. Finally, the higher costs of materials and equipment are factors that result in increased levels of expenditure in grades 11 and 12. These considerations are reflected in the weights that the committee proposed for grades 9-12, which were 50% higher than those for grades 3 and 4; they were 80% higher for students in grade 11; and 100% higher for students in grade 12.

In addition to these grade-level weights, the committee proposed that there be a size adjustment factor to reflect the additional costs of provision in schools with very small enrollments. This was considered necessary to take into account the problems faced by small rural and isolated schools. The appropriate magnitude of this adjustment was estimated by the committee for the final two grades of schooling (11 and 12) only. For a school with a grade 11 and 12 combined enrollment of 500 students, the size adjustment factor might be set at 1.00. The weights would be slightly less than 1.0 for schools with an enrollment of 1,000 students, but would approach 1.2 for schools with an enrollment of 200 students.

To summarize, the committee proposed that the formula for the basic pupil allocation of the delegated schools budget contain two terms: a per capita amount weighted differentially according to the grade level of the student; and a size adjustment factor to take into account economies of scale and additional costs of provision for schools in rural areas with small enrollments. This can be represented by a general equation for calculating the entitlement of a given school for the basic pupil allocation, designated Core Funding in Victoria, as follows:

$$\text{Core funding} = f\left(\sum_{K}^{12} (w_j n_j X_1)\right)$$

in which f is a size adjustment factor, w_j is the weight for grade j, n_j is the number of students in grade j, and X_1 is the overall per capita allocation in dollars.

The above discussion applies to regular schools. Considerable work was undertaken on a comparable approach to the provision of the basic pupil allocation to special schools for students with disabilities and impairments, involving a simplified set of weights relating to different stages of schooling: 1.1 for ages 1-10, 0.9 for ages 11-15 and 1.0 for ages 16 and over. Once again, the committee proposed that a size adjustment factor be incorporated into the funding mechanism to accommodate special schools with very small enrollments (fewer than 45 students).

Component 2: Curriculum Enhancement

This component of the delegated schools budget was retained as a means of incorporating within the delegated schools budget funding for various priority programs. In 1996, this spending accounted for around 2.4% of total funding for school education, and included funds for a number of statewide initiatives and specific programs, including instrumental music programs, languages other than English, programs for Aboriginal students, and school restructure programs. It also included teacher professional development grant monies. The primary purpose of this component is to enable the government to fund strategic initiatives.

TABLE 5.3.   Funding Levels for Students With Disabilities and
                 Impairments, 1998

Level 1	$3,548
Level 2	$8,236
Level 3	$12,956
Level 4	$17,684
Level 5	$22,372
Level 6	$27,090

SOURCE: Department of Education, 1998a.

Component 3: Pupil-Specific Factors

Students with disabilities and impairments. Students with disabilities
and impairments may attend a regular school or a special school. In
1996, 10,400 students (1.3%) received additional funding under this
classification. The approach adopted within Victorian government
schools in recent years to funding students with disabilities and
impairments has been to allocate additional resources to such students following a detailed assessment using an educational needs
questionnaire that assigns eligible individuals to one of six levels of
funding (see Table 5.3). The six-level disabilities and impairments
funding formula provides resources for the following types of expenditures: teacher salaries and associated payroll tax, relief teaching,
specialized equipment, occupational therapy, physiotherapy, inter-
preter services, and nursing. The committee endorsed this approach
and recommended that it be extended progressively to all students
with disabilities and impairments enrolling in either regular or special
schools.

Students with special learning needs. This component of the delegated
schools budget targets students at risk of not making satisfactory
progress due to family or other personal circumstances. Jordan, Lyons,
and McDonough (1992) conclude that of the various ways of allocating funds for at-risk students, the most efficacious method, in terms
of stability, predictability, adequacy, efficiency, accountability, equity,
responsiveness, and nonmanipulability, is to make use of an index of
need based on a composite of indicators. It was also considered
necessary to use predictors of low achievement rather than achieve-

ment measures themselves, because direct funding of low-achieving schools could remove the incentive to strive for high achievement.

A survey of students in grades 1, 3, 5, 8, and 11 was undertaken in a sample of 83 schools to identify appropriate indicators that best predicted at-risk students. Teachers were asked to identify students whose literacy/English performance was well below that expected for their grade level. In addition, teachers were asked to provide information on more than 20 potential predictors of poor achievement in literacy/English. Useable data were obtained for 7,233 students. Using both structural equation modeling and multilevel regression modeling, it was established that the following indicators best predicted learning difficulties at school at both the primary and the secondary level in the Victorian context. Each is amenable to audit:

- Poverty: proportion of students in receipt of an education welfare payment (Educational Maintenance Allowance or AUSTUDY)
- Occupation: measure of occupational status (proportions of students living in families in which the highest breadwinner is unemployed, or is in an unskilled, skilled, white collar, or professional occupation)
- Language spoken at home: proportion of students who mainly speak a language other than English at home
- Family: measure of family status (proportions of students living with neither parent, one parent, or both parents)
- Aboriginality: proportion of students who are Koorie (from an Aboriginal background)
- Transiency: proportion of students who transfer into the school other than at the beginning of the year

In forming a composite Special Learning Needs (SLN) index, the indicators for poverty, transient, and aboriginality are given unit weightings, whereas the remaining three indicators receive a 0.5 weighting. The committee also recommended that an eligibility threshold be applied to the SLN index so that funds would be allocated only to the 30% of schools with the most at-risk students.

The implementation of the SLN index has involved the establishment of systematic and secure data collection procedures for all enrolled students in government schools in a form that can readily be verified and collated for the purposes of allocating funds. It has also required that the principle of strategic implementation be invoked

TABLE 5.4.   1998 ESL Index: Department of Education, Victoria

Level	Description	Weight	Weighting Rate
1	All ESL students not included in levels 2-4, grades K-6	1.00	$261
2	1 to < 3 years in Australian school, grades 2-6	1.29	$336
3	< 1year in Australian school, grades K-4	1.59	$416
4	< 1year in Australian school, grades 5-6	1.98	$517
5	3 to < 7 years in Australian school, grades 7-12	2.86	$746
6	1 to < 3 years in Australian school, grades 7-12	7.13	$1,860
7	< 1 year in Australian school, grades 7-12	14.26	$3,723

SOURCE: Department of Education, 1998a.

and a phasing in of the new formulas to keep gains and losses for individual schools to a maximum gain or loss of $25,000 within a given financial year.

Non-English-speaking-background students. This component of the delegated schools budget is directed at schools with large numbers of recent arrivals to Australia who do not speak English and require English as a second language (ESL) teaching. It is also directed at children from refugee families who, in addition to experiencing language problems, are likely to have experienced psychological trauma and a highly dislocated education. The committee concluded that weights for these students should reflect both stage of schooling and recency of arrival, with the highest level of additional funding going to recently arrived students in the later grades of schooling. The committee also recommended that a funding threshold should apply to the ESL index so that funds would be directed to schools with the highest need. Table 5.4 summarizes the ESL index as implemented in 1998.

Component 4: School-Specific Factors

Rurality and isolation. The geography of Australia, with its high concentration of population in the capital cities and its sparse rural populations, means that issues of rurality and isolation assume considerable significance. An important difference between rurality and isolation and other factors taken into account in the delegated schools budget is that the former applies to the total population of certain schools rather than to individual students. A further key difference is that the rationale for additional funding for rurality and isolation is related not to educational disadvantage but rather to the additional costs of provision. This has been established in a number of studies, particularly those reported in Tomlinson (1995). Thus, additional funding for rurality and isolation is justified in terms of the additional costs associated with curriculum provision, administration, and access to student support services for schools in rural and isolated locations.

In the Victorian context, rurality and isolation involve a number of distinct elements that the committee took into account in constructing an index for nonmetropolitan schools comprising an equally weighted combination of (1) distance in kilometers from the Melbourne metropolitan area; (2) distance from the nearest provincial center with more than 20,000 inhabitants; and (3) distance from the nearest school not eligible for funding as a rural or isolated school.

The committee's recommended formula for a given school was as follows:

$$\text{Location Index Funding} = \text{Base Allocation} + \\ (\text{Location Index Score} \times \text{Student Enrollment} \times \\ \text{Maximum Per Student Rate})$$

In addition to the location index, the committee recommended a separate rural size adjustment factor to take into account the additional costs associated with operating a small school in a rural area. This adjustment was recommended for primary schools with enrollments up to 200 students and for secondary schools with enrollments up to 500 students.

Premises. The premises element of the specific school factor represents just over 5% of total expenditure on school education. It covers a number of site-related costs such as the cost of contract cleaning, utilities (e.g., heating fuel, water, sewage, refuse, and garbage), maintenance of facilities and grounds, and minor works. There are separate formulas for each of these components, which are applied to data on each school site contained on a central, computer-based school assets management system (SAMS).

The premises element is a per school rather than a per student payment, although contract cleaning allocations are made on the basis of a formula that takes into account both the total area to be cleaned and the number of students occupying the premises. The formulas used are sensitive to the particular nature of each site. For example, the formula for maintenance and minor works distributes 50% of the available funds on the basis of the school's facilities entitlement area, 25% on the type of materials used in the construction of the school buildings, and 25% on the relative condition of those buildings.

Implementation

The above account of the delegated schools budget in Victoria is based on the structure proposed by the education committee (1994, 1995, 1998) and first implemented in schools in 1996. Almost all recommendations contained in the first two reports are now implemented and are reflected in the published funding arrangements for 1998 (Department of Education, 1998a). The components of the budget have been rearranged and, in some cases, given different names so that it currently structured as follows:

1. Core
   a. Leadership and training
   b. Teaching support
   c. Premises
   d. On-costs
2. Disabilities and impairments
3. Students with special learning needs
4. ESL
5. Rurality and isolation
6. Priority programs

The main set of the education committee's recommendations not implemented are those relating to the proposal that core funding be determined primarily on the basis of indexed relativities for three stages of schooling (grades K-4, 5-8, and 9-12). The committee suggested that the use of these indexed relativities be phased in over 3 years, commencing in 1998. In its response to the final report of the committee (Department of Education, 1998b), the department of education indicated that it did not intend at this stage to use additional funds available to school education to implement this new approach, but rather had decided to use the monies to fund a number of strategic initiatives aimed at improving student learning outcomes.

The most significant of these involves significant additional funding from the beginning of 1999, to assist all Victorian government primary schools to implement the Department's Early Years Literacy, formerly the "Keys of Life" program (Department of Education, 1997), aimed at improving literacy outcomes for students in the early years of primary schooling. The additional funds have been specifically targeted to cover the appointment of a literacy coordinator and the implementation of a one-to-one tutoring program such as Reading Recovery in every state primary school. The funding will be provided on the condition that schools submit plans that commit them in an ongoing way to meeting challenging, predefined standards and to implementing the Early Years Literacy program. This involves a whole school approach to improvement incorporating a number of specific design elements that were developed, implemented in 27 trial schools and evaluated as part of the Early Literacy Research Project (Crévola & Hill, 1998; Hill & Crévola, 1999).

In addition to achieving important strategic goals—improving early literacy outcomes is both a state and a national priority—the provision of these funds will also have the effect of reducing the differential between funding for primary and secondary schools and increasing relativities for the early years. The way in which the funds are being provided is also worthy of comment because it represents one of the first attempts by an Australian education system to link additional resources specifically to improved student learning outcomes and to the attainment of specific attainment targets.

Discussion

The delegated schools budgets and associated funding arrangements being developed and introduced in Australia, particularly in the state of Victoria, provide important case studies of the issues to be confronted in pursuing systemwide school reform and in ensuring as part of those reforms an equitable and cost-effective approach to school financing for government schools. Following are some general reflections on the process of reforming school finances.

First, although recent developments have involved quite dramatic reforms, they build on almost two decades of incremental change that has given schools increasing autonomy and accountability. For example, within Victoria there is a recent history of local school governance, with each school community electing a school council on which two thirds of the members are not education system employees. School councils have responsibility for developing and approving the school's charter, approving the school's budget, managing finances, and reporting on the school's performance through the annual report. They now have significant additional responsibilities for a range of staffing decisions, including involvement in and final approval of the selection of the school principal (Department of Education, 1998c).

This history has not been one of smooth or easy change. Indeed, at all points along the way, change has been hotly contested and frequently resisted. Many of the changes now being implemented were identified as desirable over a decade ago, but the political will and capacity to drive through a strong change agenda have been lacking. This leads to the second point, which is that major reform of school education requires significant political will. The scope and pace of reform in Victoria owe much to the overwhelming electoral advantage enjoyed by the current government, an advantage that cannot last forever. This in turn raises the question as to whether the changes effected thus far are irreversible and whether some future government may seek to reverse current trends and reestablish centralized control. The general view is that having given schools real control over local decision making and resources, it is unlikely that any future government would see advantage in changing direction and recentralizing unless strong evidence emerged of serious, unintended, negative consequences of the reforms.

In addition, there is the general view that school financing arrangements in Australia, which have evolved over decades, have become excessively obscure and riddled with inequities and anomalies. The prospect of fairer and more transparent systems of funding have thus generated their own momentum for reform, even when it has been pointed out that the proposed changes may involve some pain for schools that have faired relatively well under the old and less equitable funding arrangements. This leads to the third key observation, which is that fundamental reforms of school financing inevitably generate "winners" and "losers," which places real limitations on the pace of change.

It is generally not possible to reduce significantly financial allocations to schools that in the past may have been overfunded without generating an adverse political backlash. The alternative is to hold the funding levels of such schools constant until other schools have caught up, or to reduce funding to appropriate levels very gradually. This in turn implies that full implementation of new funding arrangements may take many years to effect and involve messy interim arrangements (reflecting the principle of strategic implementation).

Within the Victorian context, where change has been the most rapid, surveys over 4 years of the attitudes of representative samples of school principals indicate that principals are generally positive about the benefits associated with the reforms (Cooperative Research Project, 1994, 1995a, 1995b, 1996, 1997). Indeed, 86% of principals surveyed in 1996 indicated they preferred arrangements under Schools of the Future to those in place before the reform (Cooperative Research Project, 1997). There was an 89% approval rating for the new arrangements associated with the resources framework, including mechanisms associated with the delegated schools budget. In response to a set of questions concerned with the extent to which the delegated schools budget had built capacity within the school, principals indicated that they believed there is now a greater capacity to build a relationship between curriculum programs and resource allocation, to allocate resources to identified needs of students, and to achieve priorities as set out in the school's charter. On the other hand, in response to a further set of questions concerning the implementation of the delegated schools budget reforms, principals indicated a more negative attitude in response to questions concerning the adequacy of the time provided to adjust to the new approaches, levels of funding, and the degree of access to quality professional development for appropriate staff.

This suggests that although principals, along with most staff in schools, see merit in the reforms, they have found the pace of reform hard to accommodate and perceive that they have not had the degree of support that they ideally would have liked. This is despite the fact that there has been a massive program of professional development in place to assist principals and other staff adjust to the new arrangements. This leads to a fourth key observation, namely that it is almost impossible to overestimate the amount of professional development, training, and support services needed to sustain real reform.

Early on in the change process, when reforms were first being implemented, a large number of principals accepted the offer of a voluntary departure package and retired earlier than would normally be the case. Those who remained and those who took the place of those departing have found the changes challenging in the extreme. In other words, change has come at a considerable cost to those involved in implementing the new arrangements. But in view of the harsh reality of short electoral cycles and the reduced ability of governments to apply additional resources to smooth over the rough edges of change, are there any real alternatives to the "crash through" approach to genuine reform?

A fifth key observation is that, despite the pace and extent of the reforms thus far, the process in Australia still has a long way to go, and many issues remain to be confronted. One issue yet to be confronted in the Victorian government school context concerns the method of charging for teacher salaries. For teachers in promotional positions, schools are allocated funds and charged at actual salary costs ("actuals in, actuals out"). For the 70% of teachers not in promotional positions, schools are funded and charged at average salary costs ("averages in, averages out"). This introduces an element of inequity into funding arrangements because schools in more affluent and favored locations tend to have the more experienced teachers at the top of the salary scale. Were such schools funded on the basis of average salary costs but charged on the basis of actual expenditure on salaries ("averages in, actuals out"), they would be obliged to change the mix of their staff and employ a greater proportion of beginning teachers. In the longer term, it is preferable that all schools move to an averages in, actuals out system of funding, because this is a fairer system and also one that promotes the efficient use of resources. This approach has been adopted in Britain. In the Victorian context, this is something that would need to be phased in gradually, perhaps by extending the averages in, actuals out method to all new appointments of teaching staff made by schools, but retaining the averages in, averages out method for existing staff.

Another issue to be faced in the future development of the delegated schools budget involves approaches to funding the introduction of new information technologies in schools. Society is experiencing an awesome social and economic revolution as the Information Age becomes an increasing reality and the power of the new information technologies transforms the home, the school, and the workplace, breaking down many of the barriers that have allowed these to exist as separate worlds. For schools, the costs of buying computers, installing fiber-optic cabling, creating local area networks, linking to the World Wide Web, and providing the necessary training and support service for teaching staff are massive. Furthermore, it is not clear which are ongoing costs and which are once-off costs, nor which should be borne by the school and which should be borne by parents or the community at large. None of these costs has been properly factored into school budgets, yet there is some urgency to resolve how this should be done.

Beyond these specific issues are a set of much broader and fundamental issues, such as whether government schools can and should be given additional powers, including the authority not only to select staff but also to be the employers of their staff, for entering into local enterprise agreements, for owning the assets of the school, and for entering into partnerships and joint ventures. These issues are highly contentious and challenge the very notion of government school education. They are issues that are nevertheless being addressed, and once again have advanced the furthest in Victoria, where the parliament has enacted the Education (Self-Governing Schools) Act 1998 to enable some schools to move beyond the current framework of self-management to embrace a degree of self-governance.

The final key observation relates to the extent to which the Australian reforms to school financing, particularly as reflected in the Victorian experience, translate into educational benefits for students. The answer to this question has three parts. First, it is unlikely that the reforms to date have had a significant effect on student achievement, nor would one expect such a direct effect in the short-term. Rather, it is more realistic to expect that the effect of the reforms is to build the capacity of schools to target resources better to student learning needs and school priorities. The evidence to date is that this may already be happening. In the 1996 survey of principals (Cooperative Research

Project, 1997), 85% indicated a moderate to high gain in learning outcomes in their schools, with structural equation modeling of findings suggesting how direct and indirect links have been made between elements of the reform and learning outcomes. These links are associated, in particular, with capacity building in the personnel and professional domains, especially through professional development focusing on school priorities. Recent case study research demonstrates how these links can be made (Wee, 1999).

A second part of the answer may relate to the extent to which, even under conditions of extreme decentralization of school finances, it is good policy for systems to retain a capacity to provide additional funding to schools for strategic purposes that are not formula based and automatically allocated on the basis of inputs information, but are performance or outcomes based. A number of Australian systems have begun to implement performance-related incentive schemes for individuals, teams, or whole schools, and experience is accumulating regarding both the intended and the unintended consequences and benefits of different approaches.

The third part of the answer relates to the other aspects of the school reform agenda being pursued by school systems. These cluster around three broad areas that complement the reforms to school financing, namely reforms directed at setting high content and performance standards in the curriculum; reforms aimed at improving the professional capacity, status, and competence of teachers; and reforms designed to strengthen the accountability of schools for the way in which they use resources to improve student learning. Real improvements in educational outcomes are likely only when schools focus on change at the level of the quality of teaching and learning. There are encouraging signs that this focus on classroom teaching is emerging as the main focus of Australian education systems as they approach the new millennium.

Acknowledgments

We wish to acknowledge the substantial contributions of the other members of the education committee to the ideas contained in this chapter, namely Ian Hind, Graham Marshall, Allan Odden, and Jim Spinks. Also, we would like to acknowledge the principals and staff of participating schools of the School Global Budget Project, the

Principals Reference Group, and John Adams, the executive officer of the committee. Our colleague, Ibtisam Abu-Duhou, conducted case studies in the early stages that helped shape the research methodology.

Note

1. The board of studies is a statutory body responsible for setting curriculum standards for students in government and nongovernment schools in all years of schooling and for assessment and certification of all students in years 11 and 12, the final 2 years of schooling.

References

Australian Curriculum Studies Association. (1996). *From alienation to engagement: Opportunities for reform in the middle years of schooling.* Canberra: Author.

Blachford, P., & Mortimore, P. (1994). The issue of class size for young children in schools: What can we learn from research? *Oxford Review of Education, 20,* 411-428.

Caldwell, B. J., & Hayward, D. K. (1998). *The future of schools: Lessons from the reform of public education.* London: Falmer.

Caldwell, B. J., & Spinks, J. M. (1988). *The self-managing school.* London: Falmer.

Capelluti, J., & Stokes, D. (1991). *Middle level education: Policies, programs and practices.* Reston, VA: National Association of Secondary School Principals.

Carnegie Council on Adolescent Development. (1989). *Turning points: Preparing American youth for the 21st century.* Washington, DC: Author.

Clay, M. M. (1991). *Becoming literate: The construction of inner control.* Auckland, New Zealand: Heinemann Education.

Clay, M. M. (1993). *Reading Recovery: A guidebook for teachers in training.* Auckland, New Zealand: Heinemann Education.

Clay, M. M., & Watson, B. (1982). An in-service program for Reading Recovery teachers. In M. M. Clay (Ed.), *Observing young readers: Selected papers* (pp. 192-200). Portsmouth, NH: Heinemann Education.

Cooperative Research Project. (1994). *Base-line survey.* Melbourne: Department of Education.

Cooperative Research Project. (1995a). *One year later.* Melbourne: Department of Education.

Cooperative Research Project. (1995b). *Taking stock.* Melbourne: Department of School Education.

Cooperative Research Project. (1996) *Three year report card.* Melbourne: Department of Education.

Cooperative Research Project. (1997). *More work to be done but . . . no turning back.* Melbourne: Department of Education.

Crévola, C. A., & Hill, P. W. (1998). Evaluation of a whole-school approach to prevention and intervention in early literacy. *Journal of Education for Students Placed at Risk, 3*(2), 133-158.

Cumming, J., & Fleming, D. (Eds.). (1993). *In the middle or at the centre: A report of a national conference on middle schooling.* Canberra: Australian Curriculum Studies Association.

Department of Education. (1997). *Keys to life early literacy program.* Melbourne: Longman & Education Australia.

Department of Education. (1998a). *Guide to the 1998 school global budget.* Melbourne: Author.

Department of Education. (1998b). *Education committee for the school global budget research project launched.* Melbourne: Author.

Department of Education. (1988c). *Making the partnership work. Part 1: Roles and responsibilities.* Melbourne: Author.

Education Committee. (1994). *The school global budget in Victoria: Matching resources to student learning needs.* Melbourne: Directorate of School Education.

Education Committee. (1995). *The school global budget in Victoria: Matching resources to student learning needs.* Melbourne: Directorate of School Education.

Education Committee. (1998). *Final report of the education committee for the school global budget research project.* Melbourne: Department of Education.

Eyers, V. (1993). *The education of young adolescents in South Australian government schools: Report of the junior secondary review.* Adelaide: Education Department of South Australia.

Hargreaves, A., & Earl, L. (1990). *Rights of passage: A review of selected research about schooling in the transition years.* Toronto: Ontario Ministry of Education.

Hill, P. W. & Crévola, C. A. (1999). The role of standards in educational reform for the 21st century. In D. D. Marsh (Ed.) *ASCD Yearbook 1999: Preparing our schools for the 21st century* (pp. 117-142). Alexandria, VA: Association for Supervision and Curriculum Development.

Jordan, K. F., Lyons, T. S., & McDonough, J. T. (1992). *Funding and financing for programs to serve K-3 at-risk children: A research review.* Washington, DC: National Education Association. (ERIC Reproduction Service No. ED 342 509)

Madden, N. A., Slavin, R. E., Karweit, N. L., Dolan, L. J., & Wasik, B. A. (1993). Success for All: Longitudinal effects of a restructuring program for inner-city elementary schools. *American Educational Research Journal, 30,* 123-148.

McKenzie, I., & Taylor, S. (1995). The team solution. *Curriculum Perspectives, 15,* 23-26.

Ross, K. (1983). *School area indicators of educational need.* Camberwell, Victoria: Australian Council for Educational Research.

Schools Council, National Board of Employment, Education, and Training. (1993). *In the middle: Schooling for young adolescents.* Canberra: Australian Government Publishing Service.

Slavin, R. E., Madden, N. A., Dolan, L. J., Wasik, B. A., Ross, S. M., & Smith, L. J. (1994). Whenever and wherever we choose: The replication of Success for All. *Phi Delta Kappan, 75,* 639-647.

Slavin, R. E., Madden, N. A., Karweit, N. L., Livermon, B. J., & Dolan, L. (1990). Success for All: First-year outcomes of a comprehensive plan for reforming urban education. *American Educational Research Journal, 27,* 255-278.

Thomas, H. (1996). Efficiency, equity and exchange in education. *Education Management and Administration, 24,* 31-47.

Tomlinson, D. (Chair). (1995). *Schooling in rural Western Australia: Report of the committee to review schooling in rural Western Australia.* Perth: Ministry of Education.

Wee, J. (1999). *Self-managing schools and learning outcomes.* Unpublished thesis for the degree of Doctor of Education, University of Melbourne.

The Institution of School-Based Management in Edmonton

LLOYD W. OZEMBLOSKI

DANIEL J. BROWN

This chapter examines the conversion of the Edmonton Public Schools from centralized to school-based management during the 1970s and 1980s.[1] Using the triphasic model of change as a framework, interviews were conducted with a sample of 30 persons, including school board members, superintendents, principals, teachers, and teachers' association representatives. Interpretation of the interviews reveal a number of factors that respondents considered important for decentralization. Unlike the difficulties encountered in other efforts to introduce school-based management, the case of Edmonton shows a conflux of the right conditions. Four clusters of factors are induced from the data: sources of the initiative, support gathering, attributes of the initiative, and district context. Used with the adoption, implementation, and continuation phases of the model, the clusters provide some insights into the delegation of authority to schools. The chapter concludes with an update on school-based management in Edmonton.

Decentralization of school districts, in the form of school-based management, is attracting attention around the world (Brown, 1990; Caldwell & Spinks, 1988; Knight, 1993; Malen & Ogawa, 1988; Wohlstetter & Buffett, 1992). This interest has spawned a great deal of activity, such as the development of school-based councils in Kentucky (Steffy, 1993), planning for decentralization among American school districts (Heller, Woodworth, Jacobson, & Conway, 1989), and devolution in Chicago (Hess, 1991). (For an extensive review, see Murphy & Beck, 1995.) The general intention is to permit schools more control, or to "debureacratize them" and permit them to be more varied (Hill & Bonan, 1991; Sackney & Dibski, 1992). Bureaucratic structures are seen as being committed to uniformity and quite unresponsive to the needs of students or the wishes of teachers or parents (Lawton, 1995).

If it is assumed that such a development is a good idea and a necessary (though not sufficient) requirement to reform schools, then it is advisable to gain some understanding about how decentralization may be instituted. Unless knowledge concerning the shift to school-based management is made available, the idea may falter simply because the change itself is badly executed, regardless of the merits of the innovation itself. There have been many complaints about the change process attendant to decentralization. Districts sometimes adopt the idea superficially (Bimber, 1993; Daresh, 1992; David, 1989; Malen & Ogawa, 1988; Wohlstetter & Odden, 1992). There may be demonstrable resistance (Brown, 1990; Burke, 1992). There may be many role conflicts (Bredeson, 1992) or the continuation of policies that mandate uniformity (Daresh, 1992, Hanson, 1991; Heller et al., 1989). These problems with the process of decentralizing clearly indicate a place for studies that documents strategies that permit school-based management to be instituted without major mishaps. What is needed is an understanding of "how change occurs, and how to use this new knowledge," that is, a "good theory of changing" as Fullan (1993a, p. 392) says.

The decentralization that took place in the Edmonton public schools offers a special opportunity to explore one instance of this change process over time.[2] Edmonton undertook a substantial administrative reorganization from centralized to decentralized management between

1973 and 1989. This devolution, which remains in effect (Kuo, 1996), involved a remarkable delegation of authority from central offices to schools for decisions about resources such as the number and kinds of personnel, amounts of equipment and supplies purchased, and sometimes maintenance and utility services. A large percentage of the district's resources were affected because delegation of authority was substantial and had several direct effects. Roles of board members, central office employees, and principals changed considerably, whereas the activities of teachers were altered to a lesser degree. In contrast to similar decentralization in Great Britain, Australia, and the United States, the involvement of parents in Edmonton was less direct (Brown, 1990; Maynes, 1980). Noteworthy effects of the change included more flexibility in decision making on the part of schools, greater school accountability to the district school board, and increased parental satisfaction with schools (Brown, 1990). A special feature of Edmonton's change to school-based management was that it was voluntarily undertaken by the district and not imposed by legislation or court orders, as has been done in some large districts in the United States (Hess, 1991). As a consequence of its magnitude and longevity, this case of decentralization emerged as uniquely suited to offer some lessons for the change to school-based management.

This chapter reports on how the decentralization was managed in Edmonton. It uses the triphasic model of change as a convenient framework to organize the events and activities into adoption, implementation, and continuation periods, respectively. The triphasic model was chosen because it appeared to match the data, and the extensive literature associated with this model provided a substantial basis for inquiry into the change, as will be demonstrated. To show how the data were collected, the research method is outlined initially. After the narrative highlighting the events and key factors is presented, we offer a commentary on our understanding of the institution of school-based management.

Research Method

This study was undertaken chiefly through interviews, and used relevant documentation when available. The junior author made initial contact with a district official to gain clearance for the study and was given approval to begin the data collection. The senior author, who conducted the interviews, selected the subjects using the criterion of early involvement in the change in accordance with the rules of purposeful sampling (Bogdan & Biklen, 1982). Because a number of groups were continuously involved, senior administrators, trustees, school administrators, the local teachers association, and teachers were asked to suggest persons who had been active throughout the change to decentralized management. Nominees suggested by several persons were considered to be likely participants. The final interviewee sample consisted of 30 persons (23 males and 7 females) representative of the aforementioned groups. The 30 included two trustees, one superintendent, three associate or assistant superintendents, six central office staff members, ten principals, one teachers' association representative, six teachers, and a consultant. All interviews took place during 1989 (see Ozembloski, 1993).

Interviews with respondents proceeded in a semistructured manner. Although the questions were grounded in the literature on the triphasic model, interviewees were encouraged to elaborate and volunteer accounts of their experiences. Questions followed this general pattern:

- How was school-based management introduced?
- Who provided the major initiatives?
- What were the roles played by key personnel?
- Were there discernible stages of the change?
- What were the effects on the decision-making structure?
- What use of experts was made?
- Were there tests of the initiative?
- What was the overall time frame?
- What were some impediments and facilitators of the change?
- What were some reactions to the change?

All interviews were taped and returned to interviewees for verification. Because reliance on a single interviewer to gather information amplified the probability of personal bias, district files relevant to the innovation were accessed. Documents consisting of 550 pages of

district memoranda, minutes, and policies were checked or triangu-
lated with data from the interviews.

The interview data were analyzed using the matrix method suggested by Miles and Huberman (1984), in which respondents and their
answers are related. Analysis was guided by the general questions of
who and what, where and when, how and why, concerning the
initiative; questions were crafted to discern which main factors initiated and provided momentum for the adoption, implementation, and
continuation of the change. Categorizations of the data were undertaken to determine the emergence of themes that later formed clusters
of factors. It should be noted that the generalizations offered are
limited by the kinds of data sources selected—interviews and documents. The interview data are largely perceptual in origin and based
on a modest sample size, and need to be accepted with care. Further,
the retrospective nature of this study resulted in a separation in time
between the events and the interviews (between a few months to
about 15 years), so memories may have dimmed or filtered the observations. This is a largely descriptive account of events in Edmonton
arranged according to the three phases of the change.

Adoption

An abbreviated chronology of events during the adoption phase in
Edmonton is presented in Table 6.1. Note that the period may be
divided into two sections: the start of the incumbency of the new
superintendent (Michael Strembitsky) in Fall 1972 and the initiation
of school-based management for the seven pilot schools in Spring
1976. The first years were mostly devoted to exploration and planning; the second period focused on experimentation with the idea of
giving schools authority to allocate substantial sums of money for
personnel and material.

The inception of the change to school-based management in Edmonton was lodged in discontent with the way things were. A substantial problem was captured by a person hired to facilitate the
transition as an external change agent:

TABLE 6.1.   Main Events in Edmonton Public Schools During Adoption
                  Phase

Fall 1972	New superintendent hired
Spring 1975	System planner studies budgeting process in district
Spring 1975	Idea of school involvement meets strong opposition from district management team
Spring 1975	Superintendent proposes pilot study to board; board supports
Fall 1975	Call for volunteers for pilot; 35 come forward
Spring 1976	Seven pilot schools start
Fall 1976	System planner gathers information from other districts
Winter 1977	System planner submits negative report on current budgeting practices to board
Fall 1977	Teachers' association survey favorable to decentralization
Spring 1978	Teachers strike
Fall 1978	Progress report of pilot principals to board
Fall 1978	Redefinition of authority of central office personnel

the board knew that there was a long history for 15 years of the
people downtown getting into little rooms and dividing things
up and scratching each other's backs and doing all those things
that people do in highly centralized systems where they want to
make decisions, and basically all they were interested in is retaining power. All the power was in the center and all the work was
being done in the field. I guess we realized the Golden Rule—he
who has the gold makes the decisions and has the power. (#27:5)[3]

There was widespread dissatisfaction with that kind of practice among
many principals, according to interviewees. This problem on its own
only partially accounted for the inception of the change, however.

Many respondents remarked that the superintendent's beliefs and
personal philosophy appeared critical to the impetus during the early
adoption phase. The superintendent summarized his position concerning the importance of devolving authority to school level personnel:

Those who are closest to the point of implementation of decisions
are very often in the best position to make them and should have
a high degree of involvement in making them. Given this degree
of involvement, these decisions are going to be far superior [to]
a decision handed down elsewhere in the organization. (#30:1)

An associate superintendent endorsed the idea that the superintendent was a major actor in the initiative by saying, "Well, the prime mover was [the superintendent]; there was just no question about that. A lot of his attitudes toward decision making are inherent in the man himself and what he believes in" (#29:2).

The positive financial climate that existed in Alberta during the mid- to late 1970s was also seen as an advantage for the decentralization. Ample resources permitted decisions to be made relatively easily and avoided the severity of legal constraints associated with retrenchment. One supervisor remarked, "there was lots of money flowing around. Government grants had increased on the order of 10% to 15% per year. So this helped. There was a period of boom and one of the ways to overcome resistance was to grease the wheels of change" (#2:2).

Although resources were available, there was a teachers' strike in 1978, called in part because of dissatisfaction over the extent of central office influence in school affairs and its lack of reaction to school concerns. The strike was resolved in part by the intention to decentralize. This background was recalled by a teacher, who observed, "in a sense, the strike provided the impetus for the adoption of the concept" (#3:3).

During the adoption phase, one of two internal change agents facilitated the process by undertaking such tasks as becoming thoroughly knowledgeable about the principles of school-based management, establishing arrangements for training, working out bugs in the system, helping to plan, and heading up the pilot project for seven voluntary schools. The external change agent, hired on contract, was instrumental in providing knowledge and skill to the internal change agents. This collaboration was seen as essential to avoid misunderstanding and strife.

School board interest in decentralization during the adoption phase was also seen as a key factor. The board desired more effective and efficient allocation of resources to meet the needs of students. The board adopted a strategic planning model, which required the district to articulate goals and objectives annually. A good deal of information came to the board during this phase via principals from seven pilot project schools during their 15-minute budget presentation. This allowed board members to address an individual school's plans rather than be confined to the overall budget, providing a measure of school accountability to the board.

Principals at the pilot schools where the "experiment" took place were seen as critical during this stage. All had volunteered their schools to be pilots, but for different reasons. Some were dissatisfied with present practices; others wanted to be on the forefront of change. They demonstrated enthusiasm and generated support for the initiative by sharing their experiences throughout the district. Because their assessments were mostly positive, the innovation gained credibility with other schools. This view was endorsed by a principal, who observed, "the seven principals played a very crucial role in the adoption of the innovation. Had they not been behind the project completely, it would have gone down the tubes" (#14:6).

Part of the adoption phase involved setting up a committee of district and school personnel to monitor and facilitate the transition from the pilot program to the district level. The committee oversaw and amended the formula that allocated resources to schools. It also helped determine the respective boundaries of authority of central office personnel and principals.

Not all went well in the pilot schools, however. Many encountered difficulty with central office personnel during the adoption phase because there appeared to be little effort taken by the central office to support school-based management (see Caldwell, 1977). Incorrect information and a lack of clarity about the goals and means of implementing the initiative further complicated the transition. One reason that central office personnel may have been reticent about cooperating was because decentralization was introduced by a small group of persons who did not comprehend fully the scope or components of the initiative, let alone the details of its application. Consequently, persons who worked at the board office were not always clear about what the change meant for their roles or those of schools. For example, the finance department became known for its lack of cooperation because it would not provide data needed to determine allocation of maintenance dollars to the pilot schools. The pilot committee worked hard to resolve these problems, and despite the difficulties, support for the innovation grew until the board approved districtwide implementation of school-based management in 1980.

Clearly, the undue centralization of authority in the school board office was seen as a problem for which school-based management was a solution. The superintendent resolved to address the separation between the authority to make decisions in the central office and the responsibility for them in the schools; he was helped by the board's concern for the education of children and its desire for accountability for dollars spent. Change agents (both external and internal) and the oversight committee facilitated the shift, as did the positive assessments generated by pilot schools when they provided initial feedback on how they found the change. Such support and developments overcame the initial resistance, particularly on the part of central office personnel.

Implementation

The sequence of main events during the implementation phase is chronicled in Table 6.2. Taking place over only 2 years, this phase shows activity from the school board's "go" decision to almost all schools starting to operate under school-based management.

School board support was evident as it worked closely with the change team (the superintendent, central administration members, internal change agents, and principals). One way that the board maintained contact with the implementation process was via subcommittee meetings with groups of principals, who provided board members with the chance to learn about the particulars of the change and the problems principals faced. Feedback to the board also came from a survey (Alexandruk, 1985), and, according to a director, its "results were a very persuasive argument. It was important for the board to sense the magnitude of support by the district for the innovation, particularly the principals" (#11:11).

During implementation, the superintendent's visibility and endorsement of the innovation created a positive climate through public addresses, memoranda, and the media. The superintendent was a key actor, and his wishes were expedited by the internal change agents and other central office personnel. Change agents conducted workshops and held discussion groups that served as forums for passing

TABLE 6.2.   Main Events in Edmonton Public Schools During the
                  Implementation Phase

Fall 1978	Board approves innovation district wide for 1979-80
Fall 1978	Two pilot principals appointed as internal change agents
Winter 1979	Meetings throughout the district for all personnel
Winter 1979	Two-week block of inservice for principals
Summer 1979	Workshops for principals and central office personnel
Fall 1979	Superintendent addresses all teachers
Fall 1979	Principals establish school budgeting committees
Fall 1979	Principals meet with parents
Fall 1979	School plans reviewed by associate superintendents
Winter 1980	School funds allocated
Spring 1980	Satisfaction surveys of parents, students, and employees undertaken
Fall 1980	Districtwide implementation complete; information presented to board

on the vision of decentralization and providing skills and knowledge about school-based management and how implementation was to proceed. Central office personnel had benefited from the pilot project experience during adoption, and now provided needed information and support to the schools, such as setting indicators and establishing procedures. One pilot school principal illustrated this cooperation:

> Extensive work was done with central services both in terms of function and technical readiness. [Pilots] became set up so that the [other] schools could use us in the prescribed role . . . there was a lot of preparation. The initiative would have fallen had central services not been ready. (#5:11)

The district implementation plan devised by the change team provided an outline of the need for the process, a blueprint for preparing key actors (principals, central office staff, and teachers), and a schedule of events and actions. Although the plan was continually modified, an important part of the plan was the management cycle. It became a permanent fixture and provided a step-by-step process for the district and school to monitor the initiative and its results. Elements of the cycle were goal setting/budget preparation, budget submission and review, allocation, in-school trustee subcommittee meetings, district budget approval, satisfaction surveys, and the annual district review (R.F. #50).

School personnel were also key actors in the implementation process. Pilot school principals, who had demonstrated their commitment previously in the adoption phase, continued to be leaders during implementation. On request, they provided support to other schools through training sessions. One mentioned:

> We were invited to schools to talk. That was at the beginning of systemwide implementation. The schools thought it was important to hear how it had been done in the pilot schools, and they appreciated our input and guidance. (#16:13)

The external change agent concurred:

> Those guys did an absolutely super job at PR. The day after [the implementation] was approved, there was a big free-for-all with the TV and all this kind of stuff and I let the principals do the talking. The longer I let the principals in the pilot [schools] talk, the better off we were. The system's principals were all watching. (#27:21)

He added:

> [Pilot school principals] had to be responsible, proactive, not frightened, decisive, and possess collegial working skills. These skills were central, and if they hadn't done a reasonable job of it, implementation wouldn't have happened. (#27:24)

But what of the principals and teachers who had not participated before implementation began? They became key actors as well. The role of system principals was acknowledged to be central to the change process by a director:

> The [system] principals were key during implementation. As the principal goes, so goes the school. Anything that happens in a school is directly the result of the principal without exception, positively and negatively. He had to be the confidant, embrace the vision, convince others, show the innovation's value, risk

take, accept responsibility, be open, frank, and prepared. He had
to be able to share planning. (#13:5)

A pilot principal concurred by saying, "once you convinced [the
remaining principals] of the benefits, once that initial ice was broken,
watch out. Everybody just went for it and we never had any trouble
after that in getting people to be a part of a decision-making process,
to talk to each other" (#8:10). System principals generally developed
collaborative leadership styles voluntarily that were identified as
important to the effective progress of implementation. This collaboration was identified as an attribute of the initiative itself because it
involved school-based planning about personnel, equipment, and
supplies. As one teacher suggested, "definitely the principal was the
key. They had to be the facilitators; they had to orchestrate the implementation in the school. There were certain qualities the principal had
to have" (#21:4).

Because school-based management was mandated by the district,
teacher representatives were invited to many inservice sessions. Many
felt that decentralization had the potential to improve services to
children. It was seen by many teachers as a practical change that
would allow greater flexibility to spend money where it was needed
most. Some teachers were risk takers and possessed interest, energy,
and a positive disposition toward the change. One teacher commented, "We were told we would have more freedom and we would
know our spending capabilities. We felt there was freedom, flexibility,
and adaptability associated with the innovation. That appealed to us"
(#21:8). Although some teachers complained about the additional
workload that decision making created for them, most accepted the
change (Alexandruk, 1985).

Clearly, the change to school-based management did not proceed
unattended. It was given ample support by the board, superintendent,
central office employees, change agents, and pilot school principals
during this phase. Resistance on the part of central office staff or
uncommitted principals was seldom mentioned by the interviewees,
although their documents showed that there were a few retirements.
Remaining principals adapted to the change, collaborated with their
teachers and support staffs, and thus became within-school facilitators. When the results of the surveys were made public, consensus

TABLE 6.3. Events in the Edmonton Public Schools During the Continuation Phase

1980-89	Board endorses continuation
1982-83	Survey of principal satisfaction
1986-89	Pilot project for decentralization of subject consulting services
1986-89	Maintenance and utilities decentralized optionally

that the change was a good idea was enhanced, thus bringing more teachers on board as they began to perceive the benefits.

Continuation

An abbreviated overview of processes during the continuation phase is presented in Table 6.3. It is sparse relative to the numbers of events recalled during the adoption and implementation phases, because this phase was relatively uneventful. As the decade progressed, school-based management was modified somewhat, but also became routine for most schools.

The actors who were prominent during implementation also played key roles through the continuation phase, except for the change agents and pilot principals. The superintendent maintained his endorsements and documentation of progress through speaking engagements, memoranda, and regular progress reports on achievements. The board provided ongoing support as well. Every June, it conducted a district review of the initiative based on information collected throughout the year. The superintendent noted:

The board would consider all the indicators including the satisfaction profiles on each school produced by the parents, teachers, students, principals and the general community attitude survey results. They would review everything, and if they thought the results were favorable, they would sanction another year go-around with the initiative. (#30:7)

Central office administrators also continued to monitor school-based management. For each school, they gave preliminary approval to budgets, ensured that each engaged in goal and objective setting, and provided a direct organizational link to the superintendent. As one trustee said, the central office staff was "constantly working the allocation formulas to try to find better ways to facilitate the utility of the allocation. They build the information bases and . . . keep the concept working districtwide" (#15:10). According to one trustee, "associate superintendents who supervised about 30 schools each were deeply involved in determining whether the budget plans were in line with district objectives. . . . They were also the main channels through which two-way communication between the board, central office, the superintendent and the schools flowed" (#15:14).

The use of yearly budget plans for each school accommodated a variety of views about each school's direction. Not all schools were required to adopt decentralization uniformly by incorporating maintenance or utility functions. One principal mentioned, "the optionality helps keep the initiative in place. You take on the option when you are ready, and that's good. You don't feel like it is being forced down your throat" (#23:1). Another said, "more and more schools are opting for increased decentralized services. Some can hardly wait until certain services are put out. There is an enthusiasm in the district for it. More have come to believe" (#14:16).

As part of the continuation phase, the relationship between the district's objectives and the innovation's achievements was assessed regularly. The management cycle, mentioned above, provided a framework for systematic monitoring and evaluation. In particular, the satisfaction surveys of parents, students, the community, and district employees offered important comparisons over time. Because satisfaction scores climbed from the inception of the initiative, these surveys gave evidence that supported continuation. One particular survey that determined the degree of satisfaction on the part of principals showed that they, too, endorsed decentralization very highly. According to a supervisor, the survey,

was done by central office to determine the level of satisfaction of district principals with the initiative. There was an overwhelming endorsement, the majority had no wish to come back to the old system. The information was passed onto our trustees, and that gave them confidence to continue the initiative. (#2:2)

The evidence shows that most of the principals were willing to continue with school-based management. But were teachers? Respondents reported that teachers, under decentralization, were given more control to make professional decisions. Consultative decision making allowed them to map out goals and plans tailored to individual schools, thus providing opportunities for creative problem solving. Teachers noted that central office services had improved. Overall, teachers found that they were able to influence decision making about resources in their schools. A principal summed up his view of teacher participation by saying, "Empowerment allowed the teachers to undertake a measure of freedom . . . to exercise control over the management of school resources in the best interest of the school" (#24:6). A teacher added:

> If you did a survey and asked [teachers] if they wanted to go back to the situation that existed prior to the initiative, the majority answer would be "No!" The majority say it's better that we make the decision about how scarce resources are going to be used than someone in central office who really doesn't understand the problems we've got. (#3:15)

Although the superintendent and board continued to support the change, the contributions of the change agents and pilot principals became less important. Optionality that permitted individual school adaptation and the increasing level of teacher satisfaction with the innovation were important factors at the continuation stage. They probably had the effect of subtracting remaining resistance to the change, which was not mentioned.

The following is a precis of the triphasic change to school-based management in Edmonton. During the adoption phase, the idea of decentralization came from central office administrators who explored its application. A pilot version was established, and when a teachers' strike occurred, school-based management was seen as a partial solution to long-term problems. When decentralization was implemented, change agents moved it along, but all main actors continued to support it and ensured that all persons affected were given opportunities for participation and training. Initial feedback during implementation was mostly positive, and the financial climate permitted the innovation to be carried out. When the continuation phase arrived, all main actors remained on board, but the role of the change agents diminished. The systematic use of the management cycle provided reexaminations of decentralization and its effects. Most attributes were viewed as being favorable, and so school-based management came to be regarded as a routine way of operating the district and schools. Normal financial support to the district was sustained.

Commentary

The accounts of the change in the three phases contain many factors considered important in the literature on the triphasic model. The literature indicates that the adoption phase is concerned primarily with sharing information about the innovation (Havelock, 1973). Because personnel, organizational structures, and the use of technology all influence such information, they are key elements at this stage. Fullan (1991) notes that during the adoption phase, the advocacy of central office administrators, the use of consultants, and the imposition of problem-solving incentives are important. All three were operant in this study. Some of the literature's other factors received scarce mention by respondents. They include federal or state policy, bureaucratic incentives, and community pressure. Their absence shows that they were not necessary for the adoption of a local innovation.

Implementation, the second phase of the model, concentrates on institutional behavior and the policies that effect the change. McLaughlin and Berman (1978) comment extensively on the perils that innovations face during this period. They suggest that central office support and inservice participation/training are critical; these two factors were very strongly evident in this study. Other factors stressed in the literature included the quality/practicality of the change, evaluation of it, and board support, all of which were prominent in Edmonton. Fullan (1991) also suggests that vision and empowerment are among the factors that have a substantial effect, which they did in Edmonton. One factor noted by the literature but muted in this study is substantial resistance with resultant conflict (Elmore, 1993). This appears to have been avoided as a result of foresight and extensive efforts to communicate with all persons and groups affected by the change. For a review of attempts to sabotage decentralization in other settings, see Brown (1995).

The third phase, continuation, is the stage at which practices become routine. According to McLaughlin and Berman (1978), continuation is demonstrated by the amount of resources devoted to the innovation. Fullan (1991) observes that continuation also offers the opportunity to assess actual benefits for students, teachers, and the school more completely than in earlier phases. Throughout the continuation stage, the literature suggests that monitoring and positive evaluation will help to make the innovation routine. All these factors were weighted very strongly by the respondents in Edmonton. They also agreed that the factors operating during the two previous phases had an effect on continuation, as suggested by both Fullan (1991) and McLaughlin and Berman (1978).

This overview of the factors indicates that most were known or predictable from the literature on the triphasic model, which is considered to be applicable to all forms of managed change. This lesson is gratifying, for it suggests that if the change to school-based management is undertaken with the appropriate knowledge (a relatively complete understanding of the triphasic model), along with the requisite actions as the model suggests, then it is quite likely that a school district will be able to decentralize without major setbacks. Murphy and Beck (1995) provide an overview of failed change to school-based management attributable to superficiality of the extent of decentralization, immovable resistance, or continued bureaucracy (Burke, 1992; Daresh, 1992; Malen & Ogawa, 1988; Wohlstetter & Odden, 1992). Unlike some attempts that have faltered, the administrative change in Edmonton proceeded in a rather deliberate fashion with ample resources decentralized, diminished resistance or conflict, and a reduction in the amount of rules that constrained school-level decision making. If the span of 16 years is a measure of permanence, then it may be said that the change was successful as a result of a confluence of a host of factors. Although the individual factors are each worthy of note because they are all "bases to be covered," we found that they could be grouped according to various themes that emerged initially in the conversations with the respondents. These four themes or clusters of factors allowed us to generate a more coherent picture of the change to decentralization.

First, the source of the initiative refers to the origins of the inspiration and those who acted as advocates for school-based management. Throughout the adoption phase, the superintendent's vision, philosophy, and experience provided direction. He held a picture of how the goals of the district could be advanced by school-based management. As identified by Miles (1987), this generation and advocacy of ideas are critical for planned change. During the second phase, implementation, the sources of the initiative continued to make their contributions. The external change agent assisted in the development of the infrastructure and design of the formal implementation plans, and gave workshops for principals. The inservice training taught principals how to provide school capacity for managing the change at the school level, and prepared teachers to participate in school-level budgeting. Internal change agents provided information, worked out bugs, and helped with planning, thus performing a role indicated to be important by Huberman and Crandall (1982). During continuation, the source of the initiative diminished in importance because the change process no longer relied heavily on its initial champions.

Second, support gathering refers to the positions that key actors undertake to generate and maintain impetus for the change. Although identification of the need for change occurred during adoption, support from key actors was seen as critical to its actual manifestation. The local teachers' association, individual teachers, community members, school principals, central office staff and administrators, the superintendent, and board all supported the initiative by offering advocacy and resources. Support was also generated by the use of the pilot school reports to the board. These results agree with the conclusions of Crandall, Eiseman, and Louis (1986), Fullan (1991), and Miles (1987) that support gathering is a key component of planned change. During implementation, perhaps the most pivotal development was that support for the innovation was sustained. Pilot schools shared information with the remaining schools, thus "converting" many of them to the idea. Support from teachers was built on the perks and benefits to them. Central office administrators helped during implementation via workshops and contributed to plans, aided in group discussions, provided assistance on demand, supported principals in difficulty with the initiative, monitored progress, and acknowledged successes. These kinds of actions are accentuated by Louis and Miles (1990).

Another substantial support-gathering development was the management cycle that the district and schools employed during implementation. Principals also strongly influenced the likelihood of success during this phase by expressing a high level of interest in school-based management and sharing their enthusiasm with the teachers in their schools, thus generating grassroots support. Even though it was not as necessary as in the adoption and implementation phases, support for the change was perceived as useful during the continuation stage. Visible superintendent endorsement maintained a spirit of enthusiasm and achievement throughout the district. (Fullan, 1991, documents the importance of the CEO in supporting both implementation and continuation phases.) The board also supported school-based management through its annual review, and the management cycle became routine. Annual satisfaction surveys provided further data that showed that students, parents, and employees continued to find that decentralization worked well (Mortimore, 1988, and Odden & Marsh, 1988, identify the importance of monitoring results during change). As a consequence, the change to school-based management became institutionalized.

Third, attributes of the initiative refer to the characteristics and effects of decentralization itself. During adoption, both board and pilot principal support were generated because of decentralization's apparent flexibility and accountability. During implementation, decentralization's opportunity for school personnel to make important school-level decisions became even more evident. During continuation, teachers found that, as a result of engaging in the budget planning process, they had more control over school events affecting the needs of students. This outcome suggests that school-based management made a contribution to the core technology of schools (teaching and learning), an important aspect of any educational change (Miles, 1993). Teachers, along with administrators, chose school goals and objectives, followed the annual district guidelines, but were free to exercise some variations. The requirement to plan at the school level almost demanded a collaborative work structure as urged by Fullan (1993b). The single line of authority feature (between the school and its associate superintendent) proved extremely useful, because it expedited information exchange, clarified responsibilities, and reduced inter-school competition for resources. Another feature, the adaptation of the innovation to individual schools, was welcomed by the respondents.

Finally, context is defined as the group of factors that comprise an organization's external environment and its history. One contextual factor during the adoption phase in this study was Edmonton's stable financial climate. It allowed sufficient attention and resources to be available for the innovation (see Clark, Lotto, & Astuto, 1984). Another factor was the teachers' strike, which occurred during adoption. The fact that the strike was partly resolved by use of school-based management speaks to its relevance as a contextual influence during this phase. Context continued to play an important background role during implementation. Locally, there was a history of prior innovations in the district. Because earlier experiences were generally positive ones, this change was accommodated more readily than it might have been if other initiatives had faltered. The importance of the local history is noted by Fullan (1991). The context of the Edmonton public schools remained relatively neutral during this phase, and a stable environment prevailed.

The groupings or clusters of factors provide a simpler, more coherent structure than the disparate factors apparent from the data and the phases by themselves. Further, the first two clusters, sources and support gathering, are linked because persons and factors that served as an impetus for the change were also associated with the deliberate effort to sustain the move to decentralization. These two clusters became the levers of change, and the district leadership had the courage to grasp them. The second two clusters, attributes of decentralization and the context, may be seen as external and only somewhat subject to district influence. That is because Edmonton defined school-based management partially to suit its needs, and it wielded a measure of influence on its environment.

It is not difficult to see how aspects of any of the four clusters would vary greatly if a different version of school-based management (attributes) were introduced in a different district (context) by advocates other than the superintendent (sources), and then backed by other groups and evidence (support gathering). If the clusters hold the keys to understanding the success or failure of the change, then it is easy to imagine how decentralization would not be accepted when any one of the clusters operated to defeat it. The suggestion here is that the positive orientation of each cluster constitutes a necessary condition for the change to school-based management to take place.

As a result of our work on this case study, we assert that successful voluntary change to decentralization is possible under the right conditions. We also believe that the four clusters may be used to understand whether the voluntary change to school-based management can place in any school district. Although we have fallen far short of Fullan's good theory of changing, this study offers some guidance for similar devolutionary changes in education. Ultimately, by permitting public schools greater latitude of decision making and reducing the plethora of rules under which they operate today, we hope they may be improved.

Edmonton Since 1989

Structural changes have continued within the Edmonton public schools. One is the shift in the role of the central office toward coordination and the provision of services. Because schools have 92% of district revenues, they purchase services from the central office and pay in real dollars. Another structural change is the removal of the associate superintendent positions and their replacement by principal teams of 20 to 30 who meet regularly with the superintendent. Principals are considered to be the senior staff of the district.

The Edmonton Public School District now has a substantial number of alternate schools, partly in response to the introduction of charter school legislation in Alberta. For example, one school has a Christian emphasis for groups concerned about the place of Christian values and morality in the curriculum. Another is a military academy administered by army personnel as well as by educators. Moneys are allocated to schools wishing to start novel programs. Hence, Edmonton public schools have responded to the demands for school choice with a strategy that favors inclusion.

This successful picture is tempered somewhat by two recent developments. One is the realization that student achievement, as measured by scores on standardized tests, has not improved sufficiently. This realization led to the creation of a 4-year plan to increase scores. The other is labor strife over the board's unwillingness to provide for an early retirement option for teachers, an option already available in the neighboring nonpublic schools. Although a strike was averted when the board relented, the conflict generated a great deal of bitterness among teachers.

During the mid-1990s, Mike Strembitsky, the superintendent for many years, was replaced by Emery Dosdall, a former associate superintendent in Edmonton and superintendent in Langley, British Columbia, where he had overseen the institution of school-based management. The new superintendent spends much of his time meeting with principals, parents, students, and community leaders. He is seen as a "people person," very receptive to new ideas. The moves to flatten the district hierarchy and to include diverse schools of choice within Edmonton are attributed to him.

The provincial context has supported district decentralization throughout the last decade. The Alberta government policy involves putting money in the hands of educators in the schools and asking for accountability to increase efficiency. As a result of provincial leadership, Edmonton's variant of school-based management is a model for all public schools in Alberta to evaluate and consider for their districts.

Acknowledgments

Comments on a previous draft by Carolyn Sheilds were appreciated. The contributions of respondents in the Edmonton public schools and the support of the Social Sciences Research Council of Canada are acknowledged gratefully. Please direct all communication to the second author.

Notes

1. Edmonton is a large and complex district composed of residential, commercial, and industrial features across a wide array of socioeconomic conditions. During 1987-88, the Edmonton public schools had 73,291 students and 4,006 teachers in 190 schools. The total operating budget was $307,337,000, of which 53% was funded by the province of Alberta, 10% by provincial levy on local properties, and 37% by local taxes. The overall cost per pupil was $4,391 that year.

2. The importance of an innovation's features is stressed by writers such as Fullan (1991), Firestone and Corbett (1988), and Louis and Miles (1990).

3. This and similar codes throughout indicate the respondent and location by line number in the interview transcript. The names of the interviewees have been withheld to protect their anonymity.

References

Alexandruk, F. (1985). *School budgeting in the Edmonton Public School District.* Unpublished masters thesis, University of Alberta.

Bimber, B. (1993). *School decentralization: Lessons from the study of bureaucracy.* Santa Monica, CA: RAND.

Bogdan, R., & Biklen, S. K. (1982). *Qualitative research for education: An introduction to theory and methods.* Boston: Allyn & Bacon.

Bredeson, P. V. (1992, April). *Responses to restructuring and empowerment initiatives: A study of teachers' and principals' perceptions of organizational leadership, decision making, and climate.* Paper presented at the annual meeting of the American Educational Research Association, San Francisco.

Brown, D. J. (1990). *Decentralization and school-based management.* London: Falmer.

Brown, D. J. (1995). The sabotage of school-based management. *School Administrator, 52*(3), 8-14.

Burke, C. (1992). Devolution of responsibility to Queensland schools: Clarifying the rhetoric, critiquing the reality. *Journal of Educational Administration, 30*(4), 33-52.

Caldwell, B. (1977). *Decentralized school budgeting in Alberta.* Unpublished doctoral dissertation, University of Alberta.

Caldwell B. J., & Spinks J. (1988). *The self-managing school.* London: Falmer.

Clark, D., Lotto, S., & Astuto, T. (1984). Effective schools and school improvement: A comparative analysis of two lines of inquiry. *Educational Administration Quarterly, 20*(3), 41-68.

Crandall, D., Eiseman, J., & Louis, K. S. (1986). Strategic planning issues that bear on the success of school improvement efforts. *Educational Administration Quarterly, 22*(3), 21-53.

Daresh, J. C. (1992). Impressions of school-based management: The Cincinnati story. In J. J. Land & E. G. Epps (Eds.), *Restructuring the schools: Problems and prospects.* Berkeley, CA: McCutchan.

David, J. L. (1989). Synthesis of research on school-based management. *Educational Leadership, 46*(8), 45-53.

Elmore, R. F. (1993). School decentralization: Who gains? Who loses? In J. Hannaway & M. Carnoy (Eds.), *Decentralization and school improvement* (pp. 33-54). San Francisco: Jossey-Bass.

Firestone, W., & Corbett, H. D. (1988). Planned organizational change. In N. Boyan (Ed.), *Handbook of research on educational administration* (pp. 321-340). New York: Longman.

Fullan, M. G. (1991). *The new meaning of educational change.* New York: Teachers College Press.

Fullan, M. G. (1993a). Coordinating school and district development in restructuring. In J. Murphy & P. Hallinger (Eds.), *Restructuring schooling: Learning from ongoing efforts* (pp. 143-164). Newbury Park, CA: Corwin.

Fullan, M. G. (1993b). Why teachers must become change agents. *Educational Leadership, 50*(6), 12-17.

Hanson, M. (1991, April). *Alteration of influence relations in school-based management innovations.* Paper presented at the annual meeting of the American Educational Research Association, Chicago.

Havelock, R. G. (1973). *The change agent's guide to innovation in education.* Englewood Cliffs, NJ: Educational Technology Publications.

Heller, R. W., Woodworth, B. C., Jacobson, S. L., & Conway, J. A. (1989). You like school-based power, but you wonder if others do. *Executive Educator, 11*(11), 15-18.

Hess, G. A., Jr. (1991). *School restructuring: Chicago style.* Newbury Park, CA: Corwin.

Hill, P. T., & Bonan, J. (1991). *Decentralization and accountability in public education.* Santa Monica, CA: RAND.

Huberman, R. M., & Crandall, D. P. (1982). *Implications for action: A study of dissemination efforts supporting school improvement* (Vol. 9). Andover, MD: Network of Innovative Schools.

Knight, B. (1993). Delegated financial management. In C. Dimmock (Ed.), *School-based management and school effectiveness.* London: Routledge.

Kuo, V. (1996). *Edmonton Public School District: A case study of a district's role in supporting school reform.* Palo Alto, CA: Stanford University, Accelerated Schools Project.

Lawton, S. B. (1995). *Busting the bureaucracy to reclaim our schools.* Montreal: Institute for Research on Public Policy.

Louis, K., & Miles, M. B. (1990). *Improving the urban high school: What works and why.* New York: Teachers College Press.

Malen, B., & Ogawa, R. T. (1988). Professional-patron influence on site-based governance councils: A confounding case study. *Educational Evaluation and Policy Analysis, 10*(4), 251-270.

Maynes, W. (1980). School-based budgeting: Concerns relating to implementation. *Challenge in Educational Administration, 20*(1), 22-29.

McLaughlin, M., & Berman, P. (1978). *Federal programs supporting educational change.* Santa Monica, CA: RAND.

Miles, M. (1987, April). *Practical guidelines for school administrators: How to get there.* Paper presented at the American Educational Research Association annual meeting, San Francisco.

Miles, M. B. (1993). 40 years of change in schools: Some personal reflections. *Educational Administration Quarterly, 29*(2), 213-248.

Miles, M., & Huberman, A. M. (1984). *Qualitative data analysis.* Beverly Hills, CA: Sage.

Mortimore, P. (1988). *School matters: The junior years.* Sommerset, UK: Open Books.

Murphy, J., & Beck, L. (1995). *School-based management as school reform: Taking stock.* Thousand Oaks, CA: Corwin.

Odden, A., & Marsh, D. (1988). How comprehensive reform legislation can improve secondary schools. *Phi Delta Kappan, 69*(8), 7-11.

Ozembloski, L. W. (1993). *The process of educational change: A school-based management initiative in two western Canadian public school districts.* Unpublished doctoral dissertation, University of British Columbia.

Sackney, L. E., & Dibski, D. J. (1992, August). *School-based management: A critical perspective.* Paper presented at the seventh regional conference of the Commonwealth Council for Educational Administration, Hong Kong.

Steffy, B. C. (1993). *The Kentucky education reform: Lessons for America.* Lancaster, PA: Technomic.

Wohlstetter, P., & Buffett, T. M. (1992). Promoting school-based management: Are dollars decentralized too? In A. Odden (Ed.), *Rethinking school finance: An agenda for the 1990s* (pp. 128-165). San Francisco: Jossey-Bass.

Wohlstetter, P., & Odden, A. (1992). Rethinking school-based management policy and research. *Educational Administration Quarterly, 28*(4), 529-549.

PART III

How Schools Allocate and Use Financial Resources

SEVEN

School-Based Financing
in North America

ALLAN ODDEN

In the United States and Canada, school financing has largely addressed the issue of state-to-district formula funding. Although states
and provinces have had constitutional responsibilities for education,
each state in the United States and each province in Canada has chosen
to discharge this responsibility through local school districts. When
these systems were developed more than a century ago, their financing was generally devolved to local districts, which were given the
authority to tax local property to raise funds for their school systems.

Because the local education tax base, usually property wealth per
pupil, varied widely across districts within states and provinces, local
school districts faced different challenges in raising education revenues and spending on education programs. Low-wealth districts
often had low levels of expenditures even with high tax rates, whereas
high-wealth districts often had high levels of per pupil expenditures
even with low tax rates. School finance policy and school finance
formulas were developed to remedy these inequities, but it was not
until the end of this century that equalization formulas began substan-

tially to ameliorate the unequal abilities of local districts to raise revenues for public schools (Evans, Murray, & Schwab, 1997).

This relentless attention to interdistrict finance issues has mostly addressed financing districts (Odden & Picus, 1992; Swanson & King, 1997) and has largely ignored the issue of financing schools. But in the 1990s, these emphases have begun to change (Busch & Odden, 1997; Clark & Toenjes, 1998; Speakman et al., 1997).

Origins of Formula Funding of Schools

Several policy initiatives in the late 1980s and early 1990s began to shift attention from the district to the school site. First, states began to enact public school choice programs that allowed each child to select any public school to attend, instead of being forced to attend the neighborhood school. When students selected schools outside their school district of residence, however, states were faced with the challenge of tracking the flow of funds. To a considerable degree, states floundered in determining how to finance their new public school choice programs; their difficulty flowed primarily from their inexperience in financing schools as compared with financing districts. Unfortunately, many states created cumbersome financing transfer systems as part of public school choice, when the most straightforward way to finance such programs was simply to count the student in the school or district attended and use the regular school financing mechanism. Such an approach triggered nearly all the relevant revenue transfers (Odden & Kotowski, 1992).

The next school-based financing challenge involved charter schools. In most states, charter schools are public schools that operate largely independently from local school districts as well as from state education rules and regulations. When states enacted charter school legislation, they were even more directly faced with a finance challenge they had never addressed—how to finance an individual school site as compared to a local school district. States took many approaches to charter school financing, some quite cumbersome, when again more straightforward approaches were possible (see Odden & Busch, 1998, chapter 3).

The most significant factor that has begun to raise the issue of school-based financing in the United States is the current education reform movement, which has been called standards- and school-based education reform (Fuhrman, 1993; Massell, Kirst, & Hoppe, 1997; Smith & O'Day, 1991). This reform strategy seeks to have the top of the education system (mainly the state and district) set curriculum content and student performance standards, measure student achievement results to those standards, administer an accountability system linked to the measured results, and devolve to school sites responsibility for producing improvements in system and student performance. This strategy generally requires major changes in school curriculum, governance, management, and finance, and, however labeled, requires a school-based management system (see Odden & Busch, 1998, chapter 2).

Odden and Busch (1998) argue that this approach to education policy also requires a school-based financing system. Although this element of education financing has not been enacted by any state in the United States or by any province in Canada, it has been implemented in Victoria, Australia (see Caldwell & Hill in this volume) and England (see Odden & Busch, 1998, chapter 5). Several states, however, including Arizona, Florida, Georgia, Minnesota, Ohio, Texas, and Washington, have begun to consider incorporating a school-based financing requirement into their state education finance systems. Chapter 6 in Odden and Busch (1998) is an adaptation of a paper written for Minnesota suggesting how that state should structure the budget devolution process. Though as of December 1998, no U.S. state or Canadian province had designed or enacted such a policy, the issue is rapidly creeping onto the North American education finance agenda, and some state or province could enact such a new finance element in the near future.

Local Policy Context
for Formula Funding

On the other hand, the topic of school-based financing has not only moved onto the policy agenda of many large districts in the United States and Canada, but also has been implemented by several districts.

For nearly 20 years, the Edmonton public school system in the province of Alberta in Canada has used a weighted "per pupil" formula to provide lump sum budgets for each of its schools. Initially, Edmonton adopted this policy to improve the efficiencies of its operations, under the assumptions that schools could make more efficient decisions about how to spend resources on site needs than could the central office (Caldwell & Spinks, 1992).

During the past 4 years, however, another movement in urban education has provided a stimulus for moving to a school-based financing system. Several big cities have begun to adopt large-scale changes in their finance, management, governance, curriculum, and instructional programs as part of efforts to improve their very low levels of student performance. These cities have come to believe that minor changes in their strategies and operations would be insufficient for the large increases they need to make in their student achievement results.

Although the cities are crafting their own unique versions of standards- and school-based reforms, several decided to join with the New American Schools (NAS) and to have their schools implement one of several whole school designs that have been created by NAS. NAS offers districts and schools eight different whole school, high performance designs (Stringfield, Ross, & Smith, 1996). The curriculum, staffing, and organization of these designs are quite different from the typical American school. They produce more student achievement results and show promise for accomplishing the goal of teaching students to higher standards (Fashola & Slavin, 1997). In most districts, these programs also can be funded with dollars already in the education system (Odden, 1997; Odden & Busch, 1998).

As these districts began to implement their rather bold new initiatives, they learned that they also needed to redesign nearly all their school systems operating procedures (see Odden & Busch, 1998, chapter 8; Cincinnati Public Schools, 1996), including creating and implementing a school-based financing system. The latter was required because the cost structure and use of site resources were quite different across the different school designs, and schools needed budget authority to reallocate extant resources to the requirements of their chosen designs (Odden, 1997). Further, reports on implementation showed that school control over fiscal resources was needed for full implementation, but had not been one of the authorities that districts had provided (Bodilly, 1996, 1998). As a result, many of these districts began to create and implement new, school-based financing policies.

In sum, the district school-based financing formulas discussed in this chapter are part of large-scale, urban school district redesign and decentralization efforts, adopted for the purpose of substantially improving student achievement. These broader goals—linking decentralization to fundamental school improvement—have also been added to the decentralization and school-based financing policies in Edmonton.

Thus, all the districts discussed in this chapter are implementing school-based financing efforts as part of broader strategies to improve the performance of their education system. This rationale is quite different from the original purpose for decentralizing finance in Edmonton—simply to improve the efficiency of school operations. The overriding goal is to improve student achievement dramatically; the general management strategy is decentralization to school sites; and districts designed school-based funding formulas as part of implementing this management and school improvement strategy.

School Budgets:
Centralized and Delegated Portions

The first step in creating a school-based financing system should be to decide which functions should remain at the district and which functions should be devolved to school sites. Unlike the rather sophisticated program in England, which, from the very beginning, included this type of functional allocation (see Coopers & Lybrand, 1988; Odden & Busch, 1998, chapter 5; Thompson & Lakin, 1997), school-based financing in the United States has proceeded largely without this analysis. For example, state approaches to charter school financing, the first state-directed school-based financing initiative in the United States, focused in the initial years on whether state aid should follow the child and how local money should or should not be part of charter school financial regulations (Odden & Busch, 1998, chapter 3). This policy conversation addressed only state and local dollar distribution, with little regard for services provided or tasks to accomplish. Not until the late 1990s did the issue of functional allocation by level of the system creep into policy deliberations over charter school financing.

At the district level, which is the focus of this chapter, more attention has been given to the assignment of functions between school sites and the district office. But until recently, the discussion was driven by the perceived ease of budgeting rather than an assessment of what should be retained at the center when the district decentralizes and what should be decentralized to each school site. No district had a document that discussed the rationale for what functions should be central and what should be site as part of their new decentralization programs.

Table 7.1 shows this issue in part. The table identifies the functions that have been retained at the district office in the five districts portrayed and the percentage of the overall operating budget consumed by these functions. The second to last row shows the percentage of the operating budget devolved to school sites, and thus the percentage of the budget that is the object of the school-based financing formulas. The percentage figures are quite striking. The percentage devolved varies from 49.2% in Seattle to 80.9% in Edmonton, figures substantially below the percentage of the operating budget that is devolved to school sites in England.

Some caution must be used in reading the exact percentage figures in Table 7.1 because the definitions of functions are not precisely the same across all districts. In creating the table, care was given to the degree possible in grouping functions and areas into similar categories, but the resultant grouping and the related budget figures should not be viewed as exact. Nevertheless, the table does show the central tendencies of the school-based funding programs. All five districts retained transportation at the central office. Two of the five districts (Pittsburgh and Seattle) retained funding for special education and compensatory education, but were hoping to devolve those dollars at some time in the future. Broward was able to devolve those dollars in part by using the same weighted pupil counts as the state did in providing state aid; the same was generally true in Edmonton. All districts, except Edmonton, retained the large bulk of the central office functions of instructional and pupil support, even though it could be argued that these central office functions should be downsized as a

TABLE 7.1. Functions Retained at District Level and Percentage of Budget Retained and Devolved

	Broward	Cincinnati	Edmonton	Pittsburgh	Seattle
Functions retained (% of budget)	1997-98	Proposed 1997-98	1997-98	1997-98	1997-98
Central administration	NA	NA	6.5%	4.4%	9.0%
Logistics and other support	NA	NA	Transportation, debt, and misc. 11	25.0	Operations & maint: 4 Transp: 5.8 Food: 2.8 Other: 3.4 Total: 17
Central instruction & instruction support	NA	NA	Continuing education 1.6	2.6	E.g., special ed, Title I, bilingual ed: 13.5
Categorical grants	NA	NA	—	—	10.1
Total central office less reserves & balances	16.0%	NA	19.1	32.0	49.4
Other	Fund balance and reserves: 4.0	NA	—		General reserves: 1.4
Percent devolved to school	80.0	76.4%	80.9	68.0	49.2
School site surpluses retained & carried over to next year	NO	YES	YES	YES	YES

NA = Not available.

natural part of their decentralization strategies; these functions are addressed by most school designs. It is not clear from the data how much of the central personnel office was retained, though this is a function that largely should be devolved in a comprehensive decentralization effort. In short, although these districts decentralized a substantial portion of the operating budget, their decisions on which functions were retained at the center varied significantly, and there is ample room for more substantive analysis to determine which functions ought to be retained and which ought to be devolved.

Design of the Funding Formula

Tables 7.2, 7.3, 7.4, 7.5, and 7.6 show the components, dimensions, and indicators for the various elements of the school-based financing formulas for each of the five school districts. The data are based on analysis of budget formulas and documents from each district. All five formulas have an allocation for the 1.0 or norm student, adjustments for different grade levels, provisions for specific curriculum enhancements, numerous additions for the special needs of several categories of students, and school-specific factors as well. In other words, all five school-based financing formulas address a range of issues that relate to students, education levels, the curriculum, specific student needs, and different needs of each school building. In short, these represent quite comprehensive school-based financing formulas.

Two districts—Broward County, Florida, and Edmonton, Alberta—use a full time equivalent (FTE) pupil count and three districts—Cincinnati, Pittsburgh, and Seattle—use a simple enrollment pupil count, although Cincinnati uses an FTE count for vocational education funding. FTE pupil counts have been used for years in those states (and districts) that have a weighted pupil count for identifying and financing the extra needs of students caused by physical or mental disability, economic disadvantage, and the like. For these programs, each pupil is counted the percentage of time he or she participates in different programs, and program costs are set at a level assuming full-time provision.

These distinctions—the FTE versus the simple headcount of enrollment—must be recalled when pupil weights or extra dollars per pupil

(text continued on p. 168)

TABLE 7.2.   Relationship Among Components, Dimensions, and
Indicators in Broward County, FL

Component	Dimension	Indicator Measured for Each School
1. Basic pupil allocation		
a. Common allocation	Number of weighted full time equivalent (FTE) pupils in the school	Based on state weights and methods for determining FTE pupil counts for Florida Education Finance Program
b. Grade-level supplement	Weighted, FTE students Students in grades 4-8 represent the 1.0 weight, and funding is by weighted FTE, but base funding varies across elementary, middle and high schools	FTE pupils by grade level and by category of need, which includes basic, mainstreamed, ESL, Exceptional Programs (15 categories), and vocational 7-12 (10 categories)
2. Curriculum enhancement	Several categories, including magnet schools, vocational programs, dropout prevention	Theme based, with some small extra base funding and then extra dollars or extra teachers based on FTE counts (FTE pupil count in 10 categories, FTE pupil count)
	Several other small programs with low budgets for, e.g., reducing class size, parent outreach, DARE, SADD, arts, advanced secondary academic courses, minorities in engineering, professional development	Usually fixed dollars for program, based on unweighted FTE
3. Pupil-specific factors	Several factors:	
	a. Mainstreamed special education	FTE pupil count
	b. Teenage parent	FTE pupil count
	c. Intensive English as a Second Language	FTE pupil count
	d. Disability (15 categories)	FTE pupil count
	e. Compensatory education	Number of middle school and 10th grade pupils scoring below 18th percentile on reading & math on Stanford Achievement Test
4. Specific school factors	School size	Number of weighted FTE

TABLE 7.3.   Relationship Among Components, Dimensions, and
Indicators in Cincinnati, OH

Component	Dimension	Indicator Measured for Each School
1. Basic pupil allocation		
a. Common allocation	Number of pupils enrolled in the school	School enrollment
b. Grade-level supplement	Elementary students	Number of students
	Middle school students	Number of students
	High school students	Number of students
2. Curriculum enhancement	Major magnets: Paideia, arts enrichment, Montessori, foreign language	Number of students in magnet school
	Minor magnets: college prep, fundamental academy, etc.	Fixed amount per school
	Vocational education	Number of FTE students across all vocational education programs
3. Pupil-specific factors	None in school funding formula, considered to be handled by federal Title 1 for students from poverty backgrounds	
	Federal Title 1 program, students from poverty backgrounds	Number of students eligible for the free or reduced lunch, in categories of such students as a percentage of all students in school
	Physical or mental disability	Enrollments in nine different categories of disability, each of which has different class size maximums
4. Specific school factors	School size	Enrollment: Extra amounts per pupil for small elementary, middle and high, nonmagnet schools
	School site—base allocation	Base allocation for each school site
	Several other site-based factors	Actual expenditures in previous year

TABLE 7.4. Relationship Among Components, Dimensions, and Indicators in Edmonton, Alberta, Canada

Component	Dimension	Indicator Measured for Each School
1. Basic pupil allocation		
a. Common allocation	Number of FTE pupils enrolled in the school	FTE students FTE
b. Grade-level supplement	Elementary and middle school students (grades K-8) represent base funding	Elementary and middle FTE, determined by headcount; half-day kindergarten is counted as 0.446
	High school students (grades 9-12) are weighted 1.03	High school FTE, for which 37.5 credits equals 1.0 FTE, with 1 credit equal to 40 minutes of instruction
2. Curriculum enhancement	Several small programs for different purposes, such as reading, foreign language, high incidence of special needs, enrollment growth, new programs	
3. Pupil-specific factors	High needs:	
	a. High socioeconomic needs	Mobility, low family income according to 1991 Canada statistics
	b. Limited English proficiency	Number of students with native language other than English
	Physical or mental disability	Two categories of mild needs
		Two categories of moderate needs
		Two categories of severe needs
4. Specific school factors	Routine maintenance	Allocation based 75% on square footage of buildings and 25% on weighted enrollment

TABLE 7.5.   Relationship Among Components, Dimensions, and
                 Indicators in Pittsburgh, PA

Component	Dimension	Indicator Measured for Each School
1. Basic pupil allocation		
a. Common allocation	Number of pupils enrolled in the school	School enrollment
b. Grade-level supplement	Elementary students grades K-5 represent base funding	Number of elementary pupils
	Middle schools students grades 6-8 are weighted 1.384	Number of middle school pupils
	High school students grades 9-12 are weighted 1.505	Number of high school pupils
2. Curriculum enhancement	One middle school and two secondary magnet schools	Magnet school designation: one middle and one secondary creative and performing arts magnet; one secondary vocational-technical magnet
3. Pupil-specific factors	High needs:	
	a. Economic condition	Percentage of students eligible for federal free and reduced lunch
	b. Not residing with both parents	Percentage of students with single parents and residing in institutions, foster home, or other guardianship arrangements
	Physical or mental disability	Not now included in Pittsburgh school-based finance formula
4. Specific school factors	School size	Number of students, with adjustment for schools with fewer than 300 students

TABLE 7.6. Relationship Among Components, Dimensions, and Indicators in Seattle, WA

Component	Dimension	Indicator Measured for Each School
1. Basic pupil allocation		
a. Common allocation	Number of pupils enrolled in the school	School enrollment
b. Grade-level supplement	Elementary students grades K-3 represent base funding	Number of grade K-3 students
	Elementary students grades 4-5 are weighted 0.94	Number of grade 4-5 students
	Middle schools students grades 6-8 are weighted 0.87	Number of grade 6-8 students
	High school students grades 9-12 are weighted 0.88	Number of grade 9-12 students
2. Curriculum enhancement	No adjustment	
3. Pupil-specific factors	High needs:	
	a. Bilingual education, i.e., proficiency in English	A different extra weight by grade level for limited English proficient students
	b. Low achievement test score	A different extra weight by grade level for lowest three deciles
	c. Family poverty	Federal free and reduced lunch. A different extra weight by grade level
	Physical or mental disability	Five different levels based on severity of needs, with different weights by level and grade level
4. Specific school factors	School site	Base dollar allocation for every elementary, middle, and high school, with minimum size targets of 250, 600, and 1,000 students, respectively

representing program costs are assessed to make meaningful comparisons. For example, assume the base program cost is $5,000 per child. If a particular program costs an extra $4,000 to provide full-time, and each eligible child is in the program full-time, then that child would be weighted 1.8 (0.8 times $5,000 = $4,000). On the other hand, if the program costs $4,000 to provide but a child participates only 50% of the day (week or year), then the child would be weighted only 1.4 in an FTE pupil count, and the school would receive an extra $2,000. The cost for the same program would be set at $2,000 per student for places using an enrollment or headcount of pupils. The point is that an FTE pupil count is different in many specific ways from a headcount of students enrolled, and these differences must be considered when interpreting both student weights as well as extra per pupil amounts for special programs.

All districts make distinctions in budgeting dollars by different levels of schooling—elementary (sometimes divided between primary years and upper elementary years), middle, and high school students. Though the specific grades that these different school levels represent vary somewhat among the five districts, that variation is quite small, and usually concerns whether grade 6 is part of an elementary school or a middle school. Most high schools are 4 years and include grades 9-12.

It is important to note that none of the education level differences is related to different stages of student learning or performance benchmarks, as is true of many formulas in England and Australia (see Odden & Busch, 1998, chapters 4 and 5). Although all five districts are in the process of developing or implementing a standards-based curriculum reform program, often with content and performance standards at certain grade levels, none specifically linked differences in dollar allocations to these content or performance standards. At the same time, most of the standards that exist are for grades 4, 8, and 10. Although the grade 4 standard could be roughly equivalent to an end-of-elementary learning stage, and the grade 8 standard could be roughly equivalent to an end-of-middle-school learning stage, there are no funding distinctions related to these levels or curriculum stages, and there are no funding distinctions between the grade 10 and upper high school programs. In short, though every district provides a differential level of funding by education level, largely elementary, middle, and high school, none explicitly connects these differences to any stage of learning or any level in their curriculum standards.

Curriculum enhancement is a formula component addressed in several different dimensions. In addition, provision for curriculum enhancement varies considerably across the five districts, ranging from numerous curriculum enhancement adjustments in Broward County to no adjustments in Seattle. Three districts—Broward, Cincinnati, and Pittsburgh—provide extra money for magnet programs, which generally are part of desegregation efforts. Broward County and Cincinnati provide adjustments for vocational education programs in their high schools. Interestingly, the two districts with FTE pupil counts and a long history with weighted pupil funding formulas also have numerous additional small programs with specific curriculum emphases, all part of their school-based funding policies.

Though all five districts have not yet included funds for all major pupil-specific factors in their new funding schemes, the goal of all districts is to do so. The general goal is to include adjustments at least for students from a family with low income, students with physical or mental disabilities, students with limited English proficiency, and students achieving at a very low level. Currently, several dimensions of these pupil-specific factors are recognized. All districts have some mechanism for providing aid for disabled students, and usually those students are divided into categories that vary by the intensity of extra services provided. Though all four U.S. districts have funds from the federal Title 1 program, which provides extra resources for low-achieving students from low-income families, Broward, Edmonton, Pittsburgh, and Seattle also provide adjustments from state and local revenue sources for students from low-income backgrounds. Seattle also has an adjustment for students with low levels of student achievement, and Pittsburgh includes a family context variable—percentage of students not living in a two-parent family—that triggers extra funds. Three districts—Broward, Edmonton, and Seattle—include adjustments for students with limited proficiency in English. Finally, Broward County has a number of additional categories of special pupil needs, including being a teenage parent. In each case, the indicator generally is either the headcount or enrollment count of students with the specified special needs or a FTE pupil count. The point here is that all these programs have numerous adjustments for special student needs across several student need dimensions, even though not all the special adjustments are currently included in the school-based financing formula.

When the special students needs program dollars are not part of the school-based budget formula, however, the resources for these dimensions of student need are still often provided to school sites. For example, each school in the four U.S. districts receives a dollar allocation from the federal Title 1 program and is able to spend it as it wishes. Each school also receives resources, though staff resources if not dollar budgets, for disabled students. The point is that although not all dimensions of pupil-specific factors are included in the school-based financing formulas, the resources for those dimensions are nevertheless provided to school sites, often via another and separate formula, and often times the schools have authority over how these dollars are spent.

Finally, each district also has a component of the school-based financing formula based on specific school factors. Two major dimensions and one unique dimension are used. Broward and Cincinnati use the dimension of size, measured by the number of pupils, and have small size adjustments that provide additional funds for schools depending on their overall enrollment, usually enrollment below a certain level. Cincinnati and Seattle use the dimension of school site and provide for a base allocation for each school site; the base allocation is intended to provide an amount of administrative staff for a school. Cincinnati also has several additional school-based factors. Finally, Edmonton also uses the dimension of school site, but more specifically the level of routine maintenance needed, and adjusts all budgets by that amount.

The Pupil Component

Table 7.7 displays the allocation for the student weighted 1.0 and the grade-level weights for all other students used in each of the five school district funding formulas. The reader should take great care in interpreting these weights, especially across school districts. The amount of the budget provided to each site as a percentage of the total operating budget varies significantly. Second, even for the school budget, the base allocation provided to each site is quite large and

TABLE 7.7.   Weight 1.0 Allocation and Grade-Level Weights in Five North American Districts

	Broward	*Cincinnati*	*Edmonton*	*Pittsburgh*	*Seattle*
Allocation for student with 1.0 weight	El: $1,868 Middle: $1,931	El: $3,051 Middle: $3,488 K-8: $3,334	$3,127	$4,632 Applied to weighted pupils	$2,441 Applied to weighted pupils
	High: $1,802	High: $3,011	Applied to weighted FTE		
	Applied to weighted FTE				
	Pupil weight	*Pupil weight*	*Pupil weight*	*Pupil weight*	*Pupil weight*
Grade K	1.234 (1.00)	1.01	1.0	1.0	1.0
Grade 1	1.234 (1.00)	1.01	1.0	1.0	1.0
Grade 2	1.234 (1.00)	1.01	1.0	1.0	1.0
Grade 3	1.234 (1.00)	1.01	1.0	1.0	1.0
Grade 4	1.0 (0.83)	1.01	1.0	1.0	0.94
Grade 5	1.0 (0.83)	1.01	1.0	1.0	
Grade 6	1.0 (0.83)	1.01	1.0	1.384	
Grade 7	1.0 (0.83)	1.16	1.0	1.384	
Grade 8	1.0 (0.83)	1.16	1.0	1.384	
Grade 9	1.179 (0.96)	1.0	1.03	1.505	
Grade 10	1.179 (0.96)	1.0	1.03	1.505	
Grade 11	1.179 (0.96)	1.0	1.03	1.505	
Grade 12	1.179 (0.96)	1.0	1.03	1.505	

varies dramatically (see Table 7.10), thus reducing the amount provided by the pupil-weighted portion of the formula. In addition, the overall spending varies across the five districts, a fact that also can affect the substantive meaning of the different weights. Each affects the meaning of the grade-level weight.

With these caveats in mind, one can review the data in Table 7.7. Several observations are in order. First, the different weights apply to students in different grade levels only, that is, not specifically to students of different ages or students at different stages of the curriculum that might be reflected in the curriculum content or student performance standards. So, the practice in North America is to provide pupil weights largely by education level.

Second, four of the districts use a fully developed weighted pupil approach. Cincinnati provides a different amount for each elementary, middle, and high school student. The Broward and Cincinnati weights should be viewed with caution because the districts also provide large base allocations, which vary widely across the three levels (see Table 7.10), and also provide a very large size adjustment. The result is that it may be inappropriate to impute the differences in the allocations in Table 7.10 for Broward and Cincinnati as a pupil weight. The general conclusion, however, is that North American districts use a weighted pupil funding approach.

Third, four districts—Broward, Edmonton, Pittsburgh, and Seattle—have traditional pupil-weighted formulas, with an allocation for the 1.0 weighted students that is then applied to the number of weighted students in each school site. Broward has a slight twist to this simple approach in that the allocation applied to the weighted pupil count varies slightly among elementary, middle, and high schools.

Fourth, there are three distinct patterns for the grade-level weights: (1) weights that rise from the elementary, to middle, to high school levels; (2) weights that are the same across the three levels; and (3) weights that fall from the elementary to the secondary level. The grade-level weights in Pittsburgh follow the usual pattern of higher weights for secondary than for primary school students. Indeed, the weight is 1.0 for elementary students, 1.384 for middle school students, and 1.505 for high school students, grade-level weights for secondary students that exceed the magnitude of weights in most state-to-district finance formulas (Odden & Picus, 1992).

The weights in Edmonton also are higher in the high school than at the lower grade levels, but only very modestly so. Grade 9-12 students are weighted just 1.03 compared to elementary students, and middle school students are weighted the same as elementary school students. It would be more accurate to say that Edmonton essentially had no weights for grade-level differences.

On the other hand, the weights in Broward County (note the weights in parenthesis that peg a kindergarten student as the 1.0 student) and

Seattle are lower in middle and secondary schools than in elementary schools. In other words, Broward County and Seattle provide more revenues per pupil for young students than for older students, a practice reflecting a belief that early, intensive education for children, with the goal of developing solid literacy and numeracy expertise by the end of elementary school, is a more cost-effective use of local and state fiscal resources.

When the base allocations are factored into the Cincinnati formula, the result is a secondary allocation that is a few hundred dollars per pupil higher, that is, about 10% more. Otherwise, the data in Table 7.7 show that Cincinnati provides about the same base funding for elementary and high school students, and about 10% more for middle school students, a unique practice.

The difference in practices among these five districts is quite striking. The typical practice in spending across school levels is for higher expenditures on secondary students (Organisation for Economic Cooperation and Development, 1996). Indeed, one of the primary contentions that has emerged as governments have shifted funding to the school site has been the higher funding of secondary students (see Caldwell & Hill in this volume, and Odden & Busch, 1998, chapter 5). Yet Pittsburgh was the only district to provide such differential funding to secondary students. The other districts provided either no or very small distinctions between elementary and secondary students, or actually weighted the system in favor of elementary school students. In this sense, the grade-level weights in these five school districts represent quite different resource allocation decisions.

Although the grade-level weights adopted by these five jurisdictions cannot be taken as indicative of practice across North America, they nevertheless reflect a major fiscal value shift in the basic allocation of resources for these districts, away from the traditional bias toward higher funded secondary students and a new bias of greater funding for elementary students, particularly elementary students in grades K-3. As stated above, the rationale for this shift in the resource allocation process is to develop the basic skills early in the elementary career of a child, under the assumption that if students can read, write, and do mathematics proficiently by grade 3, then teachers at higher grades have virtually an unlimited horizon for student achievement expectations. Of course, this also reflects the obverse of this proposition—that late intervention for secondary students who have not developed good literacy and numeracy skills is not only inefficient but also very difficult to make effective.

The Curriculum Enhancement Component

These districts also provide curriculum enhancement funds for magnet schools, vocational education, foreign language, and dropout prevention programs. Broward, Cincinnati, and Pittsburgh provided extra funds for magnet schools. Broward provided about $10 million for 32 different, theme-based magnet programs at all levels—elementary, middle, and high school. Cincinnati has provided extra funds for magnet schools for several years. The district supports four major magnet themes: Paideia, Montessori (drawing from the Montessori preschool program), foreign language, and arts enrichment. The per pupil extra costs of these magnets range substantially, from a low of $374 per pupil more for the small elementary arts enrichment magnet to $1,274 per pupil more for the high school Paideia magnet, with a median amount of $834 per pupil. Cincinnati also has several minor magnet programs with funding that ranges from $10,000 to $65,000 per school. When Cincinnati fully adopts a school-based funding policy in 1999-00, it will probably retain but not expand the number of magnets. Indeed, because Cincinnati is encouraging all schools to adopt a high-performance school design, and thus become a school with a specific thematic emphasis, the notion of separate magnet schools is somewhat outmoded, but politically, the districts will find it difficult to discontinue extra magnet school funding for the magnets already created. Pittsburgh provided a smaller level of extra funding for magnet schools, ranging from an extra $11 to an extra $126 per pupil. Pittsburgh's program included only three magnets of a total of 21 school-based financed sites in 1997-98; the number of magnets could increase in the future as all schools are included in the school-based funding program.

Vocational education funding enhancements constitute the second major adjustment related to the programmatic nature of the curriculum. Extra funding for vocational education in high schools has a long tradition in North American school funding (see Odden & Picus, 1992). Broward included nine different vocational education weights in its school-based funding formula, largely following the vocational education weights used by Florida to fund each school district. The weights were 1.963 for mainstreamed vocational education programs; weights for separate vocational education programs ranged from 1.168 for exploratory programs to 1.651 for industrial arts programs. Cincinnati provided a uniform overall adjustment for vocational education that equaled a set amount per FTE across all vocational education programs. Both Pittsburgh and Seattle retained vocational education funding at the central district office, that is, did not decentralize these dollars to their high schools.

Edmonton provided funds for teaching foreign languages, with funding for 12 different foreign language programs. Funding depends on both the number of foreign language programs offered in a school and the enrollments for each. Broward County also provided an extra weight of nearly 0.5 for dropout prevention programs. A possible reason for the extensive use of student weights in Broward is that that has been the manner in which many special needs have been addressed in Florida for years. Florida has the most extensive system of pupil weighting in the entire United States (Gold, Smith, & Lawton, 1995); Broward County includes nearly all the state weights in determining each school's budget.

The Special Pupil Needs Component

The five districts created a multitude of adjustments for the special educational needs of their students. From local and state resources, they provide adjustments based on sociodemographic characteristics, achievement scores, English language fluency, and both mental and physical disability. The richness of the various adjustments indicates that there is a professional ethic among these districts to provide extra revenues so teachers can provide additional services to students who have exceptional educational needs.

Economic or Education Disadvantage

Although all four U.S. districts receive substantial funds for low-achieving students in low-income communities from the federal Title 1 program, both Pittsburgh and Seattle supplemented this provision with augmentations based on sociodemographic condition (see Table 7.8). Seattle provided extra weights for students eligible for the federal free and reduced price lunch program, a program that provides free lunch to students from a family with income below the poverty level (about $16,000 for an urban family of four) and reduced price lunches for students from families with an income up to 150% of the poverty level (about $24,000), recognizing that poverty is a general indicator of the need for additional teaching services. The weights are 0.087, 0.109, and 0.18, providing $212, $266, and $439 for elementary, middle, and high school students.

The Pittsburgh program averages the percentage of students in a school eligible for free and reduced price lunch with the percentage of students not living with both parents, multiplies that percentage times the school enrollment, and provides an extra $400 for each such student. Both of these amounts are in addition to the Title 1 school allocation, which is provided according to a different formula, and can reach $900 per pupil in high-poverty schools. Neither Broward, Cincinnati, nor Edmonton provides an additional amount based on these factors, though Cincinnati is considering adding such an adjustment.

Broward and Pittsburgh also provide extra resources for students scoring below certain levels on the district's tests of student achievement. Broward provides this enhancement only for middle and high schools, and splits the district's overall allocation of about $2 million among the numbers of students scoring below the 18th percentiles on the reading and math portions of the Stanford Achievement Test. Pittsburgh provides a small extra weight for students scoring at or below the 30th percentile. The weight is larger the lower the percentile (i.e., the lower the achievement), and the weight is larger for students in grades 9-12 than it is for students in grades K-8.

TABLE 7.8. Pupil-Specific Factors for Economic or Education Disadvantage in Five North American Districts

Broward	Cincinnati	Edmonton	Pittsburgh	Seattle
Locally funded high needs based on sociodemographic condition	NA	Title I funds %Pov$/pupil 2 210 50-60 325 60-70 375 70-80 420 80-85 500 85-90 590 90 640	Average of percentage of students: a) eligible for free/reduced lunch; and b) not residing with both parents, times enrollment, times $400 per pupil	Extra weight of 0.087 for grades K-5, 0.18 for grades 6-8, and 0.109 for grades 9-12, based on number of students eligible for free and reduced lunch
Test scores	Total district allocation of $1.938 million for non-Title I middle and high schools. Middle schools: 75% of number of students scoring below 18th percentile on reading and math portion of Stanford Achievement Test. High schools: 75% and/or reading portion of 9th grade Stanford Achievement Test	NA	NA	NA

NA = not applicable.

The dilemma in providing funding adjustments based on actual student achievement is that the funding is lost when achievement is improved. So, unless the achievement score is based on performance from another level of schooling, the workings of such a funding augmentation can sometimes be awkward.

English Language Proficiency and Disabling Conditions

Table 7.9 shows how these five districts provide extra resources for students with limited English proficiency and physical and mental disabilities. Broward, Edmonton, and Seattle make adjustments for limited English-proficient students, that is, students who need help developing English language fluency, by providing an extra weight for such students. The extra weights in all three districts are around the 25% level, but because they are applied to different base amounts, they provide different levels of extra funds, amounting to approximately $475 per pupil more for each LEP student in Broward, about $850 more per pupil in Edmonton, and $635 extra for each elementary student and just over $1,000 more for each high school student needing help learning the English language in Seattle.

The strategies these districts use for providing extra revenues for physically and mentally disabled students are the most complex. Broward and Seattle use student weights, and Cincinnati and Pittsburgh use separate formula allocations. Broward County has the most extensive list of extra weights, with elementary, middle, and high school weights for mainstreamed special education students, eight different weights for separate full-time programs, and seven different weights for part-time programs. The weights vary widely, reflecting the nature of the disability and the intensiveness of the services required.

Edmonton and Seattle have taken a somewhat less detailed approach. Edmonton provides weights in six different categories, with a less and more intense division for three levels of need—mild, moderate, and severe disabilities. They list specific handicapping conditions under each of the size weighting categories. On the other hand, Seattle has identified five categories of special needs and provides weights for just these five, sometimes but not always differentiating the weight by grade level within the category. Seattle does not

TABLE 7.5. Pupil-Specific Factors for Language Deficiency or Physical/Mental Disability

	Broward	Cincinnati	Edmonton	Pittsburgh	Seattle
Bilingual students	**Intensive English/ESL:** Grades K-3 1.254 Grades 4-8 1.267 Grades 9-12 1.288	NA	**Extra weight for ESL:** Grades K-8: 0.27 Grades 9-12: 0.24	NA	**Extra weight:** Grades K-5: 0.26 Grades 6-8: 0.41 Grades 9-12: 0.42
Special education	**Mainstream** K-3: 2.468 4-8 2.000 9-12 2.358 **Separate Programs** Ed Men Hand 2.131 Tr Men Hand 2.972 Phys Hand 3.286 Sp/Lang 2.760 Vis Hand 4.939 Em Hand 2.701 Learn Dis 1.875 Prof Hand 4.289 **Separate PT** PhysOcTher 13.723 Sp/Lang 5.266 Vis Hand 17.102 Em Hand 3.895 Learn Dis 2.772 Gifted 1.670 Hosp/Home 12.136	**Nine categories:** Vis Hand $7424 Phys Hand 7420 Dev Hand K-8 4941 9-12 3701 Mult Hand 9737 Learn Dis 4942 Beh Hand 7768 Hearing 7440 Preschool 9758 Dollar figures will be converted to pupil weights in the future	**Six levels:** Mild A—1.27 Mild B—1.29 Moderate A—2.08 Moderate B—2.35 Severe A—3.85 Severe B—5.93	NA	**Five levels:** 1—0.57 K-12 2—0.98 K-12 3—2.68 K-3 2.49 4-5 1.43 6-8 1.08 9-12 4a—3.80 K-5 3.74 6-12 4b—7.76 K-12
Teenage parent	Weight of 1.416	NA	NA	NA	NA

NA = Not applicable

179

identify a long list of the more traditional disability conditions within the five categories; it is seeking to identify the intensity of the service required rather than the label of the handicapping conditions.

Again, some care needs to be used in interpreting the different weights. Because the 1.0 weight allocation varies across these districts, the same weight triggers quite different levels of additional resources. For example, an extra weight of 1.0 in Broward would generate about $1,900 more, whereas the same extra weight would produce $3,127 in Edmonton and $2,441 in Seattle. These are very different levels of extra resources. The point here is that the extra weights themselves should not be compared across districts because the dollar levels to which they are attached are so different. The only reasonable way to compare how the districts treat students with disabilities is to calculate the dollar amounts actually provided. Further, because the Canadian dollar is worth less than the U.S. dollar in international markets, the Edmonton figures should be discounted.

For nine categories of disability, the Cincinnati plan provided an extra amount for each pupil, with constraints concerning maximum class size for each different category. The district holds the funds for more special education support, including psychologists, special education service center, tutoring, home instruction, Medicaid reimbursement, audiological services, and general services. When the program is fully implemented, Cincinnati plans to convert the dollar figures to pupil weights.

In 1997-98, Pittsburgh did not provide schools with much authority over the substantial resources in the system for students with disabilities. The district is investigating how it could devolve this budget authority, together with several other categorical program revenues, in the future, but decided for 1997-98 to retain central control over resources for special education services and programs.

School-Specific Factors

Table 7.10 shows how each district provides a base allocation to each school site and/or provides adjustments for small school size. Three districts provide base allocations—Broward, Cincinnati, and Seattle. These base allocations are quite large, ranging across all districts from

TABLE 7.10. Specific School Factors in Five North American Districts

	Broward	Cincinnati	Edmonton	Pittsburgh	Seattle
Base allocation	Elementary: $423,139 with between $10,000 and $20,000 more for every extra 75 weighted FTE above 725	Elementary: $211,140 for each elementary school, large or small	NA	NA	Elementary: $174,410
	Middle school: $839,926 with between $13,000 and $43,000 more for every extra 100 weighted FTE above 860	Middle school: $248,900 for each middle school, and $246,185 for every small middle school			Middle school: $366,738
	High school: $1,262,879 with between $36,000 and $75,000 more for every extra 100 weighted FTE above 1775	High school: $531,147 for each high school, large or small			High school: $477,670
Other school	NA	Actual prior year exp. for custodians, utilities, transportation, and carryover	NA	NA	NA
Size adjustment	NA	Elementary: $450 per pupil more in small elementary; $253 per pupil more in small middle; $778 per pupil more in small high schools. About the same differences for the major magnets.	NA	(300—number of students) times $675 per pupil	NA

NA = Not applicable

181

$175,000 at the elementary level to over $1.2 million for a high school. For an elementary school of 500 students, this provides a base of about $350 per pupil; for a high school of 1,500 students, this provides a base of $800 per pupil. In many other places with school-based financing systems, base allocations tend to be smaller and are provided to ensure that small schools have sufficient funds for a small, minimal core of administrative staff—perhaps a principal, a school secretary, and a clerk. But the size of these base allocations allows them to provide more than just a minimal, core base of administrative staff.

For all three districts, the middle and high school base allocations are substantially larger than the elementary allocations. In Broward, the middle school base allocation is nearly twice as large as the elementary base allocation, and the high school allocation is about three times the elementary allocation. In Cincinnati, however, the base allocation for middle schools is only slightly higher than that for elementary schools; the base allocation is to provide a principal, a librarian or librarians for high school, counselors at the high school level, a physical plant operator, and curriculum funds.

In Broward, moreover, the base allocation is provided for the smallest-sized elementary, middle, and high school and then increased by several thousand dollars (the amount rising by education level) for higher enrollment levels. For example, a middle school with 860 students would receive a base allocation of about $840,000. But, for every additional 100 FTE, it would receive between $13,000 and $43,000 more, the extra amount varying at different levels of the 100 student increments. The point is that larger schools receive an even larger base allocation.

The Cincinnati plan also provides several other per school allocations—actual prior year expenditures for custodians, utilities, transportation, and carryover funds. Cincinnati and Pittsburgh provide small school adjustments. The Cincinnati plan provided a higher per pupil amount for small elementary ($450), small middle ($253 per pupil), and small high schools ($778) for all regular, that is, nonmagnet, schools. Pittsburgh provided $675 per pupil for the difference between the actual school enrollment (under 300) and 300, essentially a small school enhancement. So, a school with 250 students would receive $33,750 more, and a school of 200 would receive $67,500, more modest size adjustments.

In sum, four of the districts provide either base allocations or size adjustments. Generally, these adjustments provide a high level of extra resources, much more than just to ensure a minimal administrative staff. Cincinnati provides both a base allocation and a size adjustment, and in addition provides a budget for actual site expenditures for operations activities.

Assessment and Analysis

The five school-based financing formulas discussed previously represent sophisticated innovations in school financing in North America. The formulas include allocations for the 1.0 student, grade-level enhancements, curriculum enhancements, several adjustments for specific pupil needs, and adjustments for school sites in terms of base allocations and small size augmentations.

The systems also are quite new. Although Edmonton has been implementing its school-based financing system for over two decades, the formulas in the other four districts are very recent—three were implemented for the first time during the 1997-98 school year, and the fourth—Cincinnati—is scheduled to be implemented in 1999-2000, though several pilot schools in Cincinnati had authority over their budget in 1997-98 (with the budget amount being calculated according to the traditional school staffing formulas). Given the newness of these formulas, their comprehensiveness and sophistication represent a substantial accomplishment.

Central and School Site Shares

More thought needs to be given to central functions versus site functions in at least the four U.S. districts. Because these districts are part of the New American Schools and will ultimately allow each school to select and restructure into a whole school design, they need to redesign their entire school system to one that supports a decentralized management system. As part of this process, they need to shed or at least dramatically downsize some central office functions (e.g., curriculum support, personnel, and business operations) and strengthen others (e.g., planning, evaluation and accountability, information systems) and adjust the central office budget accordingly. All other functions and their budgets should be devolved to schools. Though these districts have begun to engage in this analytic process, it should become a central focus, and the central versus site budget shares should be traceable back to these decisions. This is not now the case.

Transparency

   The Edmonton, Pittsburgh, and Seattle formulas are all public and transparent. They are on the Internet in both Edmonton (http://www.epsb.edmonton.ab.ca) and Seattle (http://sps.gspa.washington.edu/sps), and thus transparent to the entire world! All budget documents also are available in public libraries in Edmonton. On the other hand, the formulas in Broward, although public, are buried in thick budget documents and not easily accessed. It is difficult to comment on the transparency of the Cincinnati formulas because they will not be used until the 1999-2000 school year; current Cincinnati budgets are transparent, but not all formula factors are described in simple documents that are widely distributed. In 1998-99, Cincinnati will indicate to all schools what their budget would have been if they were to implement the new budgeting formula, so schools will have some advance notice for full implementation the next year.

Equity

   Because all formulas have numerous factors addressing differential site, pupil, and educational needs, it would be fair to say that they represent honest efforts to design and implement a funding system that is equitable. When Pittsburgh decentralizes its budgets for the federal Title 1 program and for special education, all five programs overall will represent comprehensive and sophisticated attempts to make school-based funding equitable across several issues. Though there could be reasonable differences concerning the exact magnitude of many of the weights and adjustments provided, it would be difficult to say that these five districts did not attempt to design fair and equitable school-based funding systems. All these school-based financing systems aggressively recognize a variety of special circumstances.

Perhaps the most unexpected equity element of the formulas is the weighting in favor of elementary students in Broward and Seattle, and the near-equal allocation across education levels in Edmonton, practices very different from the traditional higher weighting for secondary students.

Effectiveness

There should be considerable optimism that the funding devolution can help improve not only the effectiveness of the spending of education dollars but also the effectiveness of the entire education system implementing these programs. As mentioned at the beginning of this chapter, the context for the development and implementation of school-based funding is a focus on dramatically improving school achievement results. The strategies being deployed by all four U.S. districts is to decentralize funding and operations as part of a broader strategy of identifying whole school, high-performance designs, one of which is to be selected by each site. Further, the design itself—which addresses the curriculum and instruction program, classroom and school organization, and school staffing and resourcing—is what the devolved funds are intended to finance. The hope is that all the school site's resources will first be allocated to the needs of the chosen design, and that over a 3- to 5-year period, each school will restructure itself into its selected design.

Because of this specific focus, that is, linking decentralization to selection of a high performance school design, and because there is increasing evidence that these designs improve student achievement (Fashola & Slavin, 1997; Slavin & Fashola, 1998), the school-based financing plans in the four U.S. districts should be correlated over time with a rising level of student achievement. These initiatives could represent the first decentralization efforts in education that produce improved effectiveness and student achievement results.

Summary

In sum, the five districts profiled in this chapter represent impressive North American efforts to design and implement school-based financing systems. The systems not only are comprehensive and sophisticated, but they are linked to district strategic directions to improve student performance. The systems are not proffered as goals or objectives in themselves, but are part of broader education efforts to adopt high and rigorous content and performance standards, decentralize district operations to school sites, have schools select high performance designs with a rigorous curriculum program as their vision for improvement, and have schools restructure themselves into those designs over 3 to 5 years, including reallocating their resources to the needs of those designs. Hence, these school-based financing programs are strongly linked to education strategies to produce higher levels of student achievement. Because of these interconnections, it would be reasonable to expect that these programs will help lead to higher student achievement and improved productivity of these education systems.

References

Bodilly, S. (1996). *Lessons from New American Schools Development Corporation's demonstration phase.* Santa Monica, CA: RAND.

Bodilly, S. (1998). *Lessons from New American Schools' scale-up phase: Prospects for bringing designs to multiple sites.* Santa Monica, CA: RAND.

Busch, C., & Odden, A. (1997). Collection of school-level finance data [Entire issue]. *Journal of Education Finance, 22*(3).

Caldwell, B. J., & Spinks, J. M. (1992). *Leading the self-managing school.* London: Falmer.

Cincinnati Public Schools. (1996). *Students first: Strategic plan, 1996-2001.* Cincinnati: Author.

Clark, C., & Toenjes, L. (1998). Exploring alternatives for school-based funding. In W. J. Fowler, Jr. (Ed.), *Selected papers in school finance, 1996* (pp. 113-135). Washington, DC: Department of Education, National Center for Education Statistics.

Coopers & Lybrand. (1988). *Local management of schools.* London: Author.

Evans, W., Murray, S., & Schwab, R. (1997). State education finance policy after court mandated reform: The legacy of Serrano. In *1996 Proceedings of the eighty-ninth annual conference on taxation.* Washington, DC: National Tax Association, Tax Institute of America.

Fashola, O. S., & Slavin, R. E. (1997). Promising programs for elementary and middle schools: Evidence of effectiveness and replicability. *Journal of Education for Students Placed at Risk, 2*(3), 251-307.

Fuhrman, S. H. (Ed.). (1993). *Designing coherent education policy: Improving the system.* San Francisco: Jossey-Bass.

Gold, S., Smith, D. M., & Lawton, S. B. (1995). *Public school finance programs of the United States and Canada, 1993-94.* Albany: State University of New York, Center for the Study of the States.

Massell, D., Kirst, M., & Hoppe, M. (1997). *Persistence and change: Standards based reform in nine states?* (CPRE Brief No. RB-21). Philadelphia: University of Pennsylvania, Consortium for Policy Research in Education.

Odden, A. (1997). *How to rethink school budgets to support school transformation.* Alexandria, VA: New American Schools.

Odden, A., & Busch, C. (1998). *Financing schools for high performance: Strategies for improved use of resources.* San Francisco: Jossey-Bass.

Odden, A., & Kotowski, N. (1992). Financing public school choice: Policy issues and options. In A. Odden (Ed.), *Rethinking school finance: An agenda for the 1990s* (pp. 225-259). San Francisco: Jossey-Bass.

Odden, A., & Picus, L. O. (1992). *School finance: A policy perspective.* New York: McGraw Hill.

Organisation for Economic Cooperation and Development. (1996). *Education at a glance: OECD indicators.* Paris: Author.

Slavin, R. & Fashola, O. (1998). *Show me the evidence! Proven and promising programs for America's schools.* Thousand Oaks, CA: Corwin.

Smith, M. S., & O'Day, J. (1991). Systemic reform. In S. Fuhrman & B. Malen (Eds.), *The politics of curriculum and testing* (pp. 233-267). Philadelphia: Falmer.

Speakman, S., Cooper, B., Holsomback, H., May, J., Sampierie, R., & Maloney, L. (1997). The three Rs of education finance reform: Re-thinking, re-tooling and re-evaluating school site information. *Journal of Education Finance, 22*(4), 337-367.

Stringfield, S., Ross, S., & Smith, L. (1996). *Bold plans for school restructuring: The New American School designs.* Mahwah, NJ: Lawrence Erlbaum.

Swanson, A., & King, R. (1997). *School finance: Its economics and politics.* New York: Longman.

Thompson, Q., & Lakin, J. (1997). *Local management of schools and school site based financing: The experience in England and Wales since 1988.* Madison: University of Wisconsin, Consortium for Policy Research in Education.

EIGHT

Performance-Based Budgeting for Public Schools in Florida

CAROLYN D. HERRINGTON

Attempts to rationalize the budgeting process have emerged sporadically during most of this century. Spurred by attempts to curb governmental growth and enabled by the increasing analytic prowess of policy analysts and more recently the ascendant powers of information technologies, federal, state, and local governments have repeatedly sought to tame the raucous environment that besets the allocation of public resources.

Most recently, federal and state governments have become interested in the concept of *performance-based budgeting*. At the federal level, passage of the 1993 Government Performance and Results Act (emanating from Vice-President Gore's initiative to reinvent government) marks a renewed attempt to improve internal management and external accountability by requiring each agency to relate agency resources and budget requests to objective, quantifiable, and measurable goals. At the state level, a number of state legislatures are asking agencies to submit performance data in ways that legislatures can use to determine effectiveness and efficiency in meeting statutory objectives. In both federal and state cases, the goals in directing agencies to include output and outcome measures in their budget requests are to improve accountability, improve performance, increase managerial flexibility, and, perhaps most of all, regain public confidence in government.

Almost half of the states place or have plans to place some performance measures in their budget document. Florida, however, is one of the few states using performance data in the budget process. In addition, Florida is one of only two states that have created formal mechanisms for imposing incentives and disincentives based on agency performance, although neither state has begun using these mechanisms (Office of Program Policy Analysis, 1997). Though there is some evidence that interest in performance-based budgeting has peaked in a number of states, Florida is among a handful in which commitment appears to be ongoing and approaching institutionalization (Snell, 1998).

Florida's adoption of a statewide program in performance-based budgeting, known colloquially as PB^2, resulted from a citizen-led constitutional amendment enacted in 1992 calling for increased accountability for how state agencies spend tax dollars. Eventually, each of the 27 state agencies is to submit annual budget requests in which at least a portion of their budget is based on performance. The educational system is being brought into PB^2 by sectors. The community college system began the process with its 1997-98 budget request, the state university system included performance-based items in its 1998-99 budget request, and the public school system will begin with its budget request for 1999-2000.

This chapter provides (1) an overview of the history, theoretical underpinnings, and cautions behind performance-based budgeting; (2) a description of the state of Florida's ongoing efforts in this area; and (3) a review and analysis of proposals emanating from the educational sector in Florida to apply performance-based budgeting to public schooling.

Attempts to Rationalize Public Sector Budgeting

Historical Overview

Over the years, governmental budgeting has repeatedly shown to be primarily incremental and conservative and to have a limited relationship to desired outcomes. Criticisms of public sector budgeting and, in particular, its reliance on the line item as the unit of allocation, have been fierce. Wildavsky (1989) sums up the accusation of the many critics:

> From the time the caterpillar of budgetary evolution became the butterfly of budgetary reform, the line-item budget had been condemned as a reactionary throwback to its primitive larva. It has been condemned as mindless because its lines do not match programs: irrational because they deal with inputs instead of outputs; shortsighted because they cover 1 year instead of many; fragmented because as a rule only changes are reviewed; and conservative because these changes tend to be small. (p. 321)

Over the last two decades, reformers have proposed a number of changes designed to overcome the liabilities of public sector budgeting—its partisan and political nature and, in particular, its dependence on the line item. Planning, programming, and budgeting (PPB), a federal initiative in the early 1970s, was an attempt to replace a politically dominated budgeting process with rational, objective analyses. The strength of PPB lay in its emphasis on policy analysis to increase effectiveness. Programs were to be evaluated and, if found wanting, presumably replaced by alternatives designed to produce superior results. According to Wildavsky (1989), PPB, as an expression of the prevailing paradigm of rationality, was unlikely to succeed because it attempted to deny the inherently political nature of resource allocation, which relies on trade-offs and compromises.

Scholars of school budgeting have leveled the same criticism against educational budgeting practices, accusing them of being highly politicized, resistant to change, and tied to prior practice rather than best practice. Guthrie (1988) summarizes educational budget decision making in this way:

> Allocation ratios generally owe their origins variously to unexamined past practice, comparisons with similarly unscrutinized practices of surrounding school districts, collectively bargained agreements with employee unions, the pronouncements of self-serving professional associations, and the dicta of administrators. (p. 23)

School budgeting depends primarily on three components: formulaic ratios, centrally controlled budget categories, and pay scales (Guthrie, 1988). Administrators report that the formulas are inherited from their predecessors, and little relationship exists between the formulas and quality measures or costs. Teacher compensation is almost always based on the number of years employed and educational credit beyond the bachelor's degree (Guthrie, 1988), and rarely based on any direct relationship to the teacher's ability or on performance evaluations.

Current Environment

To understand the increasing saliency of interest in performance-based budgeting at the turn of this century, it is important to situate the issue in broader currents of thought that have circulated within educational policy circles over the last few decades. Several overlapping currents of thought reinforce each other and reinforce policymakers' interest in PB^2 as a policy tool for improving government.

One is the disillusion with a now two-decade-long attempt by state education policymakers to improve programs through the application of across-the-board state mandates. Responding to charges of mediocrity leveled at public schools in *A Nation at Risk* (National Commission, 1983), Florida, along with many other states, reacted with a string of policy directives intended to force higher levels of performance. These directives included lower class size, seven-period days, higher graduation requirements, and increased teacher compensation. The apparent lack of success of this approach has given credence to those who have argued that state-level mandates are inherently unproductive because across-the-board prescriptions ignore the considerable diversity that may exist at the local level and across subprograms, and restrict managerial flexibility over time as conditions change.

For policymakers, these considerations are consonant with currents of thought within the larger arenas of public policy and private sector management circles, which hold that in general, the role of central management should be rethought. This line of thinking argues that, in the public sector, state activity should be narrowed, with an emphasis on vision setting, standard setting, enabling, and, notably, performance measurement (Osborne & Gaebler, 1992). In an era of increasing public skepticism of public-sector effectiveness, this more limited and more focused role for government has an inherent appeal for elected officials. In the corporate sector, according to certain organizational analyses, U.S. companies that have successfully survived the intense global competition over the last decade have done so by creating leaner, less hierarchical, and more fluid and flexible organizational structures, and have pushed more responsibility and authority to lower units of the organization (Peters & Waterman, 1982).

Limitations of Performance-Based Budgeting

As Kirst (1988) points out, the very nature of the instructional enterprise has proven resistant to input-output analyses. The manner in which fiscal data are maintained is designed to reflect budgeting needs, not resource use. One example of the difficulty in applying fiscal data to learning outcomes is demonstrated by the fact that most of a school's resources are expended in teachers' salaries, and the level of funds is dependent, more than anything else, on average tenure of the teaching staff, which may not necessarily be related to instructional gains.

Not only is it difficult to link resources to performance, it is equally difficult to measure performance to begin with. Rockwell (1989), looking at the social indicators movement of the 1960s and 1970s, identifies a number of limitations to reliance on objective data to measure performance. According to Rockwell, the measures selected often were not of interest to key policy-making bodies or the public at large, the linkages between what the data identified as a problem and the public policy levers to intervene were often lacking, and the data were often at higher levels of aggregation than the scope of authority of the decision makers.

Second, performance-based budgeting may be facilitating a different type of politicization. Research into the use of analytical information as a support for the policy-making process and as a political strategy in itself has been investigated by social scientists over the years, and the findings from this line of research suggest that gains to be achieved may be seriously compromised. Data can be "captured" by those who must provide them, and may be far from being politically neutral (Weiss, 1989; Weiss & Gruber, 1984; Weiss & Tschirhart, 1994). Technical issues such as units of analysis, frequency of reporting, and comparability reflect different value systems, and may thwart some and advantage others. Decisions on how the data are treated, aggregated, analyzed, and arrayed may be just as critical as the actual availability of the data in determining whether they will answer policymakers' questions.

Finally, despite considerable political rhetoric regarding the need for accountability and results, there is no evidence that policymakers' reliance on policy analysis is increasing. In fact, a recent study (Lee, 1997) of policy analysis use among state legislatures found a noticeable drop between 1990 and 1995 in state budget offices conducting both productivity and effectiveness analysis and in executives using these analyses in decision making. This was the first such reported decline since 1970.

Context of Educational Reform in Florida

It is not unexpected that attempts to apply the rigors of performance-based budgeting to educational funding might surface early in Florida. Florida has a number of features supportive of information-driven policy analysis and budgeting, and has a strong record of political preference for state-level accountability systems. Florida has a highly equalized educational finance formula, a sophisticated state management information system, and an existing accountability framework that includes indicators of performance. Furthermore, the state has a small number of specific performance-based programs already in the budget that may serve as precursors for a more broadly based performance budget system.

Florida Educational Finance Program

One can argue that a highly equitable distribution of state funding is a necessary prerequisite for a performance-based funding system.

If school districts are forced to demonstrate certain levels of perform-ance to vie for funds, it is critical to any sense of fairness that the playing field be level to begin with. Florida does have one of the most equitable funding systems in the country. State law requires Florida to fund schools in a manner that promotes equity. The 1973 Florida legislation creating the current Florida Education Finance program (FEEP)

> guarantee(s) each student in the Florida public education system the availability of programs and services appropriate to his or her educational needs which are substantially equal to those avail-able to any similar student notwithstanding geographic differ-ences and varying local economic factors.

The FEEP is designed to equalize educational opportunity by distrib-uting funds to districts based on the number of full-time equivalent (FTE) students adjusted by (1) varying local property tax bases, (2) varying program cost factors, (3) district cost differentials, and (4) differences in per student cost for equivalent educational programs due to sparsity and dispersion of the student population. According to most traditional measures of interdistrict equity, Florida ranks very high (Nakib, 1998).

Management Information Systems

Florida is widely considered to have, if not the best, one of the best educational management information systems (MIS) in the country. The state committed itself to aggressive development of a comprehen-sive and highly detailed MIS in the early 1970s, at the same time it established the state finance formula. From the beginning, the MIS was designed to support school-based management and to allow for school-, district-, state-, and national-level comparisons. As manage-ment information technologies have improved over the last two decades, the state has been able to realize these objectives, and now has a fully implemented student-level database. Currently, the state has demographic and achievement data retrievable by student, as well as a broad array of finance data at the school, district, and state level. The state's current plans for performance-based budgeting are highly dependent on this already established MIS.

Offering even greater potential for data-based management is the Florida Education and Training Placement Information program (FETPIP). FETPIP collects data on students after they leave the public school program. Through individual student identification numbers, FETPIP can track the activities of students upon graduation (or dropping out). It is linked to other state databases, including postsecondary training programs, state community colleges and universities, welfare rolls, adjudication and incarceration, and private sector employment. This latter capacity, accessed through the state's unemployment insurance program, provides information on the economic sector in which the student is employed, hours of employment, and wages. Increasingly, FETPIP is employing data warehousing technologies enabling program managers and policymakers to subject the data to sophisticated queries regarding choice of employment, wage level, and continuing education of former students.

Performance-Based Accountability Systems

Florida also has a tradition of seeking greater accountability for student performance. In the 1970s, Florida passed a series of laws attempting to create a comprehensive accountability system and instituted the first large-scale state mandated student assessment system in the country (Herrington, 1995). Currently, the state's accountability system identifies 16 performance measures, requires public reporting to parents and other members of the public on how schools and their students are performing on these measures, and includes a mechanism to sanction districts and schools financially for poor student performance. The 1996 Florida legislature specifically authorized the state board to take a series of actions against school boards with respect to schools that have been designated low performing and have retained that designation for 3 consecutive years. These include (1) requiring the school board to provide additional resources if it is determined that the cause of inadequate progress was related to district policy; (2) requiring the implementation of a plan that addresses education equity problems in the school; (3) contracting for educational services; (4) reorganizing the school under a new principal who is authorized to hire a new staff; and (5) allowing parents to send their children to another district school of their choice. The legislature also authorized the state board of education to withhold state funds from a school district that has not complied with an order to take action to improve schools with low-performing students. The legislature intended that the state board use this measure only after all other recommended actions have failed to improve performance at the school. To date, no district or school has remained on the critically low-performing list for the 3 consecutive years required before state intervention is authorized.

As can be seen from the above, Florida has a long history of attempting to maintain equity in its allocation process, stimulating improvement through accountability systems that use data for analytical and for reporting purposes, and more recently trying to link performance to sanctions or rewards.

Performance-Based Budgeting
in Other State Agencies

Performance-based budgeting in Florida stems from passage of the 1994 Government Performance and Accountability Act. This act, to be phased in over a 7-year period, mandates that all state agencies provide the legislature with performance-based budget requests that include *output* and *outcome* measures, and it prescribes a method to relate appropriations to program performance and results. In 1995, the state was recognized by *Financial World* for developing "the most promising budgeting system." The 1994 law articulated several rationales for budget reform:

- Agencies need to be accountable, and their mission and goals should be clearly defined. Performance measures should be used to evaluate performance and in planning and budgeting.
- Agencies should have their performance measured and evaluated to improve coordination, eliminate duplicative programs, and provide better information to decision makers.

- Agencies should keep citizens informed of the performance and public benefits of programs.
- Agencies need incentives to be more efficient and effective and to restructure ineffective programs or eliminate unnecessary programs.
- Agencies need flexibility in using resources to be more efficient and effective.

The 1994 law also set up a process for agency implementation. As shown in Table 8.1, each state agency in Florida is to implement PB^2 over a multiyear period. In the first year, agencies propose programs to be under PB^2. After consultation with the legislature and the Office of Program Policy Analysis and Government Accountability (OPPAGA), the governor's office approves the agency measures of the program's outputs (products produced by the program) and outcomes (program results).

In the second year, the agency uses the programs and measures to develop its budget request. The request includes data on the agency's past performance and proposed performance standards for each measure. The legislature considers the request and designates the agency programs, performance measures, performance standards, and resources provided in the appropriations act.

In the third year, the agency begins operating under PB^2. Finally, in the fourth year, OPPAGA conducts a program evaluation and justification review of each PB^2 program.

Considering the program's performance, the legislature can use incentives or disincentives (such as reducing staff or budget authority) to improve or restructure the program. A critical feature in PB^2 is that it theoretically enables a state legislature to link performance information directly with the budget. PB^2 provides the legislature with data on program outputs and outcomes that it can consider when making policy and budgetary decisions about the programs. PB^2 also pushes agencies to focus on outcomes rather than outputs. For example, the state department of children and families modified its budgeting process to focus on outcomes for key client groups, rather than services offered. The agency focused on achieving outcomes, such as improving mental health status, rather than on outputs, such as the provision of a certain number of hours of counseling.

TABLE 8.1. Implemented Over a Multiyear Period for Each Agency

Fiscal Year	July	September	October	January	March/April	June
Year 1			Agency proposes program			Agency proposes measures
Year 2		Agency submits PB^2 budget request		Governor recommends PB^2 budget	Legislature passes PB^2 budget for program	
Year 3	Agency begins PB^2	Agency submits PB^2 budget request			Legislature passes PB^2 budget for program	
Year 4		Agency submits PB^2 budget request	OPPAGA conducts justification review of program		Legislature considers incentives and disincentives	

SOURCE: Office of Program Policy Analysis, 1998.

198

A key concern with performance-based budgeting is that it may hold little appeal to agency officials; it may significantly increase their analytic workload without any obvious gains. Evidence to date with agencies in Florida that have gone through this process, however, suggests that successful implementation may hold some rewards for agencies. According to a recent review, the legislature has shown a willingness to provide agencies funded under PB^2 with additional flexibility in how they can use their resources (Office of Program Policy Analysis, 1998). For example, it was found that the legislature appropriated funding with fewer line items for most of the agencies operating under performance-based budgeting. Fewer line items allow agencies more latitude in how they can use their resources; agencies were found to have used this flexibility to shift funds within their programs. In turn, agencies reported that PB^2 has allowed managers to make changes in resource use more quickly to purchase needed equipment and provide salary incentive payments.

Many problems in implementation remain, however; most important is continuing political interest in line items and inputs and hesitancy to apply incentives and disincentives. Others include (1) persistent problems with quality and type of performance information; (2) lack of activity-based costs and unit costs; (3) anxiety about holding one entity accountable for an outcome toward which several entities contribute outputs; and (4) bifurcation of premise. Are the measures to be used to hold managers accountable or to provide units to determine the amount of appropriation (Office of Program Policy Analysis, 1998)?

Performance-Based Budgeting in Education

Current Financial Incentive and
Disincentive Initiatives in Higher Education

It is widely conceded that public schooling may be the most difficult to submit to a performance-based budgeting process. For this reason, prior to the application of PB^2 to K-12 education, PB^2 was applied to the community college system and state university system budget. In 1996-97, the legislature appropriated $12 million out of a total of $700 million to be used for performance-based incentives in the community college sector. Unlike other PB^2 approaches that focus on measuring and reporting performance in relation to a set of performance standards, the legislature's approach for community colleges in 1996-97 focused on directly linking state agency performance to state funding. Specifically, this approach awarded points to community colleges based on a variety of output and outcome indicators. Community colleges received incentive funds based on the number of points they accrued. Two examples of a performance measure for the community college system are *percentage of graduates who transfer to a state university or private college* and *percentage of transfers to a state university with a grade point average at or above 2.0.* The governor's proposed standards for these two performance measures are 63.27% and 88.84%, respectively.

The state university incentive system rewards universities for improvement in graduation and retention rates and for increased productivity. The governor's 1998-99 budget recommended that $4.3 million be allocated for improvements in graduation, $2.5 million for improvements in retention, and $1.5 million for increased productivity. Examples of performance measures in the state university system might be *graduation rate for community college transfers* and *graduation rate for first time in college students.* The governor's proposed standards for those two measures are 68.70% and 65.28%, and, respectively, rates of 60.60% and 52.56% for minority and other disadvantaged students. Another performance measure is *percentage of students employed and earning $20,000 or more 1 year after graduation.* The governor's proposed standard for this measure is 56.30%.

Current Financial Incentive and
Disincentive Initiatives in K-12 Education

Even though the state department of education's official timetable for PB^2 is only now beginning, the state has been moving toward PB^2 in its public school programs on an incremental basis for a number of years. The state has enacted a number of performance-based budgeting programs in the public school budget. Currently there are six incentive funding programs: advanced placement and international baccalaureate program, vocational education, isolated high schools, remediation reduction, dropout prevention, and a school recognition program. Three were enacted prior to 1996-97.

- Advanced placement and international baccalaureate incentives: These programs award high student achievement by allowing school districts to claim additional FTE funds for each advanced placement or international baccalaureate student who meets a certain test score.
- Vocational education incentive: This incentive, established in 1994, awards funds to school districts for vocational students who (1) complete training programs for targeted occupations on the occupational forecast list; (2) complete these training programs and are subsequently employed in a targeted occupation above a certain wage threshold; or (3) do not complete the training programs but leave with a marketable skill and are subsequently employed in a targeted occupation (O'Laughlin, 1998).
- Isolated high schools: High schools that meet the following criteria are eligible for a financial incentive: (1) have students who score no less than the higher of the district or the state average on both parts of the high school competency test; (2) have no fewer than 28 students in grades 9-12; (3) are not closer than 28 miles to the next nearest high school; (4) are located in districts that levy the maximum nonvoted discretionary millage (exclusive of millage for capital outlay purposes); and (5) serve their students primarily in basic education programs. Two high schools met the criteria for isolated high school funds in fiscal year 1996-97.

The 1996 and 1997 legislatures created three new financial incentive initiatives for public schools:

- Remediation reduction incentive: This incentive, established in 1996, rewards districts for improved student scores on mathematics, reading, and writing tests, and for increased enrollment in higher-level mathematics and English classes.
- Dropout prevention/educational alternatives incentive: The dropout prevention/educational alternatives incentive, created in 1997, is designed to encourage districts to become more effective in serving students in dropout prevention programs. In 1997-98, districts earned incentives based on the number of students enrolled in the educational alternatives program in 1993-94 who (1) were still enrolled in school in 1996-97; (2) graduated by the end of 1995-96; (3) scored a 3 or above on the Florida Writes! test; (4) passed the mathematics portion of the High School Competency Test; (5) passed the communication portion of the High School Competency Test; and (6) dropped out of school.

- Florida School Recognition program: This incentive is designed to provide financial rewards to faculty and staff of schools that sustain high performance or demonstrate exemplary improvement due to innovation and effort. Schools are selected for awards based on several criteria, including student achievement data, dropout rates, attendance rates, school climate, indicators of innovation, and parent involvement. The awards are distributed to school faculty and staff based on employee performance criteria established at the district level. This program was created by the 1997 legislature, but was not appropriated any funds for the 1997-98 fiscal year; in 1998-99, $5.8 million was appropriated.

Table 8.2 summarizes Florida's current financial incentives. Florida's incentive programs target both general and special student populations, rely heavily on test scores, and are, with one exception, awarded at the district, not school, level.

Activities

In 1997, eight districts volunteered to participate in PB^2 on a pilot basis. A district advisory committee was formed of representatives from each of the pilot districts, personnel from other districts who have been identified as leaders within the field of finance, department of education personnel, and policy researchers. The committee's task was to develop a system of accountability and budgeting based on performance measures. A number of assumptions have been guiding its work:

- The PB^2 system will allow the legislature to link appropriations to specific educational outcomes
- The PB^2 system will allow decision makers to make comparisons by student, class, grade, school, district, state, other states, and other countries
- PB^2 should apply to the entire public school program, even if not applied to the entire budget. Initial suggestions from the department of education to restrict the performance-based budgeting system to a number of specific programs, such as prekindergarten or the international baccalaureate program, were not well received by the legislature
- If PB^2 were applied to the entire budget, the state might place at risk the equalization factors in its distribution formula. Therefore, PB^2 might

TABLE 8.2. Florida's Incentive Programs

Incentive Programs	Type of Students	Criteria for Earning Financial Incentive					Who Receives Funds	
		Test Score	Diploma	Job Placement	Dropout Rate	Other[1]	School District	School
Dropout prevention	At-risk	X	X		X	X	X	
Advanced placement	High performing	X					X	
International baccalaureate	High performing	X	X				X	
Performance-based incentive funding	Vocational postsec.			X		X	X	
Remediation reduction	General postsec.	X				X	X	
Isolated high school	General	X				X	X	
Florida School Recognition Program	General	X	X	X	X	X		X

SOURCE: Office of Program Policy Analysis, 1998.
[1] Other types of financial incentives criteria include factors such as enrollment in higher-level mathematics and English courses, readiness for postsecondary education, attendance rates, and performance in postsecondary programs.

better be applied to a small percentage of dollars designated specifically for that purpose

If a performance-based budgeting system is to be put into place, a number of short- and long-term issues must be resolved. The next two sections look at a number of the issues that are surfacing as the state moves forward with PB^2 for Florida's public schools, including more immediate implementation issues as well as broader philosophical issues.

Implementation and Design Issues

Attempts to draw the broad outlines of a performance-driven system are surfacing a number of design and implementation issues, such as the scope of the program, scope of funding involved, timing of consequences, and data integrity and legitimacy issues.

Scope of Application

Should PB^2 performance measures and standards be applied to all activities of the public school system? Theoretically, any input, whether material or nonmaterial, monetary or in kind, should be considered an input and would be assumed to affect the outputs and outcomes. At what point does an effort to quantify inputs outweigh the analytical power their inclusion might add? Examples are the social capital of a high-performing parent group. How might one measure its contribution and determine its contribution to the outcomes?

Scope of Funding

Should the entire $11 billion school budget be subjected to a performance-based distribution? Initial attempts by the state department to employ a categorical approach, for example, selecting specific programs that lend themselves to performance measurement (such as advanced placement courses or dropout prevention) were criticized by the legislature as not comprehensive enough, not suitable to some districts (particularly small ones that may not offer special programs such as the international baccalaureate or advanced placement courses), and not being useful enough for understanding the relationship between inputs and outcomes. Inclusion of the entire school budget risks enormous disequalization across districts and disruptions to operations within districts, however. If only nonrecurring funds not currently a part of the public school budgeting process were included, risks to the school districts of significant disruptions to the systems' operations and to interdistrict equity would be minimized, but this decision would also place the performance-based budgeting system outside of the normal operations of the budgeting process.

If the fund is to draw from existing revenue sources, three different sources of funds have been identified with progressively more intrusion into the monies currently being used to run the system. These three sources are monies currently being allocated through categorical programs, monies from new targeted incentives, and monies from the designation of a percentage of the basic student allocation formula. The first proposal would place the monies from existing state categoricals into a district performance fund. These categoricals could include the smaller ones that are currently distributed for discretionary use at the school level (approximately $24 million) or for teachers to purchase incidental materials ($13 million), as well as the larger ones, such as the $83 million currently being used for summer school programming or the $79 million designated for technology. The second option is to expand the number of programs with targeted incentives. As discussed earlier, there are already six in the budget; more could be added. The third option, and by far the most systemic and most dramatic, would be the designation of a percentage of the base student allocation. Again, the devil is in the details. To minimize disruption to the system, the base on which the percentage would be calculated would include only the increase in the base student allocation from the previous year. It has also been suggested that the base on which the percentage is calculated should not include the estimated inflation factor that was built into the base allocation.

If the most modest of these latter proposals—include only the two categoricals that involved discretionary funding for schools and for teachers—was selected, the fund would constitute approximately

0.34% of the total school budget. If all these proposals were included—all applicable categoricals, additional targeted incentives, and the increase in the base student allocation from the previous year—the fund could conceivably constitute 11.12% of the total school budget.

Relative Distribution of Funds

A point system has been proposed to help rank the districts based on performance. Examples given are a measurement system that would award 1 point for progress toward a student achievement standard (e.g., 66% of students scoring 3 or above on the state's performance-based writing assessment), 1 point for reaching or exceeding a standard, and 1 point for having no critically low-performing schools in the district.

A further variation of the proposals listed above would have two different types of funds. Distributions from one fund would be earned based on performance; the other fund would be distributed based on need, that is, a special pot of money for schools that require assistance. A related issue regarding distribution is who should receive the additional funding—the schools themselves or the districts?

Timing of Consequences

A number of alternatives have surfaced regarding the design features of the incentives and/or sanctions that would be applied to districts based on their performance. Should performance-based funds be distributed up front as an incentive and then lost if goals are not achieved or distributed after the fact as a reward?

Defining Performance Outcomes

What are the outcomes that are desired for public schooling? The committee has included all the standardized assessments required by the state: the Florida Comprehensive Achievement Tests (FCAT), which measures reading and mathematics in grades 4, 5, 8, and 10;

Florida Writes!, which is administered in grades 4, 8, and 10; and the High School Competency Test, which is a high school exit test. Other outcomes being proposed include readiness for kindergarten, promotion rates, reading readiness, safety, absenteeism, dropout rates, suspensions, and graduation rates. The committee has also discussed including postgraduation measures, such as scores on college admissions tests, job placement, scholarships earned, and admissions to postsecondary institutions. Not only are there issues regarding the reliability and validity of these assessments (Miller & Seraphine, 1998), few consider the outcomes on standardized tests sufficient measures of the objectives or the outcomes of public schooling. Valued outcomes of public schooling include performance and appreciation of the fine arts and sports and development of good character and good citizenship, among others.

Measuring Performance Gains

A particularly acrimonious issue has been the area of comparability. It has been suggested that a performance incentive system would include some comparisons of performance across schools or districts. Stronger absolute performance relative to other schools or districts and/or stronger gains compared to other schools or districts might trigger extra funding. Many district officials have been adamant, however, that virtually all comparisons across schools and across districts are invalid, except comparison of a school or district against its own past performance.

Discussions around these outcomes and the availability or quality of the data are also acrimonious at times. Some districts have better data than others. Some districts appear to achieve higher levels of performance if some measures are used rather than others. And some districts have established specific policies that result in trading off performance on one measure for performance on another. These might include adopting policies of low expulsion rates resulting in higher suspension rates, or policies regarding higher teacher salaries but also larger class size. The committee is trying to incorporate concerns regarding the availability, reliability, quality, and analytical power of data in their attempts to produce an economical list of input and output measures.

Unresolved Issues

Maintaining Equity

The need to preserve equity in the funding of public schools may limit the legislature's ability to distribute funds primarily on the basis of performance. This, in turn, could significantly reduce the effect of any efficiencies or effectiveness to be achieved from the new system. Proponents argue that financial incentives and disincentives can be used without jeopardizing equity if they affect only a small proportion of the public school budget. These assumptions, however, may seriously underestimate how profoundly a performance-oriented system is in conflict with an allocation system whose first priority is equity. A focus on performance inevitably shifts the focus from equity of inputs to equity of outcomes. As Hanushek (1994) indicates, expenditures at different sites usually yield different outcomes, due to varying degrees of efficient use, varying goals, and varying endowment of resources and organizational setups. Therefore, equitable expenditures do not necessarily amount to equitable costs.

Adequacy

The adequacy issue is even more problematic under PB^2. Many state funding programs, including Florida's, are designed to distribute funds to maintain equality of capacity among districts, but are not designed to assess the returns of such distribution. The state constitution requires Florida to provide adequately for a uniform system of free public schools. In the absence of a clear understanding of the production process that translates school inputs into student outcomes, there is no way of knowing if school expenditures are adequate, inadequate, or perhaps inefficiently managed. With a lack of knowledge about reasonable costs to provide effective educational programs capable of delivering optimal outcomes, the notion of adequacy remains obscured in a veil of funding equity with no clear conceptual framework.

Maintaining Political Support

Perhaps the greatest barriers to performance-based budgeting are political. There are few natural or easily organized constituencies for performance-based budgeting. Its implementation may prove very burdensome and its rewards very distant and vague. It is not clear that the three major players—elected officials, parents, and educators—can be convinced that the promised advantages outweigh the obvious costs.

Elected Officials

Performance-based budgeting cuts very uneasily across partisan divides. To liberals it has the attraction of promising to restore public confidence in public schooling. It also threatens to undermine equity, however, a still distant goal in most states, and, to many liberals, an unnegotiable good. Liberals are also uneasy about sanctions and fear that the most vulnerable populations might bear the brunt of a system based on performance. Conservatives, on the other hand, who usually favor greater efficiency in the delivery of public services and support the concept of reduced governmental regulation in return for improved effectiveness, are uneasy about the often massive data collection and reporting requirements of a performance-based system on grounds of both its cost and its intrusiveness.

Parents

Despite the fact that many members of the policy-making and business communities support the concept of less regulation in return for higher performance, it is less clear that parents are willing to let go of certain input controls, such as class size, in exchange for the promise of higher achievement. There is a clear clash between a performance-based system (one measured by discrete outcomes) and an accountability based system (one measured by agreed-on inputs and outputs). Parents may prefer the second.

Educators

From an institutional perspective, performance-based budgeting may have little obvious appeal to educational personnel already in the school system. Looking across all governmental programs and agencies, Wildavsky (1989) and many others underscore the very practical appeal of line-item versus program budgeting:

> Program budgeting increases rather than decreases the cost of correction error. Viewed from the standpoint of bureau interest, programs to some extent are negotiable. Some programs can be increased and others decreased, while keeping the agency on an even keel, or, if necessary, adjusted to less happy times without calling into question their existence. Precisely because the categories of line-item budgeting (personnel, maintenance, supplies) do not relate directly to programs, they are easier to change. Because money flows to objectives, budgeting by programs makes it difficult to abandon objectives without abandoning the organization that gets the money for them. (p. 321)

As Kirst (1988) points out, incremental budgeting has enormous support from political and organizational routines that have helped to preserve the existing system for many decades.

Preliminary Directions in Florida

In fall 1998, the district advisory committee was converging on a set of principles to recommend for state policy. In general, the recommendations cautioned against any widespread changes to the current system in which state resources are distributed according to FTE, not performance. The committee favored restricting any funds to be placed in a performance fund to only new and nonrecurring monies. The distribution of any funds across districts would be determined by the relative FTE count per district, not on cross-district comparative measures of performance. Within the districts, it was proposed that schools would earn or lose performance funds based on their students achieving or not achieving student performance targets. If a school fails to meet student performance targets for 2 consecutive years, the school board would then direct the use of those funds; if the district, after 2 years, fails to attain the student performance targets at the school, that school's percentage of the performance fund would be lost to the district. Other recommendations include allowing districts to redirect the school-level discretionary fund (currently at $10 per student) and the teacher discretionary fund (currently at $100 per teacher) at schools failing to meet performance targets; to grant more flexibility in how categoricals can be spent in districts that meet their performance targets; and to incorporate the performance-based budgeting process into the state's school improvement and accountability process. The district advisory committee is also recommending that the system be tested in a number of volunteer districts on a pilot basis for 2 years, with full implementation awaiting an evaluation of the pilot project during 2000-01.

The state's deliberations are far from over. The district advisory committee's recommendations, when finalized, will be forwarded to the commissioner of education, who in turn must recommend a process to the governor's office. Final action will await the spring 1999 legislative session. The state has undergone considerable turnover in political leadership as a result of the November 1998 elections. A Republican governor, Jeb Bush, has replaced the two-term Democratic incumbent, Lawton Chiles. The former commissioner of education, who appointed the district advisory committee, was Bush's running mate and is now the lieutenant governor. A newly elected commissioner of education, Tom Gallagher, will be the recipient of the committee's recommendations.

Conclusion

Two questions about performance-based budgeting are paramount. First, will political interest survive long enough to enable the process to play out completely; and second, if fully implemented, will it result in sufficient increases in effectiveness or efficiency to constitute a suitable return on investment? The answers to both are unclear. Snell (1988) reports an overall slackening in commitment from state governments to performance-based budgeting in general over the last few years. He also reports that in no state have there been promising developments regarding the public school budget. In fact, public schools have proven to be a significant stumbling block both conceptually and politically in virtually every state that has pursued performance-based budgeting. On the other hand, he notes that in a handful of states, including Florida, commitment appears to be strong, and institutionalization of some of the critical processes is advancing.

The process of defining and measuring inputs, processes, outputs, outcomes, and results can be tedious, painfully slow, and ultimately unsatisfactory. Are the gains to be achieved—more effective use of resources and greater discretion for district and school officials—worth the considerable managerial burden of accounting for expenditures according to their contribution to student achievement?

The real promise of performance-based budgeting, in my opinion, lies in the large amount of raw data it could produce on the relations between inputs and outcomes. If the system forces district finance and management information offices to create financial management systems that better track the flow of dollars into the classroom and better reveal the use of dollars in the instructional process, and if these data can be captured in a state- or district-level research and development program that explores correlations, looking behind the data to understand causal links, considerable advancements in understanding how to improve schooling could result. If the data are used only for operational purposes at the school level and not aggregated into an aggressive research and development program at the district and state levels, however, the process of improving student performance will continue to be somewhat hit or miss, and advancements in instruction will occur, as always, infrequently and sporadically.

Over the next 2 years, Florida educators and state budgeters will develop and test a performance-based system for funding public education. The proponents of PB[2] have recognized from the outset the political limitations of rationally based allocation processes and argue three circumstances that make success more likely today than in the past. First, input from all shareholders, including elected officials, educators, parents, and the business community, will go into defining the outcomes so that the system will strive for responsiveness as well as effectiveness. Although inclusion of all shareholders will invariably compromise the rational purity of the system, remaining responsive to parents' and other shareholders' concerns may also ensure enough public support to keep it alive. Second, information technologies for data collection, display, and analyses are more powerful than ever before, but are also more sensitive to policy queries. Thus, the possibility of real improvements in our understanding of how schooling works is more real. A final and perhaps the most important difference from past experiences with rationality based allocation systems is that the claims of proponents are notably more modest. PB^2 is not intended to replace the political allocation process but to support it.

References

Guthrie, J. (1988). *Understanding school budgets*. Washington, DC: Department of Education.

Hanushek, E. A. (1994). *Making schools work: Improving performance and controlling cost.* Washington, DC: Brookings Institute.

Herrington, C. (1995, March). *Persistence and evolution in state educational policy development: The case of Florida.* Paper presented at the annual meeting of the American Education Finance Association, Savannah, GA.

Kirst, M. W. (1988). The internal allocation of resources within U.S. school districts: Implications for policymakers and practitioners. In D. H. Monk & J. Underwood (Eds.), *Microlevel school finance: Issues and implications for policy* (pp. 365-389). Cambridge, MA: Ballinger.

Lee, R. D., Jr. (1997). The use of program analysis in state budgeting: Changes between 1990 and 1995. *Public Budgeting and Finance, 17*(3), 18-35.

Miller, D. M., & Seraphine, A. E. (1998, March). *Performance-based assessment and school funding.* Paper presented at the annual meeting of the American Education Finance Association, Mobile, AL.

Nakib, Y. (1998). The political economy of education finance: The context of a large, fast growing state. *Journal of Education Finance, 23,* 351-373.

National Commission on Excellence in Education. (1983). *A nation at risk: The imperative for educational reform: A report to the nation and the secretary of education.* Washington, DC: Government Printing Office.

Office of Program Policy Analysis and Government Accountability. (1997). *Performance-based program budgeting in context: History and comparison.* Tallahassee, FL: Author.

Office of Program Policy Analysis and Government Accountability. (1998). *Public schools and performance-based program budgeting: Challenges and opportunities.* Tallahassee, FL: Author.

O'Laughlin, M. (1998, March). *Performance-based incentive funding: The Florida model.* Paper presented at the annual meeting of the American Education Finance Association, Mobile, AL.

Osborne, D., & Gaebler, T. (1992). *Reinventing government.* Reading, MA: Addison-Wesley.

Peters, T. J., & Waterman, R. H. (1982). *In search of excellence: Lessons from America's best-run companies.* New York: Warner.

Rockwell, R. C. (1989). *Lessons from the history of the social indicators movement.* Background paper presented to the National Center for Education Statistics' Special Study Panel on Education Indicators.

Snell, R. (1998). Comments at a panel on performance-based budgeting at the annual meeting of the National Conference of State Legislatures, Las Vegas, NV.

Weiss, C. H. (1989). Congressional committees as users of analysis. *Journal of Policy Analysis and Management, 8*(3), 411-431.

Weiss, J. A., & Gruber, J. E. (1984). Using knowledge for control in fragmented policy arenas. *Journal of Policy Analysis and Management, 3*(2), 225-247.

Weiss, J. A., & Tschirhart, M. (1994). Public information campaigns as policy instruments. *Journal of Policy Analysis and Management, 13*(1), 82-119.

Wildavsky, A. (1989). *Budgeting: A comparative theory of budgetary processes.* New Brunswick: Transaction.

NINE

Resource Allocation in Reforming Schools and School Districts

MARGARET E. GOERTZ

MARK C. DUFFY

For the last decade, many researchers, policymakers, and educators have advocated the use of school-based management—the delegation of decision making in areas such as budget, personnel, and programs—as a way of improving educational efficiency and effectiveness (see, e.g., Malen, Ogawa, & Kranz, 1990; Mohrman & Wohlstetter, 1994). Thousands of school districts across the United States, including most of the country's largest urban systems, have implemented school-based management in at least some of their schools, and many models of high-performance schools incorporate some measure of local control (Wohlstetter, Mohrman, & Robertson, 1997). Only a few of these cases include the decentralization of budget authority—or school-based budgeting—in their school-based management structures, however.

Researchers argue that control over the school budget is essential to increasing the efficiency, effectiveness, and equity of schools. First,

215

studies conducted in the private sector have shown that decentralizing power and authority to work teams, involving employees in
making key decisions about how to organize and conduct their work,
and holding work teams accountable for results enhance organizational effectiveness and productivity (see, e.g., Lawler, 1992; Mohrman
& Wohlstetter, 1994). In the context of school-based management,
schools and their staff need the power to make allocation and expenditure decisions, access to fiscal and performance information, and
training in the budget process (Wohlstetter & Van Kirk, 1996). Second,
school-based management and budgeting structures bring the perspectives of those closest to the students to the decision-making
process, leading to decisions more focused on the interests of children.
Increasing school-level control over budgeting, hiring, and curriculum will enable schools to tailor their programs to the unique needs
of their students and their communities and provide the flexibility
needed to target resources to appropriate programs and services (see,
e.g., Clune & White, 1988; Hess, 1995). Third, in making the current
intradistrict allocation of resources more transparent to the public,
school-based budgeting and school-based financing will spark a debate regarding equity—across schools within districts and between
elementary, middle, and high schools (Odden & Busch, 1998).

At the same time, the failure of discrete education reform programs
to raise student achievement significantly, especially in high-poverty
schools, has led to the development of more comprehensive, whole
school reforms. In the fall of 1997, Congress enacted the Comprehensive School Reform Demonstration (CSRD) program to provide financial support for the implementation of comprehensive school reform
models, primarily in Title I schools.[1] Many of these new designs, such
as Robert Slavin's Success for All program and the New American
Schools (NAS) models, are staffed and structured differently from
most traditional schools; they use more classroom teachers and fewer
specialists, spend more on professional development and technology,
and group students and teachers differently. It is expected that schools
spending at or above the national average can, and should, reallocate
their resources to support these new designs. For example, Miles
and Darling-Hammond (1998) describe how five schools reallocated
teaching resources to provide smaller class sizes and more planning
time. Odden and Busch (1998) show how some schools can pay for

high-performance school designs by reducing the number of subject matter and student support specialists, and reassigning special education, compensatory education, and bilingual education staff. Yet, schools can restructure in these ways only if they have the authority to reallocate their resources (Bodilly, 1998).

In spite of calls for greater decentralization of school budget authority, we know little about the allocation of resources to and within schools and the interaction of resource allocation and educational programming decisions at the school level. To date, most research on school-based budgeting and finance has focused on the design of funding formulas in selected countries, states, and school districts (see, e.g., Caldwell & Hill, this volume; Odden, this volume; Odden & Busch, 1998; Thomas & Lakin, this volume) and on the organizational and procedural changes within schools and school districts adopting these reforms (Clune & White, 1988; General Accounting Office, 1994; Wohlstetter & Buffett, 1992; Wohlstetter & Van Kirk, 1996). A small number of researchers have examined the distribution of education expenditures by major functional categories across schools within school districts, focusing on issues of equity and productivity (Cooper et al., 1994; Rubenstein, 1997; Stiefel, Schwartz, & Rubenstein, this volume). Few studies have looked at the allocation, level, and mix of human resources within and/or across schools (Chambers, Parrish, Goertz, Marder, & Padilla, 1993; Miles, 1995; Monk, Brent, & Roelke, 1997; Stiefel et al., 1996).

This chapter uses data from a national study of reform-minded schools and school districts to explore how these entities allocate resources to build capacity for instructional reform and increased student achievement, and whether average spending schools have sufficient resources and flexibility to support new school reform models. Specifically, we address four issues:

1. How do these districts allocate resources to their schools?
2. How much and what kinds of control do their schools have over budget and personnel decisions?
3. What resource allocation patterns emerge from this decision-making structure?
4. To what extent and how do these districts and schools link resource allocation and educational improvement decisions?

Methodology

The findings reported in this chapter are part of a longitudinal study of state and local education reform in 8 states and 24 school districts conducted by the Consortium for Policy Research in Education (CPRE). The eight states—California, Colorado, Florida, Kentucky, Maryland, Michigan, Minnesota, and Texas—were selected because of their involvement in standards-based reform. CPRE then identified three school districts in each state with a reputation for pursuing innovative reforms to improve teaching and learning and to build capacity in elementary language arts and/or mathematics. Additional district sampling criteria included poverty and urbanicity. The 24 districts in the study range in size from 2,600 to more than 300,000 students, and from less than 1% to more than 95% students of color. Six of the districts have fewer than 30% of their students participating in the free and reduced school lunch program; nine have more than 60% of their students enrolled in this program. Additional data were collected from 32 public elementary schools in 11 study districts in California, Kentucky, Maryland, and Michigan. Twenty-seven of these schools participate in the federal Title I program; the average poverty rate of the 32 schools is about 63%.

Researchers visited the schools and districts in 1997-98. They interviewed 4 to 16 policymakers in each district, depending on the size and organization of the district. Respondents included superintendents, finance directors, assessment, curriculum and instruction specialists, and directors of special programs and professional development. In each school, researchers interviewed the principal, school improvement team chair (or the equivalent, where applicable), and professional development coordinator (where applicable) and collected information on the number and types of all building staff and the size and characteristics of the student body. The findings reported here are based on an analysis of interviews in the districts and schools and the school-level staffing data. The small number of schools, the sampling criteria, and the resulting sample of reform-oriented and relatively high poverty schools and districts do not allow us to generalize about schools or districts nationally. The data do provide insights into factors affecting resource allocation decisions, however.

The District Role in
Resource Allocation

The schools and districts in the CPRE study operate in diverse governance contexts. Four of the states require some form of school-based decision making (SBDM). Kentucky has the strongest decentralization legislation. Schools must establish SBDM councils with authority over curriculum, instructional programs and instructional materials, the selection of principals and teachers, school schedules, extracurricular programs, school improvement planning, and the allocation of discretionary funds. School districts and schools that meet their state accountability targets may request a waiver from these SBDM requirements (Lindle, 1997). Texas and Florida schools are also required to engage in site-based decision making, but their statutory powers are generally limited to developing and approving school improvement plans. Maryland requires all schools that have not met the state's performance standards (currently all elementary and middle schools and most high schools) to develop a school improvement plan, but the process for developing these plans is determined by the local districts. None of these state laws gives schools much budgetary responsibility. The other four states in the study have no state requirements for decentralized governance, although California has funded planning and demonstration grants to encourage schools to implement site-based management and decision-making systems.

Allocation of General Education Resources

Districts in all eight states have the option to delegate budgetary authority to their schools, but few of the districts in the study have done so. Even in districts that have decentralized instructional and some personnel responsibilities, the allocation of most resources remains a district responsibility. Districts in the study sample allocate administrative, teaching, and student support staff (e.g., nurses and counselors) using a student-to-teacher ratio (or school size) that often differs across grade span (elementary, middle, and high school). In some districts, this ratio (or cap size, as it is called in some states) reflects provisions in state general aid formulas, such as 1 teacher for every 20 or 25 students. Some states, such as California and Texas, have established class sizes limits for the primary grades (20:1 in grades K-4 and 22:1 in grades K-4, respectively) and either require (Texas) or provide monetary incentives for (California) districts to adhere to these policies. In other districts, and for other grade spans in Texas and California, class size policies reflect the interaction of district philosophy and available resources. For example, at least one district in the study allocated additional personnel units to high-poverty schools. School input into these resource allocation decisions is generally limited to consultations between principals and the superintendent or other central office staff.

The study districts generally allocate funds for instructional materials and supplies to the schools using a per pupil formula. In some districts, this formula also includes textbook monies; in other districts, textbooks are purchased centrally. The allocation of professional development funds follow one, or some combination of, three approaches: districts allocate professional development funds to schools, which then determine their own programming; the central office selects and funds professional development centrally, usually with input from school personnel; or the district provides funds to schools that may be used for multiple purposes, including professional development. In this last case, schools determine how much of this allocation should be used for training, as well as the nature of the services. For example, under state law, Kentucky districts must allocate about $100 per pupil to their schools for instructional purposes, including at least $15 per pupil in state professional development aid. Schools may, and some do, apply some of their nonprofessional development dollars to staff training.

Four districts in the study have implemented school-based budgeting, where they give their schools funds for all personnel as well as instructional materials, supplies, equipment, and professional development. One district provides an example of how this works. The central office allocates all general fund resources, including those for personnel, using a formula based on the number of students in each school (and by program for special education and bilingual education). For purposes of hiring, salaries are based on a district average. The district gives schools an allocation worksheet that shows them how much money they have received for each type of student and other allocations. Schools have some flexibility to move money among categories, but must follow state and federal guidelines for special programs. Schools are free to determine the number and composition of their faculty, and this district organizes a "teacher transfer fair" where teachers who want to change schools can apply for positions in other buildings. The district holds schools accountable for student performance on state and district outcome measures, rather than through central review of their budgets or instructional programs. Low-performing schools are subject to greater district oversight, however.

Allocation of Special Program Resources

Most of the study districts allocate personnel rather than dollars for their special education, English as a second language (ESL), and bilingual education programs. Personnel allocations are based on the number and type of students needing services in each school, usually with input from principals. In many cases, student-to-teacher ratios are set by the state (e.g., 1 resource teacher per 15 students) and vary by program category (such as resource room services vs. self-contained programs for students with different disabilities). District control over hiring differs across the sites. Principals hire special education and bilingual education teachers in some districts; in others, districts hire and assign staff because of personnel shortages, the need to assign teachers to multiple sites, or the desire to concentrate services in a few schools. Districts generally control the allocation of special education and bilingual education funds for instructional materials and professional development.

Prior to the enactment of Title I of the Improving America's Schools Act (IASA) in 1994, school districts also generally controlled the allocation of federal compensatory education funds, assigning staff and services rather than unrestricted dollars to the school site (Chambers et al., 1993; Goertz, 1988). Block grants were given only to a small number of schools that ran schoolwide programs. A schoolwide program permits a school to use funds from Part A of Title 1 and other federal programs to upgrade a school's entire educational program, rather than limiting services to a particular group of students. The IASA expanded eligibility for schoolwide programs to all Title I schools with poverty rates of 50% or higher, and the number of schools implementing these programs exploded. Close to 20,000 schools, or almost half of all Title 1 schools, now operate schoolwide programs (Unpublished data from Planning and Evaluation Services, U.S. Department of Education).

The IASA changed the nature of Title I resource allocation as well. Districts now must allocate dollars rather than human resources to Title I eligible schools, using a formula based on the number of poor students. (Districts in this study usually measure poverty by the number of students eligible for the federal free and/or reduced school lunch program.) One district, for example, has a three-tiered allocation model. Schools with 90% or more students eligible for free school lunches receive $1,000 per poor student. Schools with between 78% and 89% free lunch students receive $825 per poor student. The lowest tier, with 74% to 77% poverty, are given $500 per free lunch student. Although the average poverty rate is about 67%, district policymakers have chosen to concentrate Title I funds in the highest-poverty buildings. In contrast, another urban district with a comparable poverty rate has chosen to spread Title I funds across 60% of its schools. Its formula allocates about $310 per student to schools with the largest percentage of students receiving free or reduced school lunches, and $260 per student to schools with lower concentrations of poverty.

The Role of Schools
in Resource Allocation

Despite the trend toward SBDM, the study districts remain primarily responsible for the allocation of personnel and funds for instructional support materials and professional development; most districts grant schools only marginal budgetary authority. Schools are generally not empowered to decide how many staff they will have, how much money to use on staff as opposed to materials, or whether to cut one program to build another. School-based decisions come into play after the structure of most of the school budget, and therefore the structure of the school, has been determined by district policy. Another study of site-based budgeting in four large cities not included in the CPRE sample—Chicago, Fort Worth, New York, and Rochester—

reached similar conclusions. Schools had real discretion over less than 20% of their budgets in these districts, and most of the discretionary funds came from Title I, state compensatory education aid, and non-personnel accounts (Goertz & Hess, 1998; Iatarola & Stiefel, 1998; Moser, 1998; Peternick & Sherman, 1998). Within these constraints, what kinds of decisions can schools make, and who is involved at the school level in making these decisions?

School-Level Resource Allocation Decisions

The school's role in allocating personnel and nonpersonnel resources begins only after the district determines the number and type of staff and the level and type of discretionary funding for each building. We observed four models across the study sites. First, in those few districts with school-based budgeting, schools are free to determine how many and what kind of staff they want, and to make budgetary trade-offs between personnel and nonpersonnel resources and among programs. These districts differ, however, in how much discretion they give schools over the use of their special education and/or bilingual education resources. Second, other districts assign personnel units (FTEs) to schools, but give schools flexibility in how they will use these general education positions. In some cases, however, districts require schools to use part of their FTEs to staff art, music, and physical education positions. In the third model, schools are constrained in their allocation of general education positions, but are given discretion in how they use their categorical aid for special education, ESL/bilingual education, and Title I as long as they adhere to state and federal service requirements. For example, California allows schools to consolidate resources from designated categorical programs into a single schoolwide plan if a representative school-site council is established to manage the program. The fourth model is one of very limited flexibility. Schools are free to decide how personnel are assigned within their building, but cannot change the composition of their staff positions. These districts do not give their schools the latitude, for example, to divide one full-time staff position into two part-time positions, or to exchange subject specialists in the elementary schools, such as art, music, or physical education teachers, for either other specialists (such as reading teachers) or general classroom teachers. Staff for special needs programs are assigned by the central office.

As discussed in the preceding section of this chapter, many schools do have considerable discretion over their Title I funds. Schools that operate schoolwide programs are generally free to use these dollars according to their identified needs and subject to plans submitted to their district offices. Only one of the study districts has placed restrictions on the use of these dollars. Schools in this district must use some of their Title I funds to support an "instructional guide" position, someone who provides curricular, instructional, assessment, and data analysis support to teachers in the building. Other sites provide guidance to and/or incentives for schools to adopt particular programs to ensure more effective use of Title I funds. For example, one district is developing a menu of options that schools can choose from to use their Title I funds. These options are designed to align with the district's new priorities. Thus, the district would encourage schools interested in reducing class size to target their Title I funds on class size reductions in grades 1-3 because this is a systemwide goal. Another district has offered to pay the cost of training Reading Recovery teachers in any Title I school that selects this program.

Who Makes School-Level Allocation Decisions?

The trend toward SBDM has changed the way districts and schools make instructional, personnel, and budgetary decisions across the country. Although few states mandate the creation of SBDM committees, many call for the involvement of school personnel, community members, and parents in the development of some kind of school-level plan. The composition and responsibility of these bodies, however, varies considerably across districts and across states.

School-level councils in Kentucky have the most authority of SBDM committees in the study, with legal responsibility for the hiring of staff, curricular decisions, and design and approval of school budgets. One Kentucky principal acknowledged that his school's council has more authority than the staff. The formal role of SBDM councils is primarily advisory in the study sites outside Kentucky; the principal is responsible for budget, personnel, and curricular decisions. In

Texas, for example, school-level committees must be involved in planning, budgeting, curriculum, staffing pattern, school organization, and staff development decisions, but approve only those portions of the school plan addressing staff development needs. School accountability committees in Colorado are also advisory to the principal. In Florida, site-based management takes the form of school advisory councils responsible for determining how a portion of the FTE will be used.

Some districts encourage greater involvement by SBDM councils. In one Texas district, many schools use their SBDM councils to decide how to allocate discretionary funds, including Title I, to amend the school budget and select schoolwide reform initiatives. But central office staff feel more training is needed to empower these councils. As one respondent noted:

> The training would focus on how a campus deals with the budget. In some schools, budget authority is often held by the principal. Therefore, the rest of the staff is not sure what to do with a budget. We need to educate them on budget codes, etc. so they understand the reports. We need to let them know they are part of the decision making; it is not held in the principal's office.

In a district in another state, school site councils determine how FTEs are used in the school. They can use a portion of their FTEs to hire subject specialists or reduce class sizes, but cannot exchange staff positions for nonpersonnel resources or eliminate art, music, or physical education positions.

It is often the building principal who determines whether and how he or she shares power with other school and community members, and the principal is often ultimately responsible for the school-level decisions. In two schools in Kentucky, a state with a history of SBDM authority, principals were reported as having discretion over the allocation of personnel and nontenured staff. In another state, the principal of a school with school-based budgeting authority commented that she had "a great deal of power" to determine how teachers would be placed in the school, and was required only to consult with the school improvement team. The principal of another school identified his school's instructional needs and their effect on resource allocation decisions before going to the school improvement team (SIT), thereby giving the principal the opportunity to frame the issues and present them to the SIT for their comment. Further, it is the principal who receives information from the district, and therefore controls much of the information required in the decision-making process.

Other research raises the question of whether expanding formal decision-making power increases the perceived power of teachers, parents, and community participants in budgetary decisions. In their analysis of survey data from Chicago, Fort Worth, New York, and Rochester, Goertz and Hess (1998) found that the principal had considerable power in deciding how money is spent at the school level in these cities, regardless of the process used to develop the school budget. Even in schools where the teachers and parents (and sometimes community members) were formal participants in the school budgeting process, they and others rated their influence considerably below that of the principal, and only marginally higher than their counterparts in schools without comparable decision-making structures. One explanation for this pattern is that principals in schools with shared budget decision making take the lead in preparing the budget after receiving input from teachers. Another explanation is that teachers, parents, and community members are satisfied with their limited role. On the survey, these stakeholders reported a higher level of satisfaction with their ability to participate in their school's budget decisions than similar groups in schools without shared decision making, and over half of the respondents in Chicago said they would feel comfortable letting the principal of their school make most decisions about the budget. As Rubenstein (1997) points out in his study of Chicago, "principal-based" rather than school-based budgeting could represent an acceptable and effective distribution of authority.

Resource Allocation Patterns

In this section, we use data collected from 31 elementary schools to examine the level and type of personnel in each school and to explore factors that might explain similarities or variations in resource patterns. Table 9.1 presents the number of staff these schools employ in eight major categories: general and bilingual education teachers in self-contained classrooms; special education teachers in self-contained class-rooms; teachers of supplemental subjects, such as art, music, and physical education, as well as gifted and talented programs and computer classes; special education, ESL, and speech resource teach-ers; reading and mathematics resource teachers; instructional aides; library staff; and student support service professionals (e.g., guidance, social, psychological, and health services). The last column, Total General Resources, is the sum of all general education, bilingual education and supplemental subject teachers, reading and mathemat-ics resource teachers, library staff, and the student support services staff. All categories have been standardized to personnel per 1,000 students to control for differences in school size. The table also in-cludes information on the size of the schools and their districts and on school poverty levels and Title I status.

We face five limitations in using these data to analyze school-level resource allocation patterns. First, we do not know the per pupil expenditure levels of these schools, although most of the districts in the study spend at or below their states' average per pupil expendi-ture, and all but one state spent below the national average in 1997-98 (National Center for Education Statistics, 1998). Therefore, we cannot assess to what extent differences in resource levels reflect variation in expenditure levels. Second, we do not know how much of a school's budget is allocated to personnel versus nonpersonnel functions (such as professional development, instructional materials, and equipment). Thus, we cannot examine trade-offs between these two types of resource use. Third, in some cases, we were not able to determine the full-time equivalency of supplemental teachers or instructional aides. (These cases are marked with an asterisk in Table 9.1.) As a result, we may overstate some of these staffing levels. Fourth, we do not have consis-tent information across all schools on staff assignments, particularly those of other professional staff or instructional aides.[2] As schools make more flexible use of state and federal categorical funds and of categorically funded staff, it is increasingly difficult to assign instruc-tional staff to specific categories, such as Title I or special education. Therefore, we aggregated all instructional aides into one category, although they may be serving different groups of students (e.g., students with disabilities, limited English proficient students, and/or students with a particular learning need, such as reading) or may be funded from different revenue sources, such as the local budget, Title I, special education, and/or state compensatory education funds. Finally, these numbers are school-level averages. Thus, we do not capture variations in class size within or across grade levels.

Staffing Patterns

We first looked at the distribution of total general resources, a measure of the number of professional staff positions that schools potentially could allocate in different ways.[3] The number of general resource staff per 1,000 students ranged from a low of 36.3 to a high of 93.5, but nearly half of the schools (14) had a total of between 45 and 55 staff per 1,000 students, or 18 to 22 students per staff member. One third of the schools (10) employed between 56 and 65 staff per 1,000 students, resulting in a student-staff ratio of between 15:1 and 18:1. Two schools had staffing levels below 45 per 1,000; five schools had staffing levels in excess of 65 per 1,000. Miles (1995) found that only 60% of Boston public schools' teaching force, including special education staff, were assigned to regular classrooms. In this sample of elementary schools, between 56% and 88% of the nonspecial education staff taught in general or bilingual education classrooms; half of the schools assigned 75% to 88% of their staff to these classrooms.[4]

Table 9.1, Column 6, shows the average size of the general or bilingual classroom in the 31 schools. The modal and median class size was 25 students; class sizes ranged between 21 and 27 in two thirds of the schools. Five schools had class sizes between 17 and 20 students, whereas class sizes in the other five schools ranged from 28 to 35. There was much greater variation in the number of subject specialists and student support services staff across the sample. Disregarding the schools where the numbers may not reflect FTE counts, the number of subject matter specialists per 1,000 students ranged from less than 1 (0.8) to 10.2; about one third of the schools had a total of 3 to 5 subject matter specialists per 1,000 students, with 5 as the median number, or 1 for every 200 students. This often translated into one part-time music, one part-time art teacher, and one full-time physical education teacher per school. The level of school-level student support services resources also ranged broadly, from none in one district to more than 7 per 1,000 students in seven districts. In contrast, the level of library resources was more consistent, reflecting the allocation of between 0.5 and 1.5 FTE library staff to most schools in the study. Nineteen (60%) of the schools employed reading and/or mathematics resource teachers. Eleven of these schools had between 1 and 3 resource staff per 1,000 students; the other eight schools had between 5 and 8 staff per 1,000 students. Twenty-six of the schools employed instructional aides. The number of aides ranged from 9 to 40 per 1,000 students; the average was 21 aides per 1,000 students, or one aide for every 48 students (or two classrooms).

As discussed above, most of the districts in this study allocated instructional staff to the schools; buildings had little discretion in the numbers or types of teachers they could hire. We hypothesized that there would be little variation in average class sizes across schools within these districts, whereas schools that had school-based budgeting authority (KU1-1-3, MU1-1-3, and MU3-1-3[5]) might show different resource allocation patterns. The data do not support this hypothesis, however. There was less than 20% variation in average class size across sample schools within six of the study districts; one of these was a school-based budgeting district. Although resource allocation patterns varied across schools in the other school-based budgeting communities, we found variations in three other districts with more restrictive allocation rules.

Do other factors account for differences across schools? Table 9.2 groups the 31 schools by poverty and by enrollment. The average number of general resource staff and supplemental subject teachers has been adjusted to take into account schools where the number of supplemental subject teachers may be overstated. It appears that the highest-poverty schools in the study (76% to 100% poverty) had about 12% more resources (approximately 6 additional FTE staff) than the lowest-poverty schools (less than 50% poverty). These additional resources were allocated primarily to student support services and reading and mathematics resource teachers. The poorer schools had slightly more classroom teachers (about 1 FTE), but about one third fewer library staff (the equivalent of nearly 1 FTE staff person).

(text continued on page 233)

TABLE 9.1. Staffing Patterns in 31 Elementary Schools, 1997-98

Code	District Size Category[1]	School Enrollment	Percent Poverty	Title 1	Average Class Size	Gen Ed & Bilingual/ 1,000 Students	Special Educ. Self-Cont/ 1,000 Students	Suppl. Subjects/ 1,000 Students	Sp Ed, ESL, & Speech Resource/ 1,000 Students	Reading/ Math Resource/ 1,000 Students	Inst. Aides/ 1,000 Students	Library Staff/ 1,000 Students	Student Support Services/ 1,000 Students	Total General Resources/ 1,000 Students
CU1-1	VL	493	77.00%	x	27.39	36.51	8.11	0.81	4.06	3.04	29.61	0.00	3.25	43.61
CU1-3	VL	523	50.00%	x	20.12	49.71	5.74	3.44	4.78	1.91	16.25	1.15	2.49	58.70
CU3-1	VL	936	79.00%	x	22.29	44.87	2.14	1.92	1.07	2.67	13.46	1.07	2.24	52.78
CU3-2	VL	1137	100.00%	x	24.72	40.46	0.00	3.08	7.04	0.00	35.18	1.76	5.10	50.40
CU3-3	VL	1462	40.00%		25.21	39.67	0.00	3.08	3.42	0.00	n/a	1.03	2.39	46.17
KU1-1	L	279	23.00%		31.00	32.26	3.58	4.30	3.58	0.00	0.00	3.58	7.17	47.31
KU1-2	L	320	60.00%	x	18.82	53.13	7.81	9.37*	0.00	6.25	0.00	3.13	4.38	76.25*
KU1-3	L	573	60.00%	x	21.22	47.12	3.49	8.72*	5.24	3.49	18.32	1.75	5.24	66.31*
KS1-1	S	467	28.00%		25.94	38.54	0.00	3.43	5.78	0.00	12.85	3.21	3.64	48.82
KS1-2	S	307	50.00%	x	25.58	39.09	0.00	5.86	9.77	0.00	16.29	3.26	2.93	51.14
KS1-3	S	350	63.00%	x	26.92	37.14	0.00	2.00	7.14	5.71	20.00	2.86	3.43	51.14*
KR1-1	S	668	74.55%	x	24.74	40.42	5.99	4.49*	1.50	1.50	32.93	2.25	4.49	53.14*
KR1-2	S	360	75.00%	x	24.00	41.67	2.78	8.33*	4.17	1.39	40.28	2.78	1.39	55.55*
KR1-3	S	404	52.08%	x	25.25	39.60	0.00	3.71	5.94	1.24	39.60	2.48	2.23	49.26
MU1-1	VL	431	77.00%	x	30.79	32.48	11.60	6.96	6.96	6.96	9.28	2.32	9.28	58.00
MU1-2	VL	655	76.50%		31.19	32.06	4.58	2.75	2.44	0.00	9.16	0.00	1.53	36.34
MU1-3	VL	665	93.00%		35.00	28.57	6.02	4.51	3.01	4.51	18.80	1.50	6.02	45.11
MR1-1	S	733	43.83%	x	26.18	38.20	10.91	5.46	4.09	0.00	39.56	2.05	5.18	50.89
MR1-2	S	563	60.00%	x	18.77	53.29	3.55	5.33	9.77	0.00	21.31	1.78	3.91	64.30
MR1-3	S	734	53.00%	x	26.21	38.15	5.45	7.36	9.54	0.00	17.71	2.04	4.63	52.18
MS1-1	L	770	9.90%		27.50	36.36	3.90	8.18	0.00	1.30	0.00	1.30	3.90	51.04
MS1-2	L	544	100.00%	x	24.18	41.36	5.51	7.54	12.87	5.51	29.41	2.76	7.72	64.89

MU2-1	M	246	94.50%	×	24.60	40.65	20.33	10.16	11.79	0.00	12.20	4.07	8.54	63.41
MU2-2	M	290	99.00%	×	22.31	44.83	3.45	10.34*	5.17	0.00	13.79	1.72	8.62	65.51*
MU2-3	M	278	90.30%	×	17.38	57.55	0.00	14.38*	7.19	7.19	17.99	3.60	10.79	93.52*
MR2-1	S	297	37.00%	×	24.75	40.40	0.00	16.83*	3.37	1.68	10.10	1.68	0.00	60.60*
MR2-2	S	416	27.00%	×	23.11	43.27	0.00	8.41	5.77	1.20	10.82	3.61	0.00	56.49
MR2-3	S	275	40.00%	×	25.00	40.00	0.00	18.18*	3.64	1.82	9.09	3.64	0.00	63.63*
MU3-1	M	417	50.00%	×	21.95	45.56	7.19	1.44	0.00	0.00	14.39	2.40	4.80	54.20
MU3-2	M	211	76.00%	×	23.44	42.65	18.96	3.55	0.00	4.74	23.70	0.00	9.48	60.43
MU3-3	M	254	71.00%	×	18.14	55.12	11.81	1.77	7.87	7.87	0.00	1.97	6.69	73.43

* In these cases, the reported numbers are not necessarily by FTE and may be overstated.

[1] S= Enrollment of <10,000; M= Enrollment of 10,000-30,000; L= Enrollment of 30,000-75,000; VL= Enrollment of >75,000

TABLE 9.2. Staffing Patterns in 31 Study Schools, Grouped by Poverty Rate and Size

	# Schools	Total General Resources/ 1,000 Students[1]	General/ Bilingual Educ/ 1,000 Students	Supplement Subjects/ 1,000 Students	Library Staff/ 1,000 Students	Student Support Services/ 1,000 Students	Reading/Math Resource/ 1,000 Students	Instructional Aides/ 1,000 Students
Poverty								
0-49%	8	50.2	38.6	5.5	2.5	2.8	0.8	11.8
50-75	12	57.6	45.0	3.9	2.3	3.9	2.5	19.8
76-100	11	56.3	40.2	4.6	1.7	6.6	3.2	19.3
Enrollment								
200-300	8	60.9	44.2	4.9	2.5	6.4	2.9	10.9
301-500	10	53.5	40.7	4.1	2.6	3.5	2.6	19.3
501-1500	13	53.0	40.8	4.8	1.6	4.2	1.6	21.0

[1] Sum of general/bilingual education teachers, teachers of supplementary subjects, library staff, student support service staff, and reading and mathematics resource teachers. The average number of general resource staff and supplemental subject teachers has been adjusted to take into account schools where the number of supplemental subject teachers may be overstated.

Higher-poverty schools (more than 50% poverty) also had more instructional aides per 1,000 students.[6]

Size also has an effect on resource allocation patterns. Small schools (200 to 300 students) had, on average, 7 more FTE staff per 1,000 students than the other schools. Three of these additional staff were found in classrooms, reducing class size by an average of 2 students (from 25.1 to 23.2). The other 4 FTE staff provided additional library, student support, and mathematics and reading resources. In contrast, small schools used considerably fewer instructional aides than the larger buildings. These differences do not reflect variations in poverty across the schools; the average poverty rate for both the smallest and the largest groups of schools was about 66%. The higher level of resources may result instead from fixed allocation levels. It is difficult for districts (or schools) to assign less than 1 FTE teacher to a classroom, although the size of that classroom may be smaller than those in larger schools. Similarly, districts may not be able to allocate less than one half of a librarian or reading specialist to a school for logistical reasons.

The Case of Title I

One explanation for the different resource patterns between low- and high-poverty schools is the allocation of Title I funds. As schools implement schoolwide programs and are encouraged to blend many types of categorical funding, however, the concept of a Title I teacher or Title I aide is disappearing, making it increasingly difficult to track the use of Title I dollars. Therefore, we used data from interviews with district Title I directors and school principals, as well as from school staffing rosters, to determine how schools allocate their Title I dollars.

The schools in the sample used their Title I dollars primarily for professional development, reading resource teachers, and instructional aides. A few of the schools spent some of their Title I funds for additional classroom teachers (to lower class size), consulting teachers to provide instructional support to teachers throughout the building, computer equipment and instructional materials, and/or programs for parents.

We estimate that nearly all the reading and mathematics specialists and perhaps half of the instructional aides working in the sample of schools are supported by Title I. The other reading and mathematics specialists and instructional aides are funded by local, compensatory education and/or special education funds. Twelve of the 27 Title I schools reported that they used their specialists and their Title I-funded aides to support Reading Recovery, or home-grown versions of this program. The local programs tend to be aide based, and were developed to expand reading services to a larger number of students. One school, for example, has replaced its pull-out reading program with one where teachers and aides work side by side to deliver reading services in the classroom. Another district trains instructional aides in a district-developed, prescriptive program in reading instruction that it claims is based on the Reading Recovery model. Students work one on one with an instructional aide for one-half hour each day. A reading specialist at the school oversees the aides' work.

Instructional aides provide more general support to classroom teachers in other schools. For example, one school assigned an aide to each of its K-3 classrooms for 2 hours daily, and to its fourth and fifth grade classrooms for 2.5 hours daily. Another school assigned one aide to almost every classroom, most of which are either bilingual or sheltered English classes. Respondents justified these staffing decisions as a way to serve more children in a cost-efficient manner. For example, when asked why his school had decided to use its Title I funds for aides, one principal responded, "because six sets of hands are better than two [Title I teachers]."

Most of the schools combined their Title I professional development monies with funds from Title II of IASA, state school improvement grants, the school district, and/or local foundations to support activities focused largely on core curriculum areas, including literacy and mathematics. As discussed in the next section of this chapter, schools generally aligned the allocation of professional development resources to their school improvement plans.

The Link Between Reform
and Resource Allocation

Supporters of school-based financing argue that increasing control over their budgets will give schools the flexibility they need to target resources to appropriate programs and services. Little research exists, however, on how schools link resource allocation and program decisions, particularly those designed to increase student achievement. To address this issue, we asked district administrators in the study sites how they allocated resources to support reform, and asked school decision makers what factors, including school improvement goals, affect how money is spent in their buildings. We also asked both groups of respondents whether and how they measure the effectiveness of their resource use.

Linkages at the District Level

Across the sample, districts are setting clear expectations for student achievement through the development of district standards. They are also beginning to hold schools accountable for meeting these standards. Looking at the overall education budget, however, we found districts making few linkages between resource allocation and reform. Most of the districts' resources are allocated to their schools through a formula, in the form of either personnel units or dollars, and many districts report they have little control over how schools use these resources, particularly in communities and states with strong decentralization policies. District review of school spending varies in scope and depth across the study sites. Although some districts monitor school budgets directly, others track school expenditures when they sign purchase orders. Some districts check only for the legality of expenditures when they pay the schools' bills, however. If school budgets are reviewed at the district level, district personnel seldom interfere with the schools' decisions. As a result, some district personnel feel frustrated about their inability to ensure that school budgets are linked to school plans and that school plans and budgets are linked to district improvement goals.

Districts are moving in four directions to make tighter connections between the district improvement priorities and school-based decisions: (1) fund districtwide curricular and/or professional development initiatives; (2) use district funds to leverage school expenditures and program decisions; (3) target district resources on low-performing schools; and/or (4) restrict the budgetary authority of low-performing schools.

Several of the districts in this study use a combination of local, state, federal (e.g., Title I, Title II, Title IV, NSF), and grant monies to underwrite curriculum and professional development activities. For example, districts have adopted national curriculum projects, such as the University of Chicago Math program, Different Ways of Knowing (DWOK), and Reading Recovery, or designed their own local curriculum to meet state standards. Districts are then supporting implementation of these curricula or more general reform-oriented instructional practices through professional development and occasionally school-based instructional guides or coaches.

A few districts use central office funds and/or policies to leverage school decisions. In one district with strong instructional and budgetary decentralization, the elementary school principals and central office staff selected a national curriculum program, DWOK, that is designed to pull multiple reforms together through social studies. The schools and the district have pooled resources to pay for instructional materials and training—the schools from their professional development funds and the district from a Goals 2000 grant and a private foundation grant. More recently, the schools and district jointly funded four resource teachers to provide direct instructional support in DWOK, mathematics/science, writing, and technology to classroom teachers in all the elementary buildings. Another district, finding that the customary use of compensatory dollars for add-on programs for supplemental staff was not having a strong effect on achievement, offers schools additional funds (about $50,000 per school) only if the schools adopt a whole school reform design, such as a New American Schools model or Accelerated Schools. The intent is for these schools to use their Title I money (instead of general operating funds from the district) to maintain the programs in later years.

Several districts target additional resources to low-performing schools. Districts, particularly large urban ones, have created special offices, teams, or units to provide assistance. In most cases, these staff members provide help on an as-needed basis. At least three of the districts placed a trained teacher at each school site to provide ongoing assistance, however; one required schools to use their Title I funds to pay for this position. These teacher specialists, or instructional guides, as they are sometimes called, provide professional support for teachers, offer professional development to the entire school, serve as a curriculum resource, and/or assist with analysis of student achievement data. Some of the districts also encouraged schools to use their discretionary resources, such as Title I funds, to add a complement of aides, resource teachers, or other kinds of support staff to expand instructional capacity.

Finally, one of the decentralized districts is reevaluating the budgetary authority and control over staffing it gives its lowest-achieving schools. Concerned that some schools are using resources in the same way they did in the 1970s—"things, jobs for people, but very little impact on the lowest performing students"—central office staff have proposed a differential treatment plan. Low-performing schools would have to comply with some set of minimum budgetary standards, such as student-teacher ratios. The schools would maintain some authority over areas that fall outside these minimum standards, but would be held to stricter standards of budget oversight. Higher-performing schools would have complete budgetary control. This district is also developing options for schools' use of Title I funds that are aligned with district priorities, such as reduced class size.

Linkages at the School Level

We looked next at whether and how schools linked budgetary decisions to school goals and to data on student performance. Although there was variation across the sample, schools and districts were using achievement data to inform decision making, even in states and districts with weak and relatively low-stakes accountability systems. In most districts, central office staff provided support in data use and interpretation. Several of the study districts hired outside experts and/or trained district and school staff—even, in one case, parents—to conduct data analysis and interpretation. The superintendent in one district routinely visited schools to ask how they were interpreting outcome data and how they were using it in planning.

Schools used the data for developing remedial plans for students, planning curriculum and instruction, assigning some personnel, and/or identifying the kinds of professional development activities that might help address gaps in performance. In several of the districts, schools analyzed results from state and local assessments and examined nonacademic indicators (such as attendance and student behavior). After setting concrete goals in academic areas (e.g., increase the proficient or advanced scores on the state assessment in reading by 10%), student support services, and/or parent/community communication in their school improvement plans (SIP), school staff identified specific activities (including professional development) for meeting school goals, and determined resources to implement their plans (e.g., Title I, school professional development, and other discretionary funds). One school's SIP, for example, called for a certain number of teachers to be trained in a specific hands-on mathematics program and the development of math portfolios, and then for teachers to use math portfolios in the classroom. In this school, professional development linked to the SIP accounted for most of the teachers' state-mandated 24 hours of inservice activities. In another school, the goal of raising reading scores was addressed through the newly implemented Reading Recovery program. The SIPs did not challenge the core structure of the school, however; resource allocation decisions focused on the use of staff and nonstaff resources funded by discretionary monies.

Evaluating Reform

Although schools and districts used student data for assessing student, school, and district needs, we saw few efforts to conduct formal evaluations of the effect or effectiveness of specific reform initiatives, such as new curriculum, whole school reforms, professional development activities, class size reduction, or the increased use of instructional aides. Some instructional programs, such as Reading Recovery and Success for All, incorporate periodic testing of participants throughout the school year, but many schools relied on changes in student performance on state assessments to measure the success of their new programs. State tests, however, generate cross-sectional data on a limited number of grade levels and, in some cases, only on a sample of students.

Several districts have extended student testing beyond their state's assessment system to measure the continuous progress of individual students toward district and/or state goals and to provide instructional feedback to teachers and schools. Although some districts are adding national standardized tests, others are using district-developed end-of-unit tests, teacher-generated running records, benchmark book programs for early literacy, and performance tasks in mathematics and writing. Schools and districts face three limitations, however, in tapping these data for evaluation purposes. First, few districts have comprehensive student databases that enable administrators or evaluators to track student progress and link changes in student performance to participation in specific programs or particular classrooms. Second, most districts, particularly smaller ones, do not have the human or technical capacity to design evaluation studies and analyze large amounts of student data. Finally, most changes in resource use do not entail highly specified interventions, so it may be difficult to isolate the added value of instructional aides, instructional guides, or particular forms of professional development.

Conclusion

A major purpose of this study was to understand how and why reform-oriented schools and school districts make resource allocation decisions. The districts in this study, by and large, retain control over the allocation of most personnel and nonpersonnel resources to schools. Schools have limited control over the size and composition of their staff. In most of the study sites, schools' budgetary authority is generally limited to the expenditure of Title I, state compensatory education, instructional and professional development funds, and occasional grant monies. Yet, we can draw some lessons from these sites about how schools might choose to allocate resources under true school-based financing systems. We focus here on issues of data, staffing, and accountability.

First, schools were making data-driven decisions about how to use discretionary funds, whether for professional development or for the allocation of new staff. Schools looked at student achievement data and targeted resources on areas of low performance, generally reading (and other core curricular areas for professional development). Many of the sites in this study used their school improvement planning processes and SBDM committees to structure, if not make, these decisions.

Second, more was better. Schools viewed capacity in terms of lower student-adult ratios, rather than greater teacher expertise. When faced with limited resources, as most were, schools often chose quantity over quality; that is, they hired instructional aides instead of certified teachers to work with students and classroom teachers. This decision probably reflects the magnitude of student need in these schools— high levels of poverty, low achievement levels, and, in a few cases, numbers of students with disabilities and limited English proficiency. If schools had hired teachers rather than aides, they could have reduced class size, on average, only from 25 to 22 students. Employing an average of one aide for every 48 students, however, would enable schools to place aides in every classroom for at least part of the day. Similarly, the use of aides enabled many schools to expand reading services to considerably more students. The issue facing schools and their districts, of course, is how well prepared instructional aides are to teach students and how teachers use these aides in the classroom.

Third, schools with considerable budgetary authority generally used their resources in the same ways as schools with more limited flexibility. Schools were not exchanging subject matter specialist, library, or student support service positions for more classroom teachers, although this step could have reduced average class size from 25 to 18 (and to 16 without instructional aides) in the highest-poverty schools. These patterns may reflect a number of factors: state and federal program regulations, union contracts, the difficulty of firing colleagues or community members, and/or accepted programmatic configurations. Ironically, at the same time that states and the federal government are encouraging more flexible use of categorical funds, they are imposing other constraints, such as minimum class size or prescriptive professional development programs. Educators and parents alike support art and music specialists and either a librarian or a media center director in schools. The average level of student support services in high-poverty schools did not seem excessive; it was comparable to that recommended under the Success for All program (e.g., a social worker, a counselor, and a nurse).

Finally, as districts devolved decision-making authority to schools, they had to decide how to hold schools accountable for the efficient and effective use of their resources. Few central offices monitored school resource use directly; rather, they chose to hold schools accountable for student performance on district and/or state standards. When schools failed to show adequate progress, districts restricted schools' control over curriculum and resource allocation and provided targeted technical assistance and/or incentives for schools to adopt school reform models. The question remains, however: What is the district's role and responsibility under school-based financing systems if these interventions do not work?

Acknowledgments

Funding for this work was provided by the U.S. Department of Education's National Institute on Educational Governance, Finance, Policymaking and Management (Grant #OERI-R308A60003); the Annie E. Casey Foundation; and the Pew Charitable Trusts. Opinions expressed in this paper are those of the authors, and do not necessarily reflect the views of the National Institute on Educational Governance, Finance, Policymaking and Management, Office of Educational Research and Improvement, U.S. Department of Education; the Pew Charitable Trusts; the Annie E. Casey Foundation; or the institutional partners of CPRE.

We are indebted to the schools and districts that participated in this study and to the hundreds of teachers, administrators, and policymakers who took time out of very busy days to meet with the research staff. We would also like to acknowledge the invaluable work of the research teams: Tammi Chun, Margaret E. Goertz, Diane Massell, and Keith Look, University of Pennsylvania; Robert Floden, Suzanne Wilson, Beth Herbal-Eisenmann, Jo Allen Lesser, Sharman Oliver, and Susan Wallace-Cowell, Michigan State University; Catherine Clark and Kerri Briggs, Texas Center for Educational Research; Carolyn D.

Herrington, Florida State University; Jane Clark Lindle, University of Kentucky; Joe Petrosko, University of Louisville; and Pat Seppanen, University of Minnesota.

Notes

1. The program provides competitive grants of up to $50,000 per year per school to support the implementation of "high-quality, well-defined, and well-documented comprehensive school reform programs" (U.S. Department of Education, 1998).

2. We collected information on categories of staff not reported in Table 9.1, such as staff development personnel, instructional administrators, itinerant staff (excluding those staff providing supplementary services), and services for parents (such as family resource centers, instructional programs for family members, parenting classes, and parent liaison programs). We did not include these data in the table because of the inconsistent definition of these categories across districts.

3. We did not include special education staff in this measure because state regulations, district policies, and levels of student need often drive the use of these resources. We also excluded administrators because most of the schools with fewer than 500 students have only one administrator, the building principal.

4. We included bilingual teachers in the general education category because they serve as the equivalent of the regular education teacher for these students, and their class sizes are often comparable to those of nonbilingual students. Only four of the schools had bilingual classrooms, however. If we include special education and ESL staff in the total, the percentage of staff assigned to regular or bilingual classrooms ranges from about 44% to 82% across our schools. If we limit our analysis to teaching staff (including special education and ESL), an average of 70% of teachers in the study schools are assigned to the regular classroom. The difference in findings between our study and those of Miles (1995) may be due to considerably higher expenditure levels in Boston.

5. These codes reference the districts and schools in the study. The names of the schools and districts have been withheld to protect their anonymity.

6. A sharper contrast emerges when we look at schools with greater than, or less than, 40% poverty. Schools with poverty rates at 40% or below had an average of 7.1 instructional aides per 1,000 students, whereas schools with poverty rates above 40% averaged 20.4 instructional aides per 1,000 students.

References

Bodilly, S. (1998). *Lessons from New American Schools' scale-up phase*. Santa Monica, CA: RAND.

Chambers, J., Parrish, T., Goertz, M., Marder, C., & Padilla, C. (1993). *Translating dollars into services: Chapter 1 resources in the context of state and local resources for education*. Palo Alto, CA: American Institutes for Research.

Clune, W. H., & White, P. A. (1988). *School-based management: Institutional variation, implementation and issues for further research* (Report No. RR-008). New Brunswick, NJ: Rutgers University, Consortium for Policy Research in Education.

Cooper, B. S., Sarrel, R., Darvas, P., Alfano, F., Meier, E., Samuels, J., & Heinbuch, S. (1994). Making money matter in education: A micro-financial model for determining school-level allocations, efficiency, and productivity. *Journal of Education Finance, 20*(1), 66-87.

General Accounting Office. (1994). *School-based management results in changes in instruction and budgeting.* Washington, DC: Government Printing Office.

Goertz, M. E. (1988). *School districts' allocation of Chapter 1 resources* (ETS RR-88-16). Princeton, NJ: Educational Testing Service.

Goertz, M. E., & Hess, G. A., Jr. (1998). Processes and power in school budgeting across four large urban school districts. *Journal of Education Finance, 23*(4), 490-506.

Hess, G. A., Jr. (1995). *Restructuring urban schools: A Chicago perspective.* New York: Teachers College Press.

Iatarola, P., & Stiefel, L. (1998). School-based budgeting in New York City: Perceptions of school communities. *Journal of Education Finance, 23*(4), 557-576.

Lawler, E. E. (1992). *The ultimate advantage: Creating the high involvement organization.* San Francisco: Jossey-Bass.

Lindle, J. C. (1997). School-based decision making. In J. C. Lindle, J. Petrosko, & R. Pankratz, *Review of research on KERA, 1996.* Frankfort: Kentucky Institute on Education Research and the University of Kentucky/University of Louisville Joint Center for the Study of Education Policy.

Malen, B., Ogawa, R. T., & Kranz, J. (1990). What do we know about school-based management? A case study of the literature—A call for research. In W. H. Clune & J. F. Witte (Eds.), *Choice and control in American education, Volume 2, The practice of choice, decentralization and restructuring* (pp. 289-342). New York: Falmer.

Miles, K. H. (1995). Freeing resources for improving schools: A case study of teacher allocation in Boston public schools. *Educational Evaluation and Policy Analysis, 17*(4), 476-493.

Miles, K. H., & Darling-Hammond, L. (1998). *Rethinking the allocation of teacher resources: Some lessons from high performing schools* (Report No. RR-38). Philadelphia: University of Pennsylvania, Consortium for Policy Research in Education.

Mohrman, S. A., & Wohlstetter, P. (Eds.). (1994). *School-based management: Organizing for high performance.* San Francisco: Jossey-Bass.

Monk, D. H., Brent, B., O., & Roelke, C. F. (1997). Teacher resource use within New York state secondary schools. In W. J. Fowler, Jr. (Ed.), *Developments in school finance, 1996* (pp. 37-67). Washington, DC: U.S. Department of Education, National Center for Education Statistics.

Moser, M. (1998). School-based budgeting: Increasing influence and information at the school level in Rochester, New York. *Journal of Education Finance, 23*(4), 507-531.

National Center for Education Statistics. (1998). *Public elementary and secondary education statistics: School year 1997-98* (Report No. NCES 98-202). Washington, DC: U.S. Department of Education, National Center for Education Statistics.

Odden, A., & Busch, C. (1998). *Financing schools for high performance: Strategies for improving the use of educational resources.* San Francisco: Jossey-Bass.

Peternick, L., & Sherman, J. (1998). Site-based budgeting in Fort Worth, Texas. *Journal of Education Finance, 23*(4), 532-556.

Rubenstein, R. (1997). *School-level budgeting and resource allocation in the Chicago public schools: Processes and results.* Unpublished doctoral dissertation, New York University.

Stiefel, L., Berne, R., Goertz, M., Sherman, J., Hess, G. A., Jr., Moser, M., Rubenstein, R., & Iatarola, P. (1996). *School-level resource allocation in urban public schools. Final report to the Andrew W. Mellon Foundation.* New York: New York University, Robert F. Wagner Graduate School of Public Service.

U.S. Department of Education. (1998). *Guidance on the Comprehensive School Reform Demonstration program.* Washington, DC: Author.

Wohlstetter, P., & Buffett, T. (1992). Promoting school-based management: Are dollars decentralized too? In A. R. Odden (Ed.), *Rethinking school finance: An agenda for the 1990s* (pp. 128-165). San Francisco: Jossey-Bass.

Wohlstetter, P., Mohrman, S. A., & Robertson, P. J. (1997). Successful school-based management: A lesson for restructuring schools. In D. Ravitch & J. P. Viteritti (Eds.), *New schools for a new century* (pp. 201-225). New Haven: Yale University Press.

Wohlstetter, P., & Van Kirk, A. (1996). Redefining school-based budgeting for high involvement. In L. O. Picus & J. L. Wattenberger (Eds.), *Where does the money go? Resource allocation in elementary and secondary schools* (pp. 212-235). Thousand Oaks, CA: Corwin.

Index

CORWIN
PRESS

The Corwin Press logo—a raven striding across an open book—
represents the happy union of courage and learning. We are a
professional-level publisher of books and journals for K–12 educators,
and we are committed to creating and providing resources that em-
body these qualities. Corwin's motto is "Success for All Learners."